Portrait
of an Apostle

Portrait of an Apostle

A Case for Paul's Authorship of Colossians and Ephesians

Gregory S. MaGee

PICKWICK *Publications* • Eugene, Oregon

PORTRAIT OF AN APOSTLE
A Case for Paul's Authorship of Colossians and Ephesians

Copyright © 2013 Gregory S. MaGee. All rights reserved. Except for brief quotations in critical publications or reviews, no part of this book may be reproduced in any manner without prior written permission from the publisher. Write: Permissions, Wipf and Stock Publishers, 199 W. 8th Ave., Suite 3, Eugene, OR 97401.

Pickwick Publications
An Imprint of Wipf and Stock Publishers
199 W. 8th Ave., Suite 3
Eugene, OR 97401

www.wipfandstock.com

ISBN 13: 978-1-62032-748-7

Cataloguing-in-Publication data:

MaGee, Gregory S.

Portrait of an Apostle : a case for Paul's authorship of Colossians and Ephesians / Gregory S. MaGee.

viii + 204 pp. ; 23 cm. Includes bibliographical references and index.

ISBN 13: 978-1-62032-748-7

1. Bible. Ephesians—Criticism, interpretation, etc. 2. Bible. Colossians—Criticism, interpretation, etc. 3. Paul, the Apostle, Saint. I. Title.

BS2715.3 M35 2013

Manufactured in the U.S.A.

To my wife and children:
Emily, John, Bethany, Mark

Contents

1. The Emergence of the Exalted Apostle Theory   1
2. Paul's Identity in the Undisputed Letters   21
3. Imitation of Paul in the *Epistle to the Laodiceans* and *3 Corinthians*   63
4. Paul's Identity in Colossians   80
5. Paul's Identity in Ephesians   128
6. A Better Way   170

Bibliography   175

Index of References   191

1

The Emergence of the Exalted Apostle Theory

An Untested Theory

THIS BOOK CHALLENGES THE popular theory that in Colossians and Ephesians a well-meaning imitator, perhaps as part of an informal "school of Paul," attempts to speak using Paul's authoritative voice. This is a hypothesis that is so often restated in recent scholarship that it is arguably the default position in the field, even though the theory is relatively untested. The widely held judgment is that Paul is portrayed as an exalted, idealized apostle and prisoner in Colossians and Ephesians. Intrinsic to this position is that Paul himself did not write Colossians and Ephesians, at least not in their canonical forms. Rather, according to this view, admirers of Paul adopted a stereotyped picture of Paul in order to speak with his perceived authority in current settings. This theory, which in this book will be referred to as the "Exalted Apostle Theory," has been propagated in a variety of studies in recent decades.

J. Christiaan Beker, for instance, points to the "exalted view of Paul" and his "heroic status" in Colossians, while in Ephesians Paul is "a figure whose authority and stature have increased enormously over time" since Paul's death.[1] According to Martinus de Boer, the persona of Paul in both Colossians and Ephesians arises out of "a developing legend of Paul."[2] David Meade contends that the Paul in Ephesians has been presented as "an

---

1. Beker, *Heirs of Paul*, 68, 72.
2. De Boer, "Images of Paul," 361.

archetypical figure,"³ and Andrew Lincoln sees Eph 3:1–13 as "a device" used in order to "boost claims for the authority of the apostle's teachings for a later time."⁴ According to Leander Keck, Paul "strikes an Olympian pose" in Ephesians.⁵ For Colossians, Eduard Lohse provides this assessment: "[T]he concern is only with Paul's office, and no indication exists of a mention of the rest of the apostles, neither Peter nor the Twelve. Paul is, as *the* Apostle to the nations, the one and only Apostle."⁶ Charles Nielsen contends that the author of Colossians is "elevating the status of Paul to astonishing heights."⁷ These excerpts are representative of a perspective that has been gaining a foothold in modern studies on Colossians and Ephesians.

This book seeks to answer the claim that Colossians and Ephesians present an elevated image of Paul and employ this image to buttress the letters' authority. It will be proposed that such a view does not stand up to close scrutiny. Instead, Colossians and Ephesians reflect Paul's own understanding of his apostolic identity and ministry in a way that is consistent with the earlier letters that bear his name.

The test of any viable theory of authorship for these letters lies in the credibility of the interpretations it yields for the letters. This monograph seeks to show that interpretations based on the assumption of Paul's authorship of Colossians and Ephesians are consistently superior to interpretations positing that an admirer of Paul wrote the letters. The book thus reflects the method of historical interpretation, accompanied by an analysis of the literary relationship between works (specifically, identifying or ruling out literary dependence).

This study will look at how texts correlate with other texts that preceded them. Selected works are divided into three distinct categories. The first group consists of Paul's undisputed letters, which are Romans, 1 and 2 Corinthians, Galatians, Philippians, 1 Thessalonians, Philemon. Certain letters universally recognized as being written in Paul's name but after the time of Paul constitute the second group. The two pseudepigraphal works *Epistle to the Laodiceans* (*Ep. Lao.*) and *Third Corinthians* (*3 Cor.*) are examples of letters from early Christianity that draw on Paul's perceived authoritative status and allot a significant percentage of the material to

---

3. Meade, *Pseudonymity and Canon*, 148.
4. Lincoln, *Ephesians*, lxiii.
5. Keck, "Images of Paul in the New Testament," 341–51.
6. Lohse, *Colossians and Philemon*, 72.
7. Nielsen, "The Status of Paul," 103.

relaying a credible identity for Paul. The incorporation of Paul's identity in these letters is thus comparable to what proponents of the Exalted Apostle Theory allege for Colossians and Ephesians. The third category is comprised of the letters in question, Colossians and Ephesians. The approach of this study is to use the first group to establish Paul's understanding of his ministry and then to compare and contrast how the second and third groups adopt or reflect the themes and language of the letters from the first group.[8]

The focal point of investigation lies in the sections of discourse in which Paul's self-understanding as a minister is put forward. A successful pseudepigrapher would need to speak convincingly as Paul in those sections in order to gain a hearing in the rest of the letter. As a result, unsuccessful attempts to imitate Paul usually flounder here, as in the case of the pseudepigraphal *Epistle to the Laodiceans* and *3 Corinthians*. Passages describing Paul's ministry and calling in Colossians and Ephesians, on the other hand, stand up to rigorous scrutiny and reflect the creative and authoritative mind of Paul himself.

Comparisons among letters in the three different categories will involve attention to connections in themes, language, and context. Thematically, the complex interplay between Paul's authority and suffering in the undisputed letters will be analyzed, along with the formative influence of the Old Testament and Paul's Damascus experience on his sense of calling. Then, letters from the second and third categories will be examined to see whether they conform to the complex overall picture of Paul's apostleship as found in the undisputed letters. For language, wording from letters in the second and third groups will be measured against possible parallels from the undisputed letters. Contextually, determination will be made as to whether borrowed wording from older contexts fits naturally in new contexts.

It will be demonstrated in these comparisons that works from the second category betray their post-Pauline character in a number of ways, including incorporating only overt themes and direct language while missing more subtle connections and foundations, applying original

---

8. The Pastoral Epistles and 2 Thessalonians have been bypassed as focal points of this study. The authenticity or inauthenticity of the Pastorals and 2 Thessalonians would first need to be established with a high degree of certainty in order to apply evidence gleaned from the letters to the evaluation of Paul's portrayal in Colossians and Ephesians. Even those proponents of the Exalted Apostle Theory who detect a common effort to preserve Paul's legacy are willing to admit that Colossians and Ephesians develop this heritage differently than do the Pastorals and 2 Thessalonians.

Pauline language into contexts that are not fully suitable to the original wording, and communicating ideas that may be situated at a later point on the trajectory of developing Christian thought and expression. In contrast, the picture found in Colossians and Ephesians exhibits continuity with the complex presentation of Paul found in Paul's earlier letters, aligns well within the earliest period of Christianity in which Paul is located, and is fully appropriate to the distinct contexts of Colossians and Ephesians.

The projected significance of this investigation lies in two areas: historical and theological. First, it is expected that the book will make a contribution to the question of authorship in Colossians and Ephesians, though there are still many other factors that must be considered when assessing the character of these letters.[9] Second, the book is designed to shed light on Paul's rich comprehension of his apostolic calling, which entails ministry primarily to the Gentiles, by means of proclaiming the revealed mystery of the gospel and embodying the power of the gospel through sacrificial suffering. Many scholars exclude Colossians and Ephesians when determining the essentials of Paul's theology or treat the letters as no more than an afterthought. The undisputed letters of Paul set the foundations of Paul's self-understanding, but Colossians and Ephesians supplement this picture in significant ways.

A Survey of Works Relevant to this Study

In this section important past research will be surveyed in several general areas, followed by special consideration given to the emergence of the Exalted Apostle Theory. The general areas include the authorship of Colossians and Ephesians, the development of a Pauline school, and the motivations behind pseudepigraphy in the early centuries of Christianity.

Challenges to the Authorship of Colossians and Ephesians

The authorship question for these two captivity epistles has usually been approached by exploring the vocabulary, style, literary parallels, and theology of the letters. As early as 1838, Ernst Mayerhoff challenged the authenticity of Colossians, seeing it as dependent on the authentic

---

9. The recent publication of Ehrman's *Forged: Writing in the Name of God—Why the Bible's Authors Are Not Who We Think They Are* demonstrates that the issue of authorship in the New Testament has resurfaced as a topic of interest. In the book Ehrman disputes the authenticity of Ephesians (108–12) and Colossians (112–14).

Ephesians.[10] Comprehensive treatments of the early evolution of positions on authorship for these epistles may be found elsewhere.[11] The arguments in these studies were often characterized by appeals to theological or stylistic discrepancies between the recognized works of Paul and the letter in dispute. Works that have had an enduring place in the discussion in the question of the authorship will now be surveyed.

Edgar Goodspeed, having accepted the verdict that Ephesians was not written by Paul, offers what he believes to be a plausible historical scenario for the circumstances that gave rise to the letter. His suggestion is that Ephesians, written by a later admirer of Paul, served as an introductory work to the rest of the Pauline corpus. Ephesians was penned to help reorient people to Paul's theology and authority after a generation of Christians had neglected his works.[12] Goodspeed's explanation has acted as a catalyst for others to further examine the motives and intents of the writers of Ephesians and Colossians and thus constituted a key step in the emergence of the Exalted Apostle Theory.

Ernst Percy's book presents thorough support for Paul's authorship of Colossians and Ephesians, resisting the theories of Goodspeed and others.[13] In particular, Percy provides a response to arguments that in Eph 3:1–13 the imitator's hand is revealed. He gives alternate explanations for why Paul described his apostleship, revelation, humility, and suffering as he did.[14] With respect to Colossians, Percy devotes extensive discussion to Paul's theology of suffering in 1:24 and contends for the Pauline origin of this verse as well as for the letter as a whole.[15]

C. L. Mitton's pivotal work on the authorship of Ephesians concludes that Paul did not write Ephesians. Mitton, envisioning a scenario similar to Goodspeed's, proposes that Ephesians was penned shortly after the author, who already had access to Colossians and Philemon, came into possession of Paul's other surviving letters.[16] Mitton's argument is that the author

---

10. Mayerhoff, *Der Brief an die Colosser*, 105–6.

11. For both books see Percy, *Die Probleme der Kolosser- und Epheserbriefe*, 1–15. For Colossians, see Kiley, *Colossians as Pseudepigraphy*, 37–39. For Ephesians, consult van Roon, *Authenticity of Ephesians*, 3–36; Hoehner, *Ephesians*, 6–20.

12. See Goodspeed, *The Formation of the New Testament*, 20–32; Goodspeed, *The Meaning of Ephesians*, 10, 41–42, 73–75; Goodspeed, "Ephesians and the First Edition of Paul," 285–91.

13. Percy, *Die Probleme der Kolosser- und Epheserbriefe*.

14. Ibid., 345–47, 351–52, 379–81, 412.

15. Ibid., 128–34.

16. Mitton, *Ephesians: Its Authorship, Origin, and Purpose*, 45–54, 267.

assimilated Pauline material, most notably Colossians, in a way that is best explained by positing a post-Pauline writer. Mitton is skeptical for two major reasons of the alternative theory that Paul himself wrote Ephesians shortly after Colossians.[17] First, sentences in Ephesians sometimes appear to be composed of fragments that occur in detached sections of Colossians ("conflation").[18] Second, Ephesians adopts terms from Colossians without carrying over the original meaning of the words.[19]

Goodspeed's and Mitton's books on Ephesians also stand out in the way they seek to identify literary affinities between Ephesians and the letters that preceded them by looking at potential parallels for every verse.[20] E. P. Sanders adopts a similar approach in his seminal article on Colossians.[21] Working within space constraints, however, Sanders limits himself to representative passages in Colossians instead of looking at every passage in the epistle. In his definition of "literary dependence" Sanders allows for "quotation from memory" as well as actual incorporation of material from a written document in the writer's possession.[22] He focuses on the use of language from the earlier writings and asks whether the language in Colossians betrays the marks of someone writing in Paul's name. His conclusion is that the passages under investigation do indeed suggest the work of a well-meaning pseudepigrapher.[23]

Unlike Sanders's article, A. van Roon's book *The Authenticity of Ephesians* challenges the paradigm forged by Goodspeed and Mitton.[24] Van Roon concludes that both Ephesians and Colossians were constructed using an earlier "blueprint" written by Paul.[25] Van Roon does not suppose, however, that a later imitator was responsible for Ephesians in its final form, preferring to credit Paul with the authorship, since the letter emerged from his sphere of influence.[26] For van Roon's argument, the

---

17. Ibid., 79–81.

18. Ibid., 64–67.

19. Ibid., 83–97.

20. Goodspeed, *The Meaning of Ephesians*, 82–165; Mitton, *Ephesians: Its Authorship, Origin, and Purpose*, 118–58, 280–315.

21. E. P. Sanders, "Literary Dependence in Colossians," 28–45. Following a similar method as part of her inquiry is Leppä, *The Making of Colossians*, 59–208.

22. E. P. Sanders, "Literary Dependence in Colossians," 30.

23. Ibid., 44.

24. Van Roon, *Authenticity of Ephesians*, 435–36.

25. Ibid., 429–32.

26. Ibid., 436–37.

The Emergence of the Exalted Apostle Theory

portrait of Paul in the epistle plays an insignificant role. He mentions only briefly the "idealized picture of Paul" of Eph 3:5 that is appealed to in unnamed studies. He does not proceed to delve into this topic in any detail.[27]

In recent years there has been a call for greater objectivity in the evaluation of the authorship of Colossians and Ephesians. The use of statistically-refined models has signaled an important trend in the quest for more controlled results in the area, but it is recognized that even these studies have their limitations.[28]

In the end, research involving theological discrepancies, style variances, and literary dependence has proved persuasive to many for rejecting Pauline authorship for both Colossians and Ephesians. Today, some studies even begin with the presupposition of non-Pauline authorship for these letters. Because of the focused nature of this book and the correspondingly small sample size of the data, statistically valid measurements of linguistic style are unattainable. On the other hand, theological or literary analysis is often pertinent to the discussion. Such analysis of the material is restricted in scope to passages related to the apostolic calling and ministry of Paul.

The "School of Paul" Idea

An area that is related to authorship but not confined to Colossians and/or Ephesians is the possible existence of a "school of Paul." The hypothesis of a Pauline school has played an important role in the development of the Exalted Apostle Theory. If it is likely that disciples of Paul continued his mission after his death and that part of their work included careful study and re-appropriation of his theology, then the writing of new letters in Paul's name becomes a more reasonable scenario.

Ernst Käsemann ventured the thesis in 1949 that Col 1:12—2:3 was constructed after Paul's time in order to preserve orthodoxy by means of appeal to Paul's apostolic authority. Käsemann implies that followers of Paul were the ones responsible for insisting on both an authoritative Christian doctrine and an authoritative apostolic office that preserved and

---

27. Ibid., 389.

28. Studies of this sort include Morton and McLeman, *Paul, the Man, and the Myth*; Bujard, *Stilanalytische Untersuchungen zum Kolosserbrief*; Neumann, *The Authenticity of the Pauline Epistles*. Of these three, Neumann's work uses the most sophisticated statistical controls and arrives at the most tentative conclusions, demonstrating that with statistical analysis the process must be carried out and the results applied with due caution.

explained that doctrine.²⁹ Käsemann thus gives the portrayal of Paul in Colossians a rhetorical purpose and lays the groundwork for the idea of a school of Paul.

A key proponent of the Pauline school hypothesis is Hans Conzelmann. For Conzelmann, though, the idea of a Pauline school is quite broad. It encompasses the formal Jewish schooling Paul may have experienced, the formation of a similar Christian school under his direction, and the ongoing operation of a school after Paul's death. Conzelmann believes that disciples after Paul's death were responsible for writing letters such as Colossians and Ephesians. Though different authors were behind the different letters, their portraits of Paul share the common factors of divine calling and suffering.³⁰ Authors who endorse the Exalted Apostle Theory regularly cite Conzelmann's articles.

Scholars likewise use Hans-Martin Schenke's article on the Pauline school to support their positions. Schenke envisions a more complex and decentralized school of Paul in which disciples continued Paul's ministry as part of a vibrant mission carried out in various locales. The death of Paul was the catalyst for collecting his letters and preserving his legacy. These disciples wrote in response to diverse problems in varying contexts. Paul's surviving letters, combined with the developing legend of his life and ministry, formed the material from which letters such as Colossians and Ephesians were created.³¹

The hypothesis of a school of Paul now surfaces regularly in studies on Colossians and Ephesians.³² Proponents suppose that early disciples of Paul, either before or after his death, congregated in order to preserve and study the teachings of Paul and to reformulate those teachings in new settings. Sometimes the school proposal is tied to the image of the apostle in Colossians and Ephesians. For instance in his dictionary article on the Pauline school, James Dunn makes this connection for Ephesians, claiming that Paul comes across as "the archetypal apostle," and that the letter "sounds more and more like a eulogy penned by an admirer."³³ The school

---

29. Käsemann, "Eine urchristliche Tauftliturgie," 144.

30. Conzelmann, "Paulus und die Weisheit," 233–34; Conzelmann, "Die Schule des Paulus," 85, 88–90.

31. Schenke, "Paulus-Schule," 512–16.

32. See for instance Kiley, *Colossians as Pseudepigraphy*, 32, 90–103; Lincoln, *Ephesians*, lxx; Best, *Ephesians*, 36–40; Angela Standhartinger, "Colossians and the Pauline School," 572–73; Hay, *Colossians*, 20, 23–24; Leppä, *The Making of Colossians*, 12; R. Wilson, *Colossians and Philemon*, 34, 167.

33. Dunn, "Pauline Legacy and School," 887–93.

of Paul theory attempts to provide a credible historical setting in which Paul's theological legacy could be preserved through the creation of new letters in his name. This leads us to the topic of pseudepigraphy.

Pseudepigraphy

Pseudepigraphy is a term that describes the phenomenon of writing in another person's name, while authors of pseudepigraphal documents are typically referred to as pseudonymous writers. One specific question about pseudepigraphy that is relevant to this book is whether intentional deception is involved in ancient pseudepigraphy.

Ascertaining the presence of intentional deception in pseudepigraphal literature has significant relevance to the topic of Paul's persona in his disputed letters. The presence or absence of deception has a direct bearing on the discourse function of the material portraying the assumed author.

Some scholars seek to minimize the significance of apparent deception in the earliest instances of Christian pseudepigraphy, offering alternative suggestions for why some writers would adopt the name of a recognized authority figure. Karl Fischer identifies the time period of the writings as the decisive factor for assessing deceptive intent. He creates separate categories for New Testament pseudepigraphy and later pseudepigraphy and then exonerates the earlier pseudepigraphy from charges of ethical wrongdoing. Fischer maintains that the anonymous and pseudonymous writers of New Testament works were attempting to speak with an ecumenical perspective at a time when authoritative voices were lacking.[34]

W. J. Dalton takes a similar approach, separating "extended authorship" from "real pseudepigraphy," with the former arising shortly after the death of the implied author and the latter occurring at a later date. For Dalton, Ephesians is an example of extended authorship, since it aims simply to propagate Paul's perspective without elaborate and deceptive biographical reconstruction.[35]

David Meade's assessment of the benign motives of early Christian pseudepigraphers resembles Fischer's and Dalton's perspectives. Meade

---

34. Fischer, "Anmerkungen zur Pseudepigraphie im Neuen Testament," 76–81.

35. Dalton, "Pseudepigraphy in the New Testament," 32–33. According to Dalton the level of biographical detail in Colossians precludes it from being placed in the category of extended authorship. Dalton supposes that Colossians must be either genuinely Pauline or blatantly pseudepigraphal.

looks to Jewish canonical and apocryphal works for models of how Christian authors appropriated the authority of a prior religious figure in a contemporary setting.[36] Though Meade contends for the post-Pauline character of Ephesians (and the Pastoral Epistles) on other grounds, he uses the Jewish works to discern a possible motive for why the author presented Ephesians as Paul's work.[37] Meade concludes that "the literary attribution of Ephesians and the Pastorals must be regarded primarily as an assertion of authoritative Pauline tradition, not of literary origins."[38] Meade thus suggests that the author of Ephesians was promoting and clarifying Paul's authority rather than making a deceptive claim supporting Paul's authorship of the letter.

On the other side of the debate are scholars who emphasize the deception of early Christian pseudepigraphy. Wolfgang Speyer investigates the question of intent by differentiating among types of pseudepigraphy. Speyer first distinguishes between religious and non-religious pseudepigraphy and looks to the former as the best guide for understanding New Testament pseudepigraphy. Speyer then draws from examples of religious pseudepigraphy from the Greco-Roman world and the Jewish second temple period. Using these examples he specifies whether different types of literature were designed to deceive or simply to convey inspired thoughts through the mouthpiece of a revered religious figure. Speyer determines that most pseudepigraphal letters in early Christianity fit in the former category.[39]

Additional support for this contention is found in how pseudepigraphal documents were received in early Christianity. Early witnesses indicate that writing Christian documents under false names was denounced in early Christianity.[40] Most likely a mix of doctrinal and authorial objections to pseudepigraphy was in play among early church leaders.[41]

---

36. Meade, *Pseudonymity and Canon*, 103–106.

37. Ibid., 160–61. The rationale for the comparison is that the non-epistolary Jewish works and the disputed Pauline letters share a common desire to preserve authoritative legacy.

38. Ibid., 161.

39. Speyer, *Die literarische Fälschung im heidnischen und christlichen Alterum*, 111–68; Speyer, "Religiöse Pseudepigraphe und literarische Fälschung im Altertum," 195–263.

40. See examples in Meade, *Pseudonymity and Canon*, 204–6; Metzger, "Literary Forgeries and Canonical Pseudepigrapha," 12–15; Baum, *Pseudepigraphie*, 99–112; Wilder, *Pseudonymity, the New Testament, and Deception*, 123–53.

41. Metzger, "Literary Forgeries and Canonical Pseudepigrapha," 15.

The growing consensus, despite residual objections, is that if there are pseudepigraphal works in the New Testament, they reflect purposeful falsehood.[42] Terry Wilder's recent book provides the most comprehensive argument for this position.[43]

What does the presence or absence of deceptive motive suggest for the portrayal of Paul in pseudepigraphal or disputed letters? First, if deception is assumed, then Paul's image in the so-called Deutero-Pauline letters would be expected to align as closely as possible to the standard features of Paul's own self-expression, in order to persuade readers that Paul is the author. Second, if the pseudepigraphal letters simply extend the voice and authority of Paul beyond his own generation (and are not simply intended to deceive readers), then the likely function of the presentation of Paul would be to remind readers of Paul's authority and his relevance to their lives. Third, in the case of any letter originating from Paul, the autobiographical material would be in accord with Paul's overall agenda in the letter.

The Rise of the Exalted Apostle Theory

Despite extensive research delving into authorship, the school of Paul, and pseudepigraphy, nothing approaching a sustained, identifiable theory on Paul's post-death idealization existed in the middle of the twentieth century. Several studies in Ephesians used language suggestive of Paul's exalted status, but the references were fleeting, and nothing comparable was emerging in studies on Colossians. Lohse's relatively brief mention of the depiction of Paul's apostleship in Colossians as a possible indicator of inauthenticity served as an important catalyst for further investigation. Soon more authors published studies about Paul's image in Colossians and Ephesians as well as about the significance of Paul's portrayal in the perpetuation of his theological and sociological influence after his death. The following section tracks how the Exalted Apostle Theory has made advances in research on Ephesians, Colossians, and the broader phenomenon of Paul's legacy.

---

42. Among recent works that recognize the element of deception in early Christian pseudepigraphy are Carson, "Pseudonymity and Pseudepigraphy," 860–63; Baum, *Pseudepigraphie*, 92–93; Verhoef, "Pseudepigraphy and Canon," 95; Clarke, "Pseudonymity," 447.

43. Wilder, *Pseudonymity*. See especially the summary of his argument in 255–58.

Portrait of an Apostle

Initial Expressions of the Theory in Studies of Ephesians

Language reflecting an Exalted Apostle Theory was employed as early as 1939 by Wilfred Knox, who concurs with Goodspeed's assessment that Ephesians was crafted to introduce believers to Paul's letters and theology. Knox claims that post-Pauline writers such as the author of Ephesians were inclined "to borrow a name in order to give sanction to documents."[44] According to Knox, Eph 3:1–13 reflects "veneration" of Paul, stemming from a response to Paul's martyrdom.[45] Despite this suggestive language, Knox's work did not spark much additional discussion about the significance of the image of Paul in Ephesians.

For Mitton, the portrayal of Paul enters the discussion not as a separate category by which to evaluate the legitimacy of the work but in the course of discussing the data from Eph 3:1–13 and other sections. Mitton detects an artificial "heightening of effect" and "insincerity" in the characterization Paul in Eph 3:4 and 3:8.[46] After these fleeting comments by Knox and Mitton, interest in the possible post-Pauline esteem of Paul's ministry and authority in Ephesians lay dormant for several decades.[47]

Initial Expressions of the Theory in Studies of Colossians

The publication of Lohse's Colossians commentary in 1968, followed by a related article in 1969, marked a significant turning point in how Paul's representation relates to the problem of the authenticity of Colossians. Lohse identifies the understanding of Paul's ministry as one of the theological discontinuities between Colossians and Paul's earlier letters. According to Lohse, Paul is granted an artificial position of exclusivity as an apostle in Colossians.[48]

Also in 1968, Donald Hobson detected a portrayal of Paul "as *the* apostle *par excellence*" in Colossians.[49] In Hobson's view, the author of

---

44. W. Knox, *St. Paul and the Church of the Gentiles*, 184–85.

45. Ibid., 189.

46. Mitton, *Ephesians: Its Authorship, Origin, and Purpose*, 232–33.

47. Van Roon's passing reference to an "idealized picture of Paul" in Eph 3:5 is characteristic of the relative lack of curiosity about the topic (Van Roon, *Authenticity of Ephesians*, 389).

48. Lohse, *Die Briefe an die Kolosser und an Philemon*, 116–18, 251–54; Lohse, "Pauline Theology in the Letter to the Colossians," 215; Lohse, *Colossians and Philemon*, 72–73, 179–81.

49. Hobson, "The Authorship of Colossians," 148, 157.

The Emergence of the Exalted Apostle Theory

Colossians enhanced Paul's authority by artificially highlighting his suffering for the church, with the desired goal of speaking with a heightened authority to a post-Pauline setting.[50] Hobson's dissertation did not have the influence that Lohse's commentary did, but it revealed the growing momentum of the Exalted Apostle Theory.

In the wake of Lohse's work in particular, the presentation of Paul's ministry became a more significant factor in discussions of the authorship of Colossians. For instance, shortly after Lohse's commentary publication, Günther Bornkamm echoed Lohse's conclusion on Colossians, without further elaboration or support.[51] The status of Paul, already noted as significant in Ephesians, was beginning to attract comment in studies on Colossians as well.

The Development of a More General Exalted Apostle Theory

Interest in Paul's portrayal has expanded beyond discussions of authorship in individual letters to an exploration of how Paul's authority and teaching were reapplied to believing communities after his death. The common thread in many of these works is that the Exalted Apostle Theory is never defended systematically but rather is presupposed as part of the goal of shedding light on the process and results of the idealization of Paul.

Building upon Walter Bauer's thesis on orthodoxy and heresy in the early church[52] Georg Strecker surveys the various ways in which later authors after Paul's lifetime were responsible for expressing and defending his doctrine and image. Perceived innovations in how Paul's person and theology are portrayed in Colossians and Ephesians receive brief treatment alongside those found in the Pastoral Epistles, 2 Thessalonians, and Acts as part of an attempt to reconstruct the effects of Paul's influence in the decades following his life and ministry.[53]

C. K. Barrett refers briefly to Lohse's work in his contention that Ephesians is the product of a later disciple or school.[54] Barrett identifies in Ephesians what appears to be uncontested authority for Paul in the

---

50. Ibid., 152, 157.

51. Bornkamm, *Paul*, 242; Bornkamm also incorporated the idea of a school of Paul in his discussion of the generation that followed Paul (ibid., 86).

52. Bauer, *Rechtgläubigkeit und Ketzerei im ältesten Christentum*, 1934.

53. Strecker, "Paulus in Nachpaulinischer Zeit," 208–16.

54. Barrett, "Pauline Controversies in the Post-Pauline Period," 239–43.

universal church, with the Jewish-Gentile conflict an already settled matter.[55] He sees this as a portrait that accords well with a developing "legend" of Paul and his ministry. This legend also surfaces in the Pastoral Epistles and Acts,[56] but Colossians is still assumed to be an authentic work of Paul.[57]

Martinus de Boer's article has contributed significant fodder to the discussion of Paul's persona and legacy. De Boer identifies the major distinctives of Paul's image as reflected in allegedly post-Pauline works, including Colossians and Ephesians. Paul is set apart as the sole apostle, who verifies his calling through suffering and whose teaching is to be heeded unwaveringly.[58] De Boer operates from a descriptive standpoint, first assuming the late date of these works and then delving into the characterization of Paul and the motives behind that characterization.[59] The direction of his study is shaped by, among others, Barrett and Schenke.

D. N. Penny allots sections in different chapters of his dissertation to the portrayal of Paul in various so-called Deutero-Pauline letters. He concurs with the growing consensus that Paul comes across in Ephesians in a glamorized way.[60] Penny's thesis is that the imitation of Paul was skillful and purposeful, not merely benign, and that the activity of speaking in the name of Paul is not to be attributed to the operations of a school, since the letters ascribed to Paul pursue different goals from varying theological perspectives.[61]

Raymond Collins devotes a special section to Paul's persona in his treatment of Colossians and Ephesians as pseudepigraphy.[62] According to Collins, Paul is elevated as an exemplary prisoner, an apostle without peer, and a privileged recipient of God's mysteries in Ephesians.[63] Less overtly in Colossians, Paul comes across as an unchallenged authority figure and a memorialized martyr.[64] De Boer's article has exerted an influence in Collins work as well.

55. Ibid.
56. Ibid., 243.
57. Ibid., 239: "Ephesians is probably the oldest of the Pauline pseudepigrapha."
58. De Boer, "Images of Paul in the Post-Apostolic Period," 363–70, 378–79.
59. Ibid., 359–60.
60. Penny, "The Pseudo-Pauline Letters of the First Two Centuries," 259–66. Penny offers a similar speculation for Colossians, ibid., 346–47.
61. Ibid., 16–17, 60–61.
62. R. Collins, *Letters That Paul Did Not Write*, 166–69, 203–7.
63. Ibid., 166–69.
64. Ibid., 203–7.

Margaret MacDonald likewise builds upon de Boer's position, interacting with his article in great detail in her study of Paul's enduring influence.[65] She is interested in seeing how Paul's followers direct the work in Paul's churches after his death. For her, Colossians and Ephesians exhibit sociological traits of movements that reorient themselves after the death of the founder.[66] In her commentary on Colossians and Ephesians, MacDonald reiterates her earlier opinion of the post-Pauline origin of both letters. The elevation of Paul's status in the letters is one of the deciding factors, especially as viewed from a sociological perspective. MacDonald detects a "desire to enhance Paul's position and reputation" in Col 1:24–2:7.[67] A similar verdict is put forward for Eph 3:1–13, which "contains idealized images of the apostle that are present in Acts and other deutero-Pauline writings."[68]

Peter Müller also devotes substantial attention to the preservation and application of Paul's teaching after his death, particularly as found in 2 Thessalonians and Colossians. Müller's vision of the Pauline school spotlights its varied and unorganized character. The different branches of the "school" began with the shared pillars of Paul's own theology but then adapted them to the pressing needs of the day.[69] In Müller's discussion of what the transition period from Paul to his students looked like, the description of Paul's identity in the letters plays a central role. The portrayal in Colossians reveals the expansion of Paul's authority, which corresponds to an expanding community of believers throughout the world. Paul's status and ministry influence are enlarged so that his message and his suffering become relevant to the universal church.[70] Echoing those before him, Müller designates Paul as an apostle without peer for those in the Pauline school, because the validity of the gospel is tied to his teaching and stature.[71]

Beker engages in extended study regarding the legacy of Paul. He reiterates the assessment that the authors of Ephesians and Colossians have elevated the status of Paul. Beker believes that this portrayal of Paul

---

65. MacDonald, *Pauline Churches*, 123–26.

66. Ibid., 3, 89, 126–32.

67. MacDonald, *Colossians and Ephesians*, 8. See also ibid., 89–95.

68. Ibid., 269. See also ibid., 16, 268–73.

69. Müller, *Anfänge der Paulusschule: Dargestellt am zweiten Thessalonicherbrief und am Kolosserbrief*, 321–22.

70. Ibid., 227–32, 319–20, 323.

71. Ibid., 323.

conforms to what is seen in other places, such as Acts and the Pastoral Epistles, but that the authors of Ephesians and Colossians have been more successful in aligning their portrait with the authentic Paul of the earlier letters.[72]

According to Daniel Marguerat, the deutero-Pauline letters represent one of three avenues for continuing Paul's influence after his death. While Paul's authentic letters preserve his instruction and the canonical Acts and the apocryphal Acts of Paul reflect the memory of Paul's exploits apart from his letters, letters such as Colossians and Ephesians draw upon the image and voice of Paul from both his letters and memory to promote orthodoxy for a new generation. These deutero-Pauline letters were the product of later impersonators' extensive interaction with Paul's authentic letters.[73] The resulting picture of Paul is that of "le proclamateur par excellence" and "le destinataire privilégié" of the divine mystery in Colossians and one divinely appointed to unify Jews and Gentiles in Ephesians.[74]

Additional Research about Paul's Status in Colossians

The attention directed to the study of Paul's image in the generation following Paul is rivaled by the interest in Paul's portrayal in Colossians. Charles Nielsen shows a specific interest in Paul's image in Colossians. He takes for granted the pseudepigraphal character of the book and proceeds to articulate how the later author constructs the identity of Paul.[75] Like other scholars, Nielsen contends that the author has removed the other apostles from the picture and has accorded Paul an unchallenged position of authority.[76] The author's abrupt inclusion of Paul's self-identification in Col 1:23, the extreme assessment of Paul's suffering in 1:24, and the comprehensive scope of Paul's ministry implied in 1:25 all point to an insistence on Paul's lofty position.[77]

Walter Wilson perceives marked differences between Paul's own self-assessment and that of the pseudonymous author of Colossians, owing to the influence of popular non-Christian philosophical ideas.[78] In

72. Beker, *Heirs of Paul*, 64, 67–68, 71–72, 87–88.
73. Marguerat, "Paul après Paul," 321–23.
74. Ibid., 327–28.
75. Nielsen, "Status of Paul," 103.
76. Ibid., 107–9.
77. Ibid., 110–13.
78. W. Wilson, *The Hope of Glory*, 21.

the attempt to relay a "credible persona" for Paul, the author consults not only the prevailing image of Paul in early Christianity but also the Greco-Roman philosophical norms of the day.[79] The writer of Colossians elevates Paul's nobility in suffering and his exclusivity as a recipient of divine revelation. These characteristics adhere well to both Biblical and Greco-Roman standards for religious or philosophical sages.[80]

Angela Standhartinger interprets the assertion of Paul's suffering in Col 1:24 and his apostolic presence in 2:5 as two means by which a later student spiritualizes and universalizes Paul's ministry. Though Paul can no longer exert direct influence on the churches, through Colossians he communicates his unambiguous expectations and exhortations to the churches. The letter reads as Paul's final testament to the scattered churches that remain after his death.[81] The representation of Paul's imprisonment and suffering in Col 1:23—2:5 and Colossians 4 is best understood with Paul's martyrdom and post-martyrdom influence in mind.[82]

Jerry Sumney opts for a post-Pauline writer for Colossians and mentions the characterization of Paul's sufferings as a key component in the argument against authenticity.[83] Sumney proceeds to delve into the interpretation of Col 1:24 from the viewpoint of the letter's later origin. According to Sumney, the portrayal of Paul's suffering not only wields rhetorical force by establishing a hearing for Paul's words in the letter but also gives the readers a pattern of Christian life to mimic.[84]

Additional Research about Paul's Status in Ephesians

The degree of elaboration on Paul's status in Ephesians has not quite approached the pursuit of the similar issue in Colossians. Among those discussing the Exalted Apostle Theory as applied to Ephesians, there are even some dissenting voices who question the merits of the theory.

Rudolf Schnackenburg believes that the pseudonymous author of Ephesians has an agenda for reinforcing the unrivaled standing of Paul as an apostle. The author wishes to propagate his own expansive vision

---

79. Ibid., 64–65.
80. Ibid., 72–77.
81. Standhartinger, "Colossians and the Pauline School," 582–92; Standhartinger, *Studien zur Entstehungsgeschichte und Intention des Kolosserbriefs*, 175, 281–82.
82. Ibid., 158–75.
83. Sumney, "Paul's Vicarious Suffering Colossians," 664.
84. Ibid., 666–80.

of God's plans and the church's role in the advance of God's purposes.[85] Speaking in Paul's name, the author wants to reiterate Paul's prominence as a recipient of treasured revelation so that the author's message in Ephesians will be more readily honored and embraced as the "standard tradition."[86]

Robert Wild suggests that even though Ephesians is written falsely under Paul's name, the intent of the author in his depiction of Paul is not to deceive but to motivate. Paul is highlighted as the ideal prisoner who is not constrained by his captors but bound only to Christ. He thus speaks boldly as a free man, serving as a model for other Christians to do likewise, regardless of opposition.[87]

In his commentary on Ephesians Lincoln highlights the portrayal of Paul from the vantage point of the literary feature of the "implied author" of a document.[88] After surveying the representation of the implied author from select verses in Ephesians, Lincoln concludes that the resulting image is too forced to be the product of Paul himself. Specifically, the implied Paul of Ephesians esteems his own revelation and ministry too highly, and then overcorrects this imbalance by insisting on his own lowly status (Eph 3:8).[89]

Victor Furnish devotes a significant amount of space to how Paul's projected image in Ephesians undermines the case for Pauline authorship.[90] He believes that language especially from chapter 3 presents Paul as a "mystagogue" who occupies an indispensible position among early church leaders.[91] Even language designed to diminish Paul's status ("the least of all the saints") reveals the hand of a later imitator who venerated both the authority and the humility of the apostle.[92]

Klyne Snodgrass, a defender of the Pauline authorship of Ephesians, notes that the content describing Paul's ministry can be seen either to strengthen or to weaken the case against the authenticity of the letter. Snodgrass observes that the balance of assertion and self-effacement found in Eph 3:1–13 is compatible with testimony from Paul's earlier

---

85. Schnackenburg, *Ephesians*, 36–37, 130, 136, 143.
86. Ibid., 132.
87. Wild, "The Warrior and the Prisoner," 288–94.
88. Lincoln, *Ephesians*, lx.
89. Ibid., lx–lxiii.
90. Furnish, "Ephesians" 2:540.
91. Ibid.
92. Ibid.

letters.⁹³ On the whole, the idea of Paul as an apostle to the Gentiles and a prisoner fulfills Paul's own rhetorical agenda more reasonably than it does the goals of a later writer.⁹⁴

Ernest Best, though denying the authenticity of Ephesians, nonetheless avoids using the presentation of Paul as weighty evidence in the discussion on authorship. Slight divergences from Paul's picture in the authentic letters can be detected, but these are within the bounds of what could be expected from Paul himself.⁹⁵ Best even rejects outright the idea that the author ascribes to Paul the exalted status of either a "role model" or a "hero of the faith."⁹⁶ Best accepts the pseudepigraphal character of the letter, but does not observe the author tipping his hand in the sections that concern Paul's identity.

Peter O'Brien interacts with Lincoln, Snodgrass, and Best, echoing Snodgrass' conclusion that Paul's authorship is supported in the section. The problematic statements that place an exclusive focus on Paul on the one hand and reduce him to a lowly status on the other conform to the complex identity of Paul in his generally accepted letters.⁹⁷

Similar to Best, John Muddiman does not embrace Pauline authorship for the letter as a whole but does reject the idea of an artificially glamorized Ephesian portrait of Paul. His conclusions stem from the perspective that Ephesians is the product of careful redaction of an authentic Pauline letter to the Laodiceans.⁹⁸ From this viewpoint, some of the material (for instance, much of Eph 3:1–13) reflects the genuine Paul, while the hand of a later editor can be detected throughout (for instance, in 3:5, 9–11).⁹⁹ The redaction was not undertaken for the purpose of elevating Paul but nonetheless reflects a "post-apostolic perspective" in some cases.¹⁰⁰

Resisting the trend towards skepticism about exalted apostle arguments for Ephesians, Gregory Sterling revisits the issue of how after his lifetime, Paul's influence is promoted in pseudepigraphal letters.¹⁰¹ He argues that order to construct a credible persona for Paul, the author of

---

93. Snodgrass, *Ephesians*, 26.
94. Ibid., 27.
95. Best, *Ephesians*, 40–44.
96. Ibid., 43.
97. O'Brien, *Ephesians*, 34–36.
98. Muddiman, *Ephesians*, 20–24.
99. Ibid., 145–64.
100. Ibid., 29, 154.
101. Sterling, "From Apostle to the Gentiles to Apostle of the Church," 74–98.

Ephesians relied heavily on Colossians, especially in his presentation of the revealed mystery entrusted to Paul and others.[102] According to Sterling, the subtle changes the author of Ephesians made to content from Colossians and to prevailing tradition about Paul's relationship to the other apostles help demonstrate the author's intention to grant Paul "pride of place in the revelation of God's mystery."[103]

Clinton Arnold finds that the sections of the letter that describe Paul's calling and ministry are best taken at face value. He summarizes his skepticism towards those who have proposed alternate interpretations for the material related to Paul in the letter: "[E]xplanations I have read of this material by those who affirm pseudepigraphy are not at all compelling."[104]

Summary of Studies Pertaining to the Topic

Numerous other authors have made the claim, often without extensive substantiation, that Colossians and/or Ephesians depict an artificially pronounced view of Paul. Often scholars insist that the pseudonymous authors hoped to speak authoritatively under Paul's name and thus presented Paul according to their idealized memory of him. Unlike Lohse, who used data from biographical sections in Colossians to challenge the origins of the letter, many scholars in recent decades have used the assumption of pseudepigraphy to further illuminate the authors' shaping of Paul's image for their purposes. Recent skepticism by Snodgrass, Best, Muddiman, and O'Brien about the strength of exalted apostle arguments in Ephesians may signal a change in perception, though a similar turn has yet to surface in studies on Colossians.[105] The debate over Paul's image in studies on Colossians and Ephesians calls for detailed inspection of the key passages in order to determine whether Paul's portrait more likely reveals the imprint of an imitator or exhibits the self-perception of Paul himself.

---

102. Ibid., 76–89.

103. Ibid., 88.

104. Arnold, *Ephesians*, 46–47.

105. Works that post-date the studies of Snodgrass, Best, Muddiman, and O'Brien and are still supportive of the Exalted Apostle Theory include MacDonald, *Colossians and Ephesians*; Standhartinger, "Colossians and the Pauline School"; Standhartinger, *Studien zur Entstehungsgeschichte und Intention des Kolosserbriefs*; Harding, "Disputed and Undisputed Letters of Paul," 162; Sumney, "Paul's Vicarious Suffering Colossians"; Sterling, "From Apostle to the Gentiles to Apostle of the Church"; Marguerat, "Paul après Paul."

2

Paul's Identity in the Undisputed Letters

Paul in His Own Words

This chapter will explore the contours of Paul's apostolic calling and ministry as revealed in his undisputed letters. The complex picture of Paul emerging from these letters is comprised of several important components, which are established by select biblical passages.[1] In later chapters, literary similarities between some of these passages in the undisputed letters and passages in either non-Pauline or disputed letters will be examined in more detail. The goal of the chapter, however, is to understand the overall picture Paul painted of his calling and ministry.

There is a group of interlocking themes that relate to Paul's calling as an apostle of Christ. These themes include the account of Paul's revelation from Christ on the road to Damascus, his sense of God's grace in choosing and empowering him, the revelation of the mystery of the gospel to Paul, the Old Testament foundations of Paul's ministry perspective, Paul's standing as an apostle in relation to the other apostles, and Paul's ministry through suffering and imprisonment. One topic that is not examined in a separate section, but is analyzed as it surfaces in the other sections throughout the chapter, is the Gentile-orientation of Paul's ministry. Though the rest of the themes have significant overlap with one another, for the purposes of this chapter they will be examined in separate sections.

---

1. Some of these components are further attested in Luke's account of Paul's ministry in Acts, but the NT sources for this chapter of the book will be restricted in scope to the actual letters of Paul.

Portrait of an Apostle

Paul's Account of His Damascus Road Experience

Paul's Damascus road call is an appropriate place to start, since he recognized this experience as uniquely formative in his ministry direction. In Paul's letters, this episode is depicted primarily in Gal 1:11–17.[2] Paul aims to defend the divine origins of his gospel and apostleship in this passage. He does so by pointing to his encounter with Christ on the road to Damascus.

The whole passage, especially Gal 1:11–12, reiterates an emphasis begun in Gal 1:1, where Paul states that God, and not any human authority, gave him his status as apostle. Paul's assertion in Gal 1:11–12, that Jesus himself gave Paul the gospel message, defines the argument he will unfold in the verses that follow.[3] Paul is insistent that his ministry arises not from human but from divine authority. The similar wording in Gal 1:11–12, this time applied to the gospel and revelation (ἀποκάλυψις Ἰησοῦ Χριστοῦ)[4] received by Paul, suggests that Paul's gospel, apostleship, and revelation are intricately connected to one another and to the Damascus road event. In no uncertain terms, Paul asserts that God supernaturally bestowed this calling and message upon him.

Paul also speaks of this calling and encounter with Christ as having arrived through the grace of God (1:15). Paul views his appointment to ministry as a product of grace because he recognizes that he had been an unlikely candidate for such a privileged task. In his prior aggressive opposition to the church and pursuit of advancement in Judaism (Gal 1:13–14), he had revealed his loyalties quite clearly. Only an abrupt, divine act of grace, ordained from before his birth, had altered the course of Paul's life and ministry (1:15). This sudden change of direction conforms to the accounts of Paul's Damascus road experience in Acts. The topic of God's grace to Paul will receive further attention in the next section.

The grace of God on the way to Damascus is mentioned within the context of the revelation of God's son (1:16). The infinitive clause

---

2. The event is also recounted in Acts 9:3–19; 22:1–21; 26:12–18.

3. See Betz, *Galatians*, 59; Matera, *Galatians*, 55.

4. The phrase "revelation of Jesus Christ" most likely highlights Jesus as the giver of revelation, since this best completes the thought begun in 1:11b–12a (with "Jesus Christ" being parallel to "man" as an agent of revelation) and best accords with the symmetry familiar from 1:1 (see Ridderbos, *The Epistle of Paul to the Churches of Galatia*, 63; Longenecker, *Galatians*, 23–24). Even if it is determined that Christ is not highlighted as the one doing the revealing in the Galatians passage but is instead the content of the revelation, Paul's experience on the road to Damascus may still be called an encounter with Christ (Gal 1:1; 1 Cor 9:1; 1 Cor 15:8).

Paul's Identity in the Undisputed Letters

ἀποκαλύψαι τὸν υἱὸν αὐτοῦ ἐν ἐμοί completes the verb εὐδόκησεν from 1:15. This verb has God as its subject, though the manuscript testimony is divided as to whether God is mentioned explicitly.[5] Either way, the head verb highlights God's initiative as a key feature of Paul's call.[6] The infinitive clause is open to several interpretations. First, Paul might be referring simply to God's revelation of Christ to Paul, with the preposition ἐν reinforcing the dative ending and indicating that Paul is the indirect object of the clause.[7] Second, ἐν might entail its more common locative nuance ("in"), emphasizing the inward quality of Paul's apprehension of the revelation, though not necessarily to the exclusion of a tangible, outward event.[8] Third and less likely, the preposition might carry an instrumental sense ("by" or "through"), so that Paul is designated as the vessel for displaying Christ to the nations.[9] Whatever the interpretation, the clause reiterates that Paul beheld Christ in a special act of revelation during his journey to Damascus. The content of this revelation will be examined more closely later in this chapter.

The purpose for God's revelation to Paul is stated simply as preaching Christ among the Gentiles. Paul thus attributes the source of his Gentile mission to his Damascus experience. This focus on the Gentiles is repeated in Gal 2:2, 7, 8. Central to Paul's self-concept is his divinely bestowed calling to bring the gospel to the Gentiles.

Less explicit allusions to the Damascus road event are found elsewhere in the undisputed letters.[10] Among these passages 1 Cor 9:1 and

---

5. According to a reasonable interpretation of the internal evidence, ὁ θεός was likely added to make explicit what was already implied in the sentence (see Metzger, *A Textual Commentary on the Greek New Testament*, 521–22).

6. Sandnes, *Paul—One of the Prophets?*, 59.

7. Proponents of this view include BDF §220; Ridderbos, *Epistle of Paul to the Churches of Galatia*, 64; Bockmuehl, *Revelation and Mystery*, 136; Martyn, *Galatians*, 158.

8. This option is preferred by Bruce, *Galatians*, 93; Best, "The Revelation to Evangelize the Gentiles," 16; Fung, "Revelation and Tradition," 26; Toit, "Encountering Grace," 81–82.

9. A view such as this seems to be favored by John Goldingay, who speaks about Paul's mandate to "embody" the message he proclaims (Goldingay, *God's Prophet, God's Servant*, 129).

10. Potential candidates for inclusion are 1 Cor 9:1; 15:8; 2 Cor 4:6; Phil 3:12 (Bockmuehl, *Revelation and Mystery*, 136–37; Toit, "Encountering Grace," 73–74). In 2 Cor 4:6, Paul's comment about being enlightened by the glory of God in the face of Christ might allude to his experience on the way to Damascus (note Paul's description of his ministry in the surrounding material, including 2 Cor 4:5), or it might refer

15:8 most likely refer to Paul's Damascus road encounter. Both references are brief. In 9:1, Paul's purpose is to supplement the description of his apostleship. His mention of seeing the Lord is tied closely to his identity as an apostle. His vision of the Lord most likely points to his experience on the road to Damascus. In 1 Cor 15:8 Paul contends that the risen Christ appeared to him, just as he had to other apostles. The claim once again is used to establish the basis of Paul's apostleship. This comment generates a recollection of Paul's past as a persecutor, along with gratitude for God's grace in calling him despite that past (1 Cor 15:9–10). Given the similar collection of themes in Gal 1:13–16, this passage is best interpreted as a reference to Paul's Damascus transformation. Both of these passages support the notion that much of Paul's self-perception as an apostle and minister stems from his certainty of having met with Christ unexpectedly on the way to Damascus.

God's Grace Shown in Paul's Calling and Ministry

As seen already in Gal 1:13–15 and 1 Cor 15:9–10, Paul marvels at God's gracious selection of him as an apostle, in spite of his history as a persecutor of the church. In Gal 1:13–14, Paul submits both his opposition to the church and his zealous commitment to Judaism as evidence of his being a surprising choice for God's selection for Christian ministry.[11] The mention of grace in Gal 1:15 underscores the point that God's calling was totally unmerited and unprovoked by Paul's track record. Galatians 1:23–24 further supports this understanding, since there Paul's turnabout from persecutor to advocate is cause for surprise and results in crediting God for the change. The focus on grace in Gal 1:15 supports the larger argument of the divine origin of Paul's gospel and apostleship.

The passage in 1 Cor 15:9–10 illustrates a similar point, with the first two of three references to grace signifying Paul's unanticipated reception

---

more generally to the Christian's knowledge of Christ (see the similar wording applied generally in 2 Cor 4:4). For Phil 3:12, the remarks describe Paul's own situation, but the verse lacks any explicit language of Christ being seen or revealed, so the association with the Damascus road vision remains uncertain.

11. Philippians 3:6 also makes a connection between zeal and persecuting the church, though in that context, Paul is highlighting how the apparent benefits of his old life are now understood as nothing in the light of knowing Christ. The unexpected grace of Paul's apostolic calling is not the primary interest in that passage, even though some interpreters detect an indirect allusion to the Damascus road in 3:12 (Kim, *Origin of Paul's Gospel*, 3; Bockmuehl, *Revelation and Mystery*, 136–37).

of his apostolic ministry. Paul's first reflection on God's grace in 15:10a is provoked by a recollection of his unworthiness as an apostle, based on his prior attempts to hinder God's work (1 Cor 15:9). A second mention of grace in 15:10a refers back to this grace of calling. But then an additional feature of God's grace to Paul is shown to arise in Paul's ongoing ministry in 15:10b. God's selection of Paul has been vindicated in the results of his ministry, which in turn is attributed to God's work through Paul. God's grace thus serves to launch Paul's ministry and to give it success.

Paul also highlights God's grace of calling Paul to ministry in passages other than those explicitly concerned with the Damascus road event. In Gal 2:9, the apostles in Jerusalem are reported to have acknowledged God's grace in Paul's calling. Though Paul does associate grace with salvation elsewhere (Gal 1:6; 2:21; 5:4; 1 Cor 1:4; 2 Cor 4:15; 6:1; 8:9; Rom 5:2, 15, 17), this is an instance in which Paul connects grace with his ministry mandate.[12] The preceding verses contend that Paul has been entrusted with the gospel to the uncircumcised (Gal 2:7) and that his ministry resembles Peter's apostleship (2:8), so the topic of Paul's ministry is clearly in view. In particular, Paul's ministry is oriented towards the Gentiles (2:8–9). Paul describes his ministry to the Gentiles as a product of God's grace.

In 1 Cor 3:10 Paul uses a phrase resembling the one from Gal 2:9 (κατὰ τὴν χάριν τὴν δοθεῖσαν μοι) to describe his labor of ministry. This occurrence reflects Paul's propensity to give God the credit for any constructive service Paul accomplishes (see also Rom 15:18; 1 Cor 15:10; 2 Cor 1:12). This suggests that for Paul, though grace often indicates his calling in contrast to his past as a persecutor, in some settings it highlights the source of Paul's ongoing ministry success. This latter aspect of grace is also tied closely to giftedness in ministry (see Rom 12:6). The reference to a foundation (θεμέλιος) sheds additional light on Paul's specific ministry contribution and gift. He views his calling in terms of breaking new ground, which is consistent with a Gentile-oriented ministry (see 2 Cor 10:14–16; Rom 15:20).[13] In short, the reference to grace in this verse emphasizes God as the source of Paul's success, and foundational ministry (especially to the Gentiles) as the essence of his calling.

Related to the grace behind ministry success is the grace for personal endurance in the midst of hardship in Phil 1:7. Grace appears to be applied

---

12. For Paul, his own salvation and ministry calling were realized at the same time on the journey to Damascus (with Schütz, *Paul and the Anatomy of Apostolic Authority*, 134; Fung, "Revelation and Tradition," 32).

13. See Munck, *Paul and the Salvation of Mankind*, 49; Fee, *The First Epistle to the Corinthians*, 137–38.

specifically to a ministry context in this passage, according to Paul's reference to his imprisonment and defense and confirmation of the gospel. The description of the Philippians being "co-sharers" with Paul of God's grace in this ministry context suggests that through the Philippians' support of Paul they are becoming sharers with Paul in the grace he experiences in his ministry. Most likely then, the grace in view here is not the grace of salvation but the grace upholding Paul (along with the Philippians) in ministry.[14] Paul once again recognizes that God's support is essential for helping him carry out his ministry.

Romans 1:5 exhibits a likely relationship between God's grace and Paul's calling. Grace and apostleship are paired together and described as having been received through Christ. It is likely that Paul intends to characterize the grace of his ministry under the broader category of the endowment of gifts to all believers.[15] Paul's specific gift is carried out in the ministry of apostleship. The stated purpose for this endowment of grace is to foster the obedience of faith among the Gentiles. Coupled with Rom 1:13, Paul insinuates that the scope of his Gentile ministry encompasses a sense of stewardship for Gentile congregations that did not originate from his ministry.[16] Nothing indicates that Paul has his misguided past in view here, as is the case in Gal 1:13–16 and 1 Cor 15:9–10.

Unlike the instance in Rom 1:5, the grace in Rom 12:3 is restricted to Paul alone. Paul draws on his gracious calling in order to deliver a direct and authoritative challenge to his readers. This reference to grace has the effect of reminding the Romans of both Paul's apostolic authority and his unworthiness to have received that calling.[17] At the same time, Paul then proceeds to affirm the similar grace working among the Roman believers (Rom 12:6–8), as they exercise their gifts in ministry.[18] For Paul, the experience of grace is not limited to his own ministry, yet grace is manifested

14. The verbal form of grace (χαρίζομαι) surfaces in this very context in 1:29. See Hawthorne, *Philippians*, 23; Schenk, *Die Philipperbriefe des Paulus*, 105; Fee, *Philippians*, 91; Bockmuehl, *Philippians*, 63.

15. See BDF §280; Byrne, *Romans*, 40.

16. Clark, "Apostleship," 52.

17. With Cranfield, *Romans*, 2:612; Fitzmyer, *Romans*, 645; Moo, *Romans*, 760. Contrary to Best, "Paul's Apostolic Authority?," 9, Paul's apostolic authority, while not mentioned explicitly in this passage, may be assumed throughout the letter, given the way Paul introduces himself in the letter in terms of his apostleship (1:1, 5) and applies his apostleship directly to the Gentiles (1:5; 11:13). This same reasoning can also be employed for the mention of grace and its connection to authority in Rom 15:15–16.

18. Dunn, *Romans*, 2:720. Byrne also summarizes nicely the relationship between Christian gifts and Paul's apostleship (Byrne, *Romans*, 40).

uniquely in his ministry, based on the specific calling he received from God.

Later in Romans (15:15–16), Paul once again connects grace with his authoritative stance towards his readers.[19] Paul presents this reception of the grace of God as his basis for exhorting his readers. He perceives that this grace has been given for the sake of his ministry to the Gentiles. Paul draws upon his gracious calling, given by God, for ministry to Gentiles as the basis of his confident authority towards them. In the process of exercising his authority towards the Gentile Christians in Rome, Paul demonstrates his assumption that his ministry extends to all Gentiles, and the wording of Rom 15:16 confirms this perspective. Using the language of priestly service, Paul explains that his offering to God consists of the fruit of his ministry among the Gentiles (Rom 15:16). This is further echoed in Rom 15:18, where Paul attributes the "obedience of the Gentiles" to the work of Christ through Paul's ministry. God's grace compels Paul to fulfill this ministry with all diligence (Rom 15:18–19). Thus, the operation of God's grace in Paul is seen in effective ministry to Gentiles, such as those believers meeting together in the Gentile city of Rome. In conclusion, God's grace for Paul both establishes the legitimacy of his ministry to Gentile believers and empowers him for ongoing service to the Gentiles.

The sum of these verses on God's grace reveals several facets of God's gracious endowment of ministry to Paul. First, in several cases grace is mentioned in the context of God's dramatic reversal of Paul's orientation towards God's work. Second, grace is used to refer to the divine origins of Paul's apostolic calling and thus carries a strong connotation of authority. Third, grace at times refers to the divine source of Paul's ongoing ministry fruitfulness. Fourth, Paul's ministry received by grace is often tied to the goal of reaching the Gentiles. Finally, the grace received brings with it Paul's obligation to carry out his ministry faithfully. In chapter 5 of this book the emphasis on grace in Eph 3:1–13 will be analyzed in relation to these passages and the perspectives on grace reflected in them.

---

19. The wording once again echoes Gal 2:9; 1 Cor 3:10; and Rom 12:3. There also may be parallels to Rom 1:1–15. Based on a common emphasis on Paul's apostleship and ministry to the Gentiles, Rom 1:1–15 and 15:14–33 have been seen as parallel segments within the structure of the letter (Chae, *Paul as Apostle to the Gentiles*, 21, 38–39).

Revelation and Mystery

Closely associated with Paul's Damascus experience and calling is God's revelation of the mystery of the gospel. As part of his calling to ministry, Paul believed that he had received divine revelation about God's saving work through Christ (see Gal 1:11–12). Paul felt obligated to impart this revealed insight, which he sometimes called a "mystery" (μυστήριον), to those he taught. As a minister, Paul was not operating according to his own whims but was constrained by the calling God had initiated and the truth God had revealed to him and other chosen ministers.

Because of the frequent appearance of μυστήριον in Colossians and Ephesians and the charge by some that the sense of the word has undergone modification when compared to Paul's original understanding, Paul's use of this term in his undisputed letters will receive extended treatment in this section.[20] Though Paul follows no fixed pattern in discussing the mystery in his undisputed letters, the composite testimony derived from the various passages provides a template against which to evaluate the relevant passages from Colossians and Ephesians.

Paul discloses revelation using the language of mystery in 1 Cor 2:7; 4:1; 15:51; Rom 11:25; 16:25–26.[21] The term also arises in 1 Cor 13:2 and 14:2, but within those contexts, Paul speaks of mysteries broadly as a description of divine knowledge, and the topic of Paul's calling is not under investigation. The term also surfaces frequently in the disputed Pauline letters (Eph 1:9; 3:3, 4, 9; 6:19; Col 1:26, 27; 2:2; 4:3; 2 Thess 2:7; 1 Tim 3:9, 16), though these verses will not be considered in this section. The topic of Paul's understanding of the revealed mystery has attracted extended treatment in works from recent decades, with the consensus position being that Paul's concept of mystery derives from the Jewish conception of

---

20. For the claim that μυστήριον carries a different sense in Colossians and Ephesians, see for example Mitton, *Ephesians: Its Authorship, Origin, and Purpose*, 88–90; E. P. Sanders, "Literary Dependence in Colossians," 39–40.

21. The textual uncertainty of Rom 16:25–26 will be explored later in this section. Another possible occurrence of μυστήριον in 1 Cor 2:1 will not be examined in detail, since as suggested by relatively weak external support, the term most likely does not occur in Paul's original letter. Even if it were acknowledged to be the original reading, Paul's lack of elaboration on the term in that verse would hinder efforts to fully understand Paul's conception of the mystery from this verse alone. At most, if original to 2:1, mystery would refer to a divine message associated with the work of Christ on the cross (2:2), and Paul's inclusion of the term would demonstrate his propensity to incorporate the term as shorthand for his gospel.

divine truth to which humans gain access only through divine revelation.²² The content of the mystery is related particularly to Christ's death and resurrection, along with the saving benefits of Christ's work in the lives of believing Jews and Gentiles.

Sometimes Paul incorporates the idea of mystery in his letters to underscore the entire breadth of Christ's work and its implications. This is the case in 1 Cor 2:7; 4:1, and Rom 16:25–26.

In 1 Cor 2:1–16, Paul relates the mystery to God's wisdom, a wisdom that can only be discerned by the Spirit among the mature. This "wisdom in mystery" consists of a proclaimed message about Christ and his cross, by which believers are assured of an eschatological victory. In 1 Cor 2:7 Paul enlists the concept of mystery to further describe divine wisdom.²³ Bockmuehl observes parallels between this wording and that which is found in Jewish literature, concluding that 1 Cor 2:7 conforms to the Jewish notion of mystery as that of God's disclosed salvific plans.²⁴ Following ἐν μυστηρίῳ is τὴν ἀποκεκρυμμένην, which modifies either the entire phrase (θεοῦ σοφίαν ἐν μυστηρίῳ) or simply σοφίαν. Either way, in the concept of hiddenness, Paul begins to unpack what it means that God's wisdom is ἐν μυστηρίῳ.²⁵ God's "wisdom in mystery" involves a hidden dimension, because God has withheld the knowledge of its contents.

But does Paul in this passage understand truth to be concealed with regard to time or to audience, or perhaps to both? Some scholars make the case that the revealed/hidden division in this passage separates the spiritually discerning from the spiritually dull, not present disclosure of truth from past hiddenness.²⁶ Paul makes this chief concern clear in the contrast presented in 1 Cor 2:6–16. Paul begins by specifying that God's wisdom

---

22. Bockmuehl understands correctly that this divine revelation encompasses both the Christ event and Paul's (and other mediators') divinely enabled apprehension of its significance (Bockmuehl, *Revelation and Mystery*, 133–37). The Jewish precedent for the role of mediators in the dissemination of the mystery is found in passages such as Dan 2:18–19, 30, 47, where Daniel is the mediator, and 1QpHab 7:1–2, where the Teacher of Righteousness receives and imparts the revelation.

23. The phrase ἐν μυστηρίῳ modifies either the preceding verb λαλοῦμεν or the noun σοφίαν. The resulting difference is not drastic, though the preferred understanding in this section is the latter of the two options.

24. Bockmuehl, *Revelation and Mystery*, 161.

25. As pointed out by Raymond Brown, the association of mystery with wisdom occurs in Jewish literature known to Paul (Brown, *"Mystery" in the New Testament*, 41–42).

26. See Merklein, *Das kirchliche Amt nach dem Epheserbrief*, 168; Grindheim, "Wisdom for the Perfect," 698–701; Garland, *1 Corinthians*, 96.

has been designed for reception by the spiritually mature (οἱ τέλειοι).[27] Paul then expounds upon the differentiation between those who reject and accept God's message. God's revealed wisdom through Christ has not been ascertained by the powerful of this age (1 Cor 2:8), as demonstrated by their crucifixion of the Lord. In contrast to the worldly representatives' oblivion to God's truth, believers apprehend God's revelation in Christ by God's Spirit (1 Cor 2:10).[28] Paul further specifies the Spirit's role in disclosing truth in 2:11–13.[29] The primary contrast between the spiritually perceptive and the spiritually blind is once more articulated in 2:14–16. In view of the impressive contextual support for this perspective, it is likely that this demarcation is the main topic in the context.

This conclusion, however, does not rule out all concern for an underlying pattern that distinguishes past hiddenness from present disclosure. Paul's discussion of the gospel here assumes an unveiling of this mystery in the present age, even if the main emphasis remains on the Spirit's work in the process.[30] It is clear that Paul sees himself as a mouthpiece for announcing God's wisdom in mystery in this passage (see the first person language of 2:4–7, as well as Paul's mention of preaching as the vehicle of salvation in 1:21). Finally, a marked transition from past hiddenness to present revelation is reinforced in the contrast between truth concealed in 2:9 and truth revealed in 2:10. Therefore, God's wisdom in mystery is revealed in Paul's generation through the preaching about Christ and the cross.

Paul's mystery is based on the cross but also points to eschatological horizons. Paul's thesis starting in 1 Cor 1:18 has been that God's wisdom

---

27. The meaning of τέλειος here denotes those who receive God's word by the Spirit as opposed to those who are spiritually resistant. When Paul chastises the Corinthians for their immaturity in 1 Cor 3:1–3, the rebuke carries a sting precisely because they demonstrated maturity by receiving Paul's message in the first place, but their subsequent actions suggest otherwise. See Grindheim, "Wisdom for the Perfect," 702–9; Carson, "Mystery and Fulfillment," 416–17.

28. The surrounding context (especially 2:9 and 2:12) suggests that in 2:10 all believers rather than chosen ministers are recipients of the Spirit's revelation (agreeing with Robertson and Plummer, *First Epistle of St. Paul to the Corinthians*, 43; Fee, *First Epistle to the Corinthians*, 109; Grindheim, "Wisdom for the Perfect," 705; *contra* Kim, *Origin of Paul's Gospel*, 77; Bockmuehl, *Revelation and Mystery*, 164–65).

29. These three verses illustrate the dual components of how God's wisdom is received by listeners (2:11–12) and the role of messengers in proclaiming the truth (2:13). This dual emphasis is consistent with the two threads seen throughout the passage.

30. See Carson, "Mystery and Fulfillment," 417–18.

in the cross represents his power to bring eternal salvation to believers.[31] Paul continues a discussion of the eschatological benefits of God's wisdom in 1 Cor 2:7b. Since before the beginning of time God designed his work in Christ with a view towards the believer's ultimate benefit. In contrast to believers who will possess eschatological blessings in Christ, the rulers of the age have crucified the Lord of glory (1 Cor 2:8). In other words, they tragically appraised Christ as worthless even though he was actually the power of God and the wisdom of God (1:24) and was himself destined for glory.[32] Paul captures the beauty and eschatological orientation of this divine and hidden wisdom with a free rendition of one or more OT passages in 1 Cor 2:9.[33]

In this passage as a whole Paul's description of wisdom ἐν μυστηρίῳ encompasses the spiritually perceived significance of Christ's saving work on the cross (1 Cor 2:2; 1:18). Though Paul proclaims God's eternal wisdom as definitively located in Christ and his crucifixion, it is the reception and understanding of this message among others that Paul discusses at greater length. The idea of mystery in this passage is tied closely to wisdom, the work of the Spirit, the significance of the cross, and the promise of glory for the believer. The subtle implication of the passage is that Paul is a spokesperson responsible for proclaiming God's mystery.

In 1 Cor 4:1, the plural form "mysteries" surfaces in a passage describing Paul's stewardship from God. The significance of the plural form

---

31. Note the emphasis on power and salvation in 1 Cor 1:18, 21, 24.

32. Similarly, Robertson and Plummer note that the phrase highlights "the contrast between the indignity of the Cross and the majesty of the victim" (Robertson and Plummer, *First Epistle of St. Paul to the Corinthians*, 40). Kim suggests that the title "Lord of glory" recalls Paul's encounter with Christ on the road to Damascus (Kim, *Origin of Paul's Gospel*, 79).

33. The contrasting tone of the conjunction ἀλλά, which introduces the OT wording, probably communicates an ironic rebuke to the rulers of this age, who when they crucified Jesus were oblivious to the fact that Jesus was the means of God's deliverance for the people. In Isa 64:2–3 (MT), the passage most likely shaping the saying Paul adopts, the prophet begins by highlighting the unexpected character of God's past display of power in the days of Moses (64:2). This reminiscence of God's unanticipated deliverance in the past directs the prophet in 64:3 to the God who is characterized by his unforeseen and unparalleled work for the sake of those who wait for him (see Watts, *Isaiah 34–66*, 335; Oswalt, *Isaiah: Chapters 40–66*, 622–23). For Paul, it is obvious that this deliverance was granted in the person of the "Lord of glory" (1 Cor 2:8). At some point in early Christianity, either before or after Paul's time, the first part of the quotation began to circulate as a set phrase, and it appears in places such as *Gos. Thom.* 17 and 1 *Clem.* 34:8 (Kremer, *Der Erste Briefe an die Korinther*, 59; Lindemann, *Der Erste Korintherbrief*, 67).

Portrait of an Apostle

of the word is difficult to ascertain, since later occurrences in the plural may not be relevant to the meaning in 4:1.[34] The suggestion that the plural accords well with a steward's responsibility to oversee multiple areas is as good as any.[35] The immediate context depicting Paul's ministry in 1 Cor 4:1 suggests that the mysteries relate to the content of Paul's gospel.[36] But the passage highlights the enactment of Paul's ministry rather than the content of his message, so Paul may speak of mysteries generally here, without any specific component of the mysteries squarely in view. Instead, Paul refers to any truth relevant to God's will, as revealed to Paul and other ministers of the gospel.

The mysteries reflect the intersection of the divine and human spheres. On the one hand, the mysteries of 4:1 are regarded as God's mysteries, so they are divine in origin. On the other hand, the mysteries are truths that are now granted to human messengers. The title of steward (οἰκονόμος) indicates that God's mysteries are things that have been entrusted to Paul.[37] This concept supports Paul's contention that he must answer to God for the faithfulness of his service (1 Cor 4:2–5). Paul elaborates on this idea of stewardship later in 1 Cor 9:16–17, where he brings attention to his obligation to please God in his service. In short, 1 Cor 4:1 portrays Paul's relationship to the mysteries of God without divulging the exact contents of the mysteries. Paul identifies himself as one of the appointed custodians of God's divine revelation.

The third passage yielding a broad meaning for mystery is found in Rom 16:25–26. Many scholars dispute the authenticity of the doxology (16:25–27).[38] External and internal factors must be taken into account when making judgments about authenticity. With regard to manuscript evidence, skeptics of the Pauline origin of the doxology point primarily to its inconsistent placement in various ancient manuscripts. But while the witnesses preserve different locations for 16:25–27, the material is still

---

34. While the mention of mysteries in 1 Cor 4:1 carries the plural form found in the references in 1 Cor 13:2 and 14:2, the later verses arise in the course of discussion that is markedly different from the discourse of 1:10–4:23.

35. See Kremer, *Der Erste Briefe an die Korinther*, 83; Lindemann, *Der Erste Korintherbrief*, 96.

36. See Barrett, *First Epistle to the Corinthians*, 99–100; Fee, *First Epistle to the Corinthians*, 159; Kremer, *Der Erste Briefe an die Korinther*, 83.

37. For a discussion of οἰκονόμος in 1 Cor 4:1–2, see Reumann, "Οἰκονομία—Terms in Paul," 160–61.

38. See Cranfield, *Romans*, 1:6–8; Dunn, *Romans*, 2:913; and many others.

present in the vast majority of extant manuscripts and versions.[39] The list of witnesses is particularly impressive for the doxology's location at the end of Rom 16.[40] Definitive conclusions for what led to the relocation, subtraction, or addition of the doxology are elusive.[41] Any plausible reconstruction of the textual history of the ending of Romans that assumes the originality of the doxology is not without problems.[42] The lack of a plausible explanation for what gave rise to the diverse manuscript testimony if the original form of Romans was Rom 1:1—16:27 casts some degree of doubt on the Pauline origins of Rom 16:25–26.[43]

From an analysis of the style and wording of the doxology, arguments may be put forward for both positions. On the one hand, certain verbal and thematic correspondences between 1:1–5 and 16:25–26 create a sense of coherence in the letter as a whole, suggesting that 16:25–27 was an essential part of the original letter. The connections include the gospel, the prophets and the Scriptures, the obedience of faith, and ministry among or unto all the Gentiles. On the other hand, the benediction of 16:20 (or 16:24) is a more typical way for Paul to end a letter, and some of the vocabulary in the doxology is considered non-Pauline.[44] Arguments from language and style are notoriously subjective, and the presuppositions regarding the dating of other Pauline letters make the issue in this case especially problematic.[45] When all is considered, the support from early

39. The exceptions are F, G, 629, a couple of old Latin versions, and manuscripts known by Jerome.

40. Manuscripts supporting this location include P61, ℵ, B, C, 81, 1739, 2464, and a variety of versions. D also contains this reading, though Metzger argues that based on an altered format of writing that begins in verse 25 in D, it is likely that Rom 16:25–27 was absent in the manuscript from which the scribe of D was copying (Metzger, *Textual Commentary on the Greek New Testament*, 471–72).

41. For judicious treatments of relevant factors in the evaluation of the location of the doxology see Bruce, *Romans*, 26–30; Guthrie, *New Testament Introduction*, 417–425. Bruce and Guthrie both favor the view that Paul included the doxology in his original letter.

42. For extensive analysis of this puzzle, see Gamble, *Textual History of the Letter to the Romans*, 96–132, 141.

43. Agreeing with Collins, the lack of uniformity in the location of the doxology is the most persuasive evidence against the view that Paul originally included the doxology in his letter (R. Collins, "The Case of a Wandering Doxology: Rom 16,25–27," 295).

44. See for instance Gamble, *Textual History of the Letter to the Romans*, 123; Jewett, *Romans*, 998–1002.

45. For a brief critique of the style and language arguments, see Marshall, "Romans 16:25–27—An Apt Conclusion," 172. Many studies on the language of the doxology

manuscripts and the thematic connections that point towards authenticity are somewhat counteracted by likely reconstructions of the passage's history. Given the resulting doubts about the authenticity of the passage, its contribution to Paul's thought will be assessed with caution.

The passage portrays a gospel that is revealed in the unveiling of the mystery. The essence of the gospel (εὐαγγέλιον) and Christian preaching (κήρυγμα) is summarized by a detailed depiction of the revealed mystery of Christ. According to the passage, the previously hidden mystery has now been revealed. This characterization is consistent with Paul's description of mystery in 1 Corinthians and elsewhere in Romans, though the division between past hiddenness and present revelation is more marked here.

In the bulk of Rom 16:26, a description of the reception of the mystery is put forward, with the main assertion that the mystery has been made known. The author submits that the grasp of the mystery's significance arrived through the prophetic Scriptures[46] and according to God's authoritative decree. This pairing introduces a tension that fits within the wider Pauline balance between continuity and discontinuity with regards to the gospel's relationship to the OT Scriptures.[47] As Rom 16:26 continues, it is indicated that the purpose of the revelation of the mystery is to engender the obedience of faith among all the Gentiles, echoing language from Rom 1:5.[48] Such wording in Rom 16:25–26 shows that the revealed mystery entails a specific application for Gentiles, which is consistent with Paul's apostleship to the Gentiles (Rom 11:13). On the whole, the passage portrays a revealed mystery that is equivalent to Paul's gospel and preaching. By divine initiative and in continuity with past revelation, the mystery is unveiled for the purpose of fostering faith among the Gentiles.

---

begin with the debatable assumption that Ephesians, Colossians, and the Pastoral Epistles are post-Pauline (Elliott, "The Language and Style of the Concluding Doxology to the Epistle to the Romans," 124–30; R. Collins, "The Case of a Wandering Doxology," 297–303; Byrne, *Romans*, 461).

46. The prophetic writings designate the OT Scriptures (Dunn, *Romans*, 2:915; Bockmuehl, *Revelation and Mystery*, 207–8; Fitzmyer, *Romans*, 754; Moo, *Romans*, 940; Carson, "Mystery and Fulfillment," 423).

47. See Marshall, "Romans 16:25–27," 181; Carson, "Mystery and Fulfillment," 423. The rootedness of Paul's own commissioning within the OT Scriptures will be examined in the next major section.

48. Both passages in turn may allude to Gen 49:10, where Jacob envisions the subjugation of the nations to Judah's royal descendant (Beale, *John's Use of the Old Testament in Revelation*, 239–41).

In contrast to the all-encompassing descriptions of mystery in the passages above, 1 Cor 15:51 and Rom 11:25 incorporate the term μυστήριον to highlight one aspect of the broader notion of mystery.[49] In 1 Cor 15:51 Paul attests to the mystery of the bodily resurrection. As in previous passages, the mystery is understood to be revealed in Paul's proclamation of it. It is no longer inaccessible knowledge.[50] Once again, the mystery has continuity with past revelation, since the bodily resurrection was referred to or alluded to in passages such as Dan 12:2, Isa 25:8; 26:19, and Hos 13:14.[51] But Paul's talk of mystery signals that he is now offering a more complete understanding of the resurrection. The resurrection, which is patterned after Christ's death and resurrection and is tied to Christ's return, has implication for both those who are dead and those who are alive at Christ's *parousia*.[52] Specifically, since flesh and blood cannot inherit the kingdom of God (15:50), living believers, along with the dead, will receive glorified bodies at Christ's return.[53]

Two observations are in order about how this passage relates to other mystery sections. First, the eschatological dimension of mystery in this passage corresponds to the eschatological focus in 1 Cor 2:6–16. Second, in comparison to the general uses of mystery discussed earlier, the mystery here transmits a specific detail of God's revealed plans, but this important detail is still based on the central events of Christ's life, past and future.

In Rom 11:25–27, Paul imparts the mystery that for a season God is including the Gentiles in his plan of salvation before consummating the fulfillment of his promises to Israel.[54] This is presented as truth that

---

49. See Carson, "Mystery and Fulfillment," 414.

50. *Contra* Thiselton (*First Epistle to the Corinthians*, 1295), who detects a primary or exclusive reference to the inscrutability of the truth Paul is sharing.

51. The second and fourth of these verses are brought into the discussion in this passage by Paul himself in 1 Cor 15:54–55.

52. Christ's death and especially his resurrection form the basis for the whole discussion in 1 Cor 15. The relevance of Christ's return is indicated in 1 Cor 15:23 and implied in 15:51–52 (especially considering the parallels to 1 Thess 4:13–17).

53. See Fee, *First Epistle to the Corinthians*, 799; Thiselton, *First Epistle to the Corinthians*, 1295. This interpretation assumes the originality of the text attested by B, Ψ, 048, 075, 1881, the majority text, and others for 1 Cor 15:51 (see Metzger, *Textual Commentary on the Greek New Testament*, 502; Fee, *First Epistle to the Corinthians*, 796; Thiselton, *First Epistle to the Corinthians*, 1293).

54. Agreeing with the majority of recent commentators, "Israel" denotes the physical descendants of Israel (Cranfield, *Romans*, 2:576–77; Hafemann, "The Salvation of Israel in Romans 11:25–32," 53; Fitzmyer, *Romans*, 62–24; Moo, *Romans*, 720–22; Schreiner, *Romans*, 614–15; Byrne, *Romans*, 350; Osborne, *Romans*, 305–6; *contra* Wright, *The Climax of the Covenant*, 250).

the readers had not previously grasped. Though the broad background of God's salvation through Christ is present in these verses, it is the specific timing and direction of God's work that is magnified.[55] In particular, the mystery involves the place of Jews and Gentiles in God's saving plans. Paul sees the mission to the Gentiles being brought to completion before salvation for Israel is realized.[56] God's promises to the Jewish people are not eradicated but instead facilitated by ministry progress among the Gentiles.[57] Once again, Paul emphasizes continuity with God's redemptive patterns from the past, using a conflation of OT passages to support his assertions. But it is the reality of God's intervention through Christ in human history that brings the order and timing of God's work into clearer focus. In addition, as a chosen herald of God's revelation, Paul plays a part in the revelation of the mystery by speaking authoritatively about matters that were previously hidden from view. Once again, the passage discusses events with eschatological significance.

The overall testimony of the passages depicting the revelation of the mystery in relation to Paul's ministry is that Paul viewed himself as an agent of God in proclaiming the full implications of Christ's advent, death, resurrection, and return. Paul draws upon patterns of expectation shaped by the Old Testament but contends that the clear significance of God's work in history has been hidden in the eternal plans of God until God has disclosed them by means of the revelation of Christ, the ministry of

---

55. Christ and his saving work on the cross are understood as the means of Israel's ingathering in this passage (Viard, *Épître aux Romains*, 248–49; Fitzmyer, *Romans*, 620).

56. The fullness of the Gentiles may draw upon Jewish eschatological notions found in literature contemporary to Paul's letters (Fitzmyer, *Romans*, 621–22; Moo, *Romans*, 718–19; Osborne, *Romans*, 305). Paul's own ministry is an essential part of God's revealed plans for Jews and Gentiles, since he is an apostle to the Gentiles (Rom 11:13) and spares no effort to reach all of the Gentiles in his sphere of ministry (see Rom 15:19, where the related verbal form πληρόω surfaces in relation to Paul's accomplishment of his ministry among the Gentiles). The parallel to the πλήρωμα of the Jews in Rom 11:12 has also been noted (Spencer, "Metaphor, Mystery and the Salvation of Israel in Romans 9–11," 124).

57. This agrees with the view that the ὅτι that introduces the substance of the mystery points to the whole of 11:25 and 11:26a, so that Israel's initial rejection of the gospel, the Gentiles' subsequent reception, and the resulting salvation of Israel are all in view (See Cranfield, *Romans*, 2:574; Carson, "Mystery and Fulfillment," 419–21). Furthermore, the οὕτως of 11:26 functions non-temporally with an anaphoric force, so that Paul refers to antecedent material (especially 11:25) in order to indicate the manner of Israel's salvation (Cranfield, *Romans*, 2:576; Wright, *The Climax of the Covenant*, 249–50; Moo, *Romans*, 719–20; Osborne, *Romans*, 305).

Paul's Identity in the Undisputed Letters

approved messengers such as Paul, and the work of the Spirit in illuminating God's truth to believers. 1 Corinthians 2:6–16 relates the mystery to God's wisdom, future glory, and the work of the Spirit, while 1 Cor 4:1 attaches Paul's stewardship of the mystery to the picture. Several instances examine the eschatological aspect of the mystery. From Rom 11:25–27 and, if it is admitted into evidence, Rom 16:25–26, the inclusion of the Gentiles in these redemptive plans is one component of the revelatory content of the mystery.

The Old Testament Foundation to Paul's Ministry to the Gentiles

Even though Paul's encounter with Christ and his reception of the revealed mystery occurred suddenly and without any expectation on Paul's part, his ministry was nonetheless rooted in Israel's past. Paul's self-understanding is grounded in the OT background of the ministry of the servant figure of Isaiah 40–66. Paul confirms this backdrop most explicitly in Gal 1:15–16, 2 Cor 6:2, and Rom 15:21.[58]

To begin, Gal 1:15–16 is shaped by the consecration language of Isa 49:1, 5–6. In the literary context of Gal 1–2, Paul is defending the divine origins of his calling and his gospel. His service to God is not a result of his own choice and initiative but of God's sovereign selection of him before birth. This selection corresponds to the consecration of the servant of Isaiah.

The connections from Gal 1 to Isa 49:1–6 are stronger than to Jer 1:5, which speaks of Jeremiah's prophetic call. In addition, there are many more major references elsewhere in Paul's letters to Isa 40–66 than to Jeremiah, so the primary influence on Paul's thinking is likely Isa 49.[59] In particular, the phrase ἐκ κοιλίας μητρός μου from Gal 1:15 parallels the LXX reading of Isa 49:1. This is followed in Gal 1:15 by a form of καλέω,

---

58. Acts 13:47; 26:16–18 add additional support to the notion that these OT passages shaped Paul's identity. Acts 13:47 quotes Isa 49:6 as justification for Paul and Barnabas' mission to the Gentiles. In a more indirect reference, Acts 26:16–18 arguably picks up on light and darkness imagery found in Isa 42:6–7, as well as the language of appointment for a mission to the Gentiles (v. 6).

59. Holtz, "Zum Selbstverständnis des Apostels Paulus," 325–30. See also Webb, *Returning Home*, 129. Witherington favors Jer 1:5 as the primary source for the allusion, while allowing for the relevance to Paul's wording of Isa 49:1–6 as well (Witherington III, *Grace in Galatia*, 105).

a verb that also occurs after ἐκ κοιλίας μητρός μου in Isa 49:1.[60] A look at the broader context of Isaiah 49 will reveal other ways Paul likely drew upon the passage.

In the overall structure of Isaiah 40–66, a shift in directions occurs at the beginning of chapter 49.[61] This turn is seen clearly in the changing portrayal of the servant. No longer a mere "passive servant," as in the preceding chapters, he is "that servant who was introduced at the beginning of the previous section (42:1–9), who will be God's agent to bring his covenant to the people and his justice to the nations."[62] This servant no longer appears to be equated with the people of Israel as a whole, but rather is an individual representing Israel.[63] Israel has failed in its role as a servant, so the text introduces God's specially chosen servant who will fulfill Israel's role.[64]

Chapter 49 begins with an address to "islands" and "peoples from afar," which foreshadows the focus on the nations in 49:6–7.[65] The speaker proceeds to emphasize his calling as Yahweh's servant ("the LORD called me from the womb; from the body of my mother he named me"), in wording that echoes previous similar occurrences in earlier chapters (Isa 41:8–9; 42:1; 43:1,10; 44:1,21,24; 45:4). The nature of the servant's ministry is reemphasized in verse 2, with a focus on the mouth of the servant as his key weapon. Thus the servant's role as a herald of God's message is at the forefront of this passage.

Verse 3 shows the ultimate purpose of the servant's ministry: as God's servant, he was appointed to put God's glory on display. A representative function of the servant is in view here, with a chosen individual standing in for Israel, who had failed in living out its calling to glorify God.[66]

---

60. Jeremiah 1:5 shares the words κοιλία and μήτηρ, though not in the same combination or forms as in Gal 1:15. It does, however, include an emphasis on the nations, which is also reflected in Gal 1:16. Holtz cautions, however, that Jeremiah's ministry to the Gentiles lacked the saving purpose that is found in the servant of Isaiah's mission (Holtz, "Zum Selbstverständnis des Apostels Paulus," 328).

61. Wilcox and Paton-Williams, "The Servant Songs in Deutero-Isaiah," 80–81.

62. Oswalt, *Isaiah 40–66*, 286–87.

63. This common view is held by Goldingay, *The Message of Isaiah 40–55*, 371; Oswalt, *Isaiah 40–66*, 291–92; Childs, *Isaiah*, 384–85; Seitz, "'You Are My Servant,'" 128.

64. Wilcox and Paton-Williams, "Servant Songs," 92; Gignilliat, *Paul and Isaiah's Servants*," 73–74, 86.

65. Goldingay, *The Message of Isaiah 40–55*, 366.

66. The identification of the servant with Israel in this verse would seem to support the position that Israel as a whole is still the referent of the title. But the overall context

The ongoing reality of Israel's failure to heed God's message provoked the servant to discouragement, as reflected in verse 4. The language of the LXX here (κενῶς ἐκοπίασα) is most probably echoed in a number of Paul's letters.[67] The contrast between a glorious calling and lack of visible success prompted the servant to renew his trust in God and his obedience to God's calling ("my reward is with my God").

Verse 5 reiterates the servant's prior calling from verse 1 ("the Lord, who formed me from the womb to be his servant") and also expands on it. In this verse the new identity of the servant as an individual rather than corporate Israel emerges most clearly. The servant's prophetic ministry is to be directed to Israel, with the goal of bringing back and gathering Israel to Yahweh. At the end of the verse, the servant responds in gratitude and wonder about the nature of his calling. The significance of the servant is found in his role as God's chosen instrument.

The servant's calling is not limited to Israel but is expanded to encompass the nations in verse 6. The term "salvation," so common in Isa 40–66, is now extended to both Israel and the nations. Yahweh is entrusting the servant with a ministry of salvation that will stretch to the ends of the earth. The precise relationship of the servant to God's salvation is rendered differently in various translations.[68] The resulting meaning includes possibilities spanning from the servant carrying the message of salvation to the servant embodying salvation in his person. An interpretation on the latter end of the spectrum draws support from the servant's role as more than a messenger, as displayed in 42:1–7, and from the brief reference in 49:7 to the servant being the focal point of a watching world in the midst of his humiliation and exaltation.[69] This theme receives more extended

---

of chapter 49 weakens this view, so the term Israel in this verse should be understood in a "predicate" rather than "vocative" sense (Wilcox and Paton-Williams, "Servant Songs," 93; see also Seitz, "Isaiah 40–66," 429; Goldingay, *The Message of Isaiah 40–55*, 369; Gignilliat, "2 Corinthians 6:2," 152). Wilcox and Paton-Williams note the scant textual support for the hypothesis that "Israel" was a later insertion ("Servant Songs," 90), *contra* Westermann, *Isaiah 40–66*, 209.

67. Gal 2:2; 1 Thess 2:2; 1 Cor 15:10, Phil 2:16; 2 Cor 6:1.

68. Some modern English versions translate the Hebrew clause להיות ישועי literally as "to be my salvation" or something similar (KJV, NKJV, HCSB). Similarly, the LXX has εἶναί σε εἰς σωτηρίαν. Others translate the clause along the lines of "that you may bring" (NIV, NLT, NET). Still others opt for God's salvation as the understood subject, rather than the servant, with a translation such as "that my salvation may reach" (NRSV, NASB, TNIV, ESV).

69. For the argument from 49:6–7 specifically, see Oswalt, *Isaiah 40–66*, 2:294–95.

treatment in Isa 52:13–53:12.[70] On the other hand, there is enough ambiguity with the clause to allow for a more general understanding of the servant as the bearer of God's saving work and message.[71]

Paul's call to ministry in Galatians 1 parallels the experience of the servant of Isa 49:1–6 in many ways. As was seen previously, Gal 1:11–16 Paul contends for the divine source of Paul's calling by incorporating wording similar to what is repeated in Isa 49:1, 5. Beyond the similarities in wording are conceptual affinities. Paul's calling entails a ministry of proclamation of the gospel (Gal 1:6–9, 11), resembling the "sharp sword" of the mouth that characterizes the servant's appointment (Isa 49:2). Paul recognizes that his sole concern is to please God with his ministry (Gal 1:10), just like the servant looks to God for his reward (49:4). Paul's ministry does not exclude the Jews but reaches beyond them to the Gentiles (Gal 1:16; 2:2, 8–9), in keeping with the expanded scope of the servant's ministry (Isa 49:6).[72] Paul still recognized Christ's work as the centerpiece of God's saving action for humanity (as indicated in Gal 1:4) and understood Christ's person and work as the content of his message (Gal 1:7, 16). But Paul so closely identified himself with Christ (see Gal 2:20) that he appears to have adopted the servant mission of Isa 49:1–6, though this calling is mediated through Christ's own unique sacrifice.

As seen from the preceding discussion, the prophetic call of the OT as represented particularly in the commission of the servant of Isa 49:1–6 shaped Paul's expectation of what his ministry encompassed. Paul draws from Isaiah 49 once again in 2 Corinthians 6:2. The analysis of Isa 49:1–6 already provided applies to 2 Corinthians 6 as well. The additional relevance of Isaiah 49 is explored beginning in Isa 49:7.

Isaiah 49:7 raises the prospect of suffering as an essential aspect of the servant's ministry, in addition to a calling already including proclamation (seen especially from 49:2).[73] The servant's humiliation, which is not

---

70. Though Paul would have applied this vision of the servant to Christ rather than to himself, it is possible that he understood his ministry from the perspective of being united with Christ in his suffering and glory, and thus sharing in the calling of the servant (Gal 2:20; 2 Cor 4:10–12; Phil 3:10–11). Paul's ministry of suffering will be further discussed later in this chapter.

71. Paul may have appropriated this more general perception out of deference to Christ's unique sacrificial work in God's plans, or he may have embraced the idea of embodying God's message through suffering, which represented his identification with the sufferings of Christ.

72. Paul's continued concern for the Jews emerges clearly in Rom 9–11.

73. If Isa 49:6 implies the servant's embodiment of salvation in his ministry, then 49:7 may simply be extending that line of thought.

developed extensively in this passage, is shown in a reversal of fortunes to result in glory, since surrounding rulers will ultimately pay homage to God's servant.[74] The conclusion of the verse with a reminder that God has chosen the servant demonstrates that the servant's certain future of exaltation is based on his certain calling. Until that day of honor, the conjunction of Isa 49:2 and 49:7 foreshadows the fact that suffering and proclamation are harmonious elements of the servant's ministry.

The next verses (8–13) are grouped with the preceding ones (1–7) through the connecting formula "Thus says the LORD."[75] At the hinge point of verse 8, Yahweh announces his intention to strengthen his servant for the purpose of bestowing salvation, with the effects of the salvation transforming both Israel and the nations of the world (v.6–7, 12–13). In 49:8a, Goldingay observes that the "religious freight" of the phrases "favorable time" and "day of salvation" is represented in the terms "favorable" and "salvation," rather than on the time markers.[76] The verbs exist in the perfect tense in the Hebrew, and may be characterized as "prophetic perfects"[77] or "perfects of certainty,"[78] indicating the promised realization of actions that are yet to unfold. Following verse 8a, the message proclaimed through the servant is couched in vivid language that may be grouped with the new exodus imagery found throughout Isa 40–66.[79] In view is God's glorious intervention in the land and in the lives of the people. The section ends in a universal call to praise with a mention of comfort that ties the passage to the greater themes of Isa 40–66, which began with a call of comfort from God.

Paul's use of Isa 49:8 in 2 Cor 6:2 fulfills two aims. First, 2 Cor 6:2 reflects that through Christ's death and resurrection, the day of salvation promised by God in Isaiah 40–66 has arrived, demanding full reception.[80] In the events of the death and resurrection of Christ, Paul sees the fulfillment of God's plans to redeem Israel and reconcile the world to himself.[81]

---

74. Later, in Isa 52:13—53:12, a similar note of triumph (52:13) precedes a more complete characterization of the servant's suffering, which is required for the sins of the nation. Gignilliat notes that in Isa 49:7 "the conceptual linkage to 52.13—53.12 echoes loudly" (Gignilliat, *Paul and Isaiah's Servants*, 74).

75. Childs, *Isaiah*, 386.

76. Goldingay, *The Message of Isaiah 40–55*, 376.

77. Webb, *Returning Home*, 139; Oswalt, *Isaiah 40–66*, 395.

78. Motyer, *The Prophecy of Isaiah*, 391.

79. Childs, *Isaiah*, 387; Webb, *Returning Home*, 133–36.

80. See the prior emphasis on this theme in 2 Cor 5:14–17.

81. Paul envisions the effects of this fulfillment reaching the whole world—Jews

This is supported earlier in the discourse, when Paul uses the time markers μηκέτι (v.15), ἀπὸ τοῦ νῦν and οὐκέτι (v.16), the pair of clauses τὰ ἀρχαῖα παρῆλθεν, ἰδοὺ γέγονεν καινά and the announcement of καινὴ κτίσις (v.17) to signal the abrupt change taking place in history as a result of Christ's death and resurrection.[82]

Second, 2 Cor 6:2 confirms that Paul understands his ministry through the lens of Isaiah 49. The broader context supports this as well. Paul's calling conforms to the servant's calling, since he serves God (5:11-13) and is motivated by Christ's love (5:14). His message of salvation aligns with the servant's message to Israel and the nations, since he proclaims that God is bringing about a new creation by reconciling the world (Jews and Gentiles) to himself through the forgiveness of sins (5:17-21). His discouragement over laboring in vain (6:1) corresponds to the servant's.[83] Finally, Paul's experience of God's support in the midst of suffering and dishonor follows the servant's pattern (6:8-10).

Though Paul is related typologically to the servant it is only through the transforming presence and pattern of Christ.[84] Christ is the genuine fulfillment of the servant of Isaiah, especially in reference to the saving effects of his suffering for the sins of the people in Isa 52:13-52:12. Paul identifies himself with the servant of Isaiah, but even more he identifies himself with Christ-with his death, and with his resurrection.[85] This is clear from the immediate context in 2 Cor 5:14-17, as well as from other passages in 2 Corinthians such as 1:5 and 4:7-11. Paul's identification with the servant of Isaiah is filtered through the person and work of Christ.[86]

---

and Gentiles alike. Isaiah 49 itself introduces us to this expanded mission (Goldingay, *The Message of Isaiah 40-55*, 376).

82. Several passages in Isaiah 40-66 may have played a role in shaping Paul's association of a new creation with a defining point in history (Isa 42:9-10; 43:18-19; 48:6; 65:17). For a further discussion of the possible influence of Isaianic thought on Paul's perception of the new creation in this passage, see Hafemann, "Paul's Use of the Old Testament in 2 Corinthians," 252; Webb, *Returning Home*, 121-28; Wilk, "Isaiah in 1 and 2 Corinthians," 150.

83. The phrase μὴ εἰς κενόν modifies the reception of the grace. Isa 49:4 uses the cognate word κενῶς to describe the servant's despondency over Israel's failure to heed God's message of salvation, making an echo of Isa 49:4 in 2 Cor 6:1 possible (see Hays, *Echoes*, 225).

84. See Cerfaux's treatment of Paul's complex relationship to both the Isaianic Servant and Christ (Cerfaux, *Études d'Exégèse et d'Histoire Religieuse*, 448-49, 453).

85. Ibid., 453.

86. Cerfaux rightly observes that Paul's identification with Christ's suffering and

In Rom 15:21, the distinction between Paul as the messenger and Christ as the sacrificial servant is clearer. Paul quotes Isa 52:15 to support his aspiration to reach Gentiles with the gospel of Christ. The verse is situated in the larger context of Isa 52:13–53:12, where the subject is the suffering and vindication of God's servant. Oswalt identifies the two main themes of the passage as being "the contrast between the servant's exaltation and his humiliation and suffering, and the contrast between what people thought about the Servant and what was really the case."[87] In Isa 52:13–15 in particular, the prophet describes the reaction of nations and kings to the surprising status of God's servant.[88] They will be "startled" and will close their mouths in astonishment.[89] The comparative construction in the MT suggests that the response to the servant's exaltation (52:15) will mirror the reaction people had to the servant's troubling humiliation (52:14).[90] Chapter 53 then reports the suffering to be endured by the servant prior to being exalted.

In Rom 15:21, Paul adopts the wording of the LXX, though there may have been a rearrangement of words, with ὄψονται being placed at the front of the phrase for emphasis.[91] The LXX has a different emphasis from what is found in the original Hebrew in Isa 52:15b, but the overall point

---

death reflects a larger pattern of Christians sharing in the sufferings (and death) of Christ (ibid., 444). Similarly, Beale points to the believer's participatory identification with Christ as the basis for Paul's assumption of the Isaianic Servant's ministry from Isa 42 and 49 (Beale, *John's Use of the Old Testament in Revelation*, 231).

87. Oswalt, *Isaiah 40-66*, 376.

88. This reading understands the nations and kings, rather than a group within Israel (see Childs, *Isaiah*, 413), as those who experience the new appreciation of the servant.

89. The parallelism in the first two lines of Isa 52:15 and the primary emphasis in the broader context suggests a meaning of "startle" rather than "sprinkle" for the hiphil form of the verb נזה. Supporting this position are Blenkinsopp, *Isaiah 40-55*, 346–47; Childs, *Isaiah*, 412–13; Seitz, "Isaiah 40–66," 463. Childs rejects the solution of textual corruption and instead opts for an alternate meaning of the root, corresponding with the LXX translation of "surprise" (Childs, *Isaiah*, 412–13). Baltzer prefers "sprinkle" but not with the cultic overtones (Baltzer, *Deutero-Isaiah*, 400). Seifrid sees a "salvific, cultic action" arising from the idea of sprinkling (Seifrid, "Romans," 691; see also Motyer, *The Prophecy of Isaiah*, 425–26).

90. See Oswalt, *Isaiah 40-66*, 379; Brueggemann, *Isaiah 40-66*, 142; Childs, *Isaiah*, 412.

91. Codex Valentinus and some later minuscules preserve this reading, which may have been changed in other manuscripts in order to bring the NT into complete conformity with the LXX (Cranfield, *Romans*, 2:765; Dunn, *Romans*, 2:856; Jewett, *Romans*, 902, 916; contra Wilckens, *Der Brief an der Römer*, 3:121).

is similar in both places: unexpected truth about the servant's ultimate destiny will be acknowledged by those who were previously unaware of his outcome.[92]

Paul picks up this theme as an expression of his determination to proclaim the good news of Christ to those who have not heard it. Paul's prior reference to Christ in 15:20 implies that he identifies Christ as the servant described in Isa 52:13—53:12.[93] On the basis of this correlation Paul makes a parallel between the announcement of the servant's exaltation and the spread of the good news of Christ. Even though in Isa 52:15 the news is not explicitly positive for the nations, for Paul, the message is interpreted as good news for the nations because of the inclusion of the Gentiles in the work of Christ.[94] Isaiah 42:6, 49:6, 51:4 are probable grounds within Isaiah for Paul's conviction. In those passages, the servant's appointed ministry to Israel is promised to bring the nations into relationship with God.[95]

But why does Paul envision the participation of a human agent in the process of disseminating the news of the suffering servant's triumph and glorification? Two excerpts from the material surrounding Isa 52:13–15 surface as possible catalysts for Paul's perspective. Earlier in Isa 52, the prophet extols the virtues of the messengers of God's good news of salvation (Isa 52:7). Paul had already quoted this verse earlier in his letter to the Romans (10:15). Immediately following this reference (in 10:16), Paul cites Isa 53:1 as an expression of the lack of positive response to the message of good news. The passage quoted in Rom 15:21 (Isa 52:15) is enclosed by verses pointing to a message delivered by human agents.[96]

---

92. Whereas in the Masoretic Text the focus is placed on the exalted state of the servant, in the LXX, the focus is more on those who become aware of the servant's condition. These two features are not in opposition in either passage, but the weight is shifted towards the audience in the LXX. The LXX also indicates overtly that the message concerns the servant.

93. Cranfield, *Romans*, 2:765; Moo, *Romans*, 898; Schreiner, *Romans*, 770; Wagner, *Heralds of the Good News*, 335; Jewett, *Romans*, 917. Dunn leaves the door open to equating both Paul and Christ to the Servant of 52:15 (Dunn, *Romans*, 2:866).

94. Some commentators discern a benevolent tone in Isa 52:15 (Young, *The Book of Isaiah*, 3:339; Baltzer, *Deutero-Isaiah*, 400), while others detect a foreboding sense (Watts, *Isaiah 34-66*, 230; Chae, *Paul as Apostle to the Gentiles*, 31). Most likely, the emphasis is not on the implications for the nations but rather on the widespread recognition of the servant's stunning status (Westermann, *Isaiah 40-66*, 259-60; Brueggemann, *Isaiah 40-66*, 142).

95. See Goldingay, *God's Prophet, God's Servant*, 94, 132-33.

96. Wagner, *Heralds of the Good News*, 335.

Paul's Identity in the Undisputed Letters

Paul assumes this role of a messenger by "fulfilling" the gospel of Christ to Gentiles spread around the Roman world (Rom 15:19).[97]

A survey of the OT contribution to Paul's ministry mindset reveals that more than any other section of Scripture Isa 40–66 played a significant role in shaping Paul's self-perception. The picture in that section of a divinely appointed messenger charged with both announcing with words and manifesting through sacrificial actions the salvation of God to Jews and Gentiles was well suited to Paul's understanding of his own ministry. Paul recognized the unique fulfillment of God's saving plans in the person of Christ, and through his own calling entered into association with Christ in the challenge of bearing hardship for the sake of God's mission and with the hope of God's approbation.

Paul and the Other Apostles

Next is the topic of apostolic authority and Paul's relationship to other apostles and tradition. Key passages include Gal 1:1, 17; 2:1–10; 1 Thess 2:6–7; 1 Cor 1:1; 9:1–6; 15:1–11; 2 Cor 1:1; 11:5; 12:11–12; Rom 1:1; 11:13. Paul speaks with a combination of authority and humility when discussing his apostolic calling. He recognizes the legacy of the original apostles and other apostles while defending the validity of his own apostleship.[98] This balance between independence and common ground in his standing with other apostles sets the standard for later presentations of this dynamic in the letters examined in chapters three, four, and five of the book.

In several of his letters, Paul identifies himself as an apostle from the outset (Gal 1:1; 1 Cor 1:1; 2 Cor 1:1; Rom 1:1). The opening in Gal 1:1 is the most forceful assertion of Paul's apostleship. The divine authorization behind Paul's apostleship is the intended message, and the antithetical construction (οὐκ ἀπ' ἀνθρώπων οὐδὲ δι' ἀνθρώπου ἀλλὰ διὰ Ἰησοῦ καὶ θεοῦ πατρός) drives home the contention more powerfully. This wording is consistent with the argument Paul makes throughout the rest of Gal 1. The opening statements in 1 Cor 1:1 and 2 Cor 1:1 are similar to one another. In both cases, Paul's apostleship is placed in a genitive relationship with

---

97. Schreiner defines "fulfillment" here as Paul's completion of "his goal of establishing churches in virgin territories" (Schreiner, *Paul, Apostle of God's Glory in Christ*, 60). Note also the connection to the fullness of Gentiles as one component of the mystery of Rom 11:25.

98. See Clark, "Apostleship," 56–63, for an analysis of how Paul uses the term "apostle" to refer to other ministers.

Portrait of an Apostle

Jesus Christ (or Christ Jesus) and is qualified as being dependent upon the will of God. This qualification represents a different way of stressing the divine origins of Paul's apostleship, and the emphasis is reinforced in 1 Cor 1:1 by the possible inclusion of κλητός before ἀπόστολος.[99] In Rom 1:1, Paul submits that he is called as an apostle (κλητὸς ἀπόστολος), which communicates the fact that God is the source of Paul's ministry and authority. Paul's apostleship is followed immediately by his perception of being set apart for the gospel, demonstrating the close association between his apostleship and the gospel.

Taking the greetings from the four letters as a group, it is likely that Paul mentions his apostleship at the beginning of the letters for three main reasons. First, Paul saw his apostleship as central to his identity. Second, the divine bestowal of his apostleship serves as his basis for addressing the churches in an authoritative manner. Third, Paul's apostleship supports the validity of his gospel, which is always a chief concern in his letters.[100] Beyond these three shared characteristics, questions about Paul's apostleship and his gospel continue to surface in Galatians, so the initial identification of Paul as an apostle foreshadows a primary theme in the letter.

After offering his gospel as the standard against any corrupt imitation (Gal 1:6–9) and as part of a sustained defense of the divine origin of his gospel in Gal 1:6—2:10, Paul provides a brief glimpse of his standing relative to the other apostles in Gal 1:17 when he mentions visiting the "apostles who were before me" (τοὺς πρὸ ἐμοῦ ἀποστόλους). Bruce is correct in observing that the phrase "is temporal; it does not denote precedence in status."[101] Instead, the phrase groups Paul with the other apostles, stressing the common standing among them.[102] Thus Paul is neither detached from nor inferior to the other apostles. For Paul, independence entails possessing an apostolic legitimacy that does not rest on the authorization of other Christian leaders but does keep him aligned with their mission and message.

---

99. The bulk of the manuscript evidence supports the presence of κλητός in the verse, though significant early witnesses P61, A, and D omit the term. The inclusion may be influenced by Rom 1:1, or the omission may be explained as a scribal error.

100. For a discussion of how the gospel regulated Paul's apostleship, rather than the other way around, see Dunn, *The Theology of Paul the Apostle*, 572.

101. Bruce, *Galatians*, 94. See also Longenecker, *Galatians*, 34; *contra* Dunn, *Galatians*, 68–69.

102. See Ridderbos, *Epistle of Paul to the Churches of Galatia*, 65. Clark rightly determines that this group consisted of "primarily the twelve" original apostles of the church (Clark, "Apostleship," 51).

As Paul proceeds to develop his argument of independence from, yet association with, the other apostles, he recounts in Gal 2:1–10 a meeting in Jerusalem with leaders of the early church, including James, Cephas, and John (Gal 2:2, 6, 9). Paul's purpose was to present his gospel to them in order to garner their backing of his ministry to the Gentiles. Paul makes a fine distinction between the respected leaders and those who had been opposing Paul's ministry, insisting that his gospel did not need approval from the latter group (2:2–5). But even with the recognized leaders, Paul takes pains to point out that though they affirmed Paul in his mission, they did not modify or supplement his message (2:6–9). The ultimate authorization for Paul's ministry and gospel rests with God alone. Even the leaders themselves are reported to have acknowledged the divine design of Paul's ministry, since they identified both that God had entrusted Paul with the gospel to the uncircumcised and that this commission was evidence of God's grace to Paul (Gal 2:7–9). All parties involved had affirmed that Paul's gospel ministry to the Gentiles was on par with Peter's ministry to the Jews (note the use of the comparative adverb καθώς in 2:7), with Paul using the term apostleship to describe both (2:8). The contribution of this passage to the focus of this book is that it attests to a balance between Paul's cooperation with the other apostles and his determination to defend his calling as being unconnected to their blessing or the initiative of any human source. While Paul gives the greater emphasis to his independence from the early church's hierarchy in Gal 1–2, he still associates himself with the other apostles, with the common bond of the gospel tying them together.[103]

A relatively brief contribution to the topic of Paul's apostleship occurs in 1 Thess 2:6–7. There, in the middle of his recollection of his ministry to the Thessalonians, Paul connects apostleship with authority.[104] Paul's standing as an apostle carries the potential of acclaim arising from the possession of apostolic authority.[105] But out of sincerity of motive and a desire to please God, Paul has bypassed an authoritative approach even

---

103. An attempt to reconcile the main emphasis in Gal 1–2 with a representative passage giving preference to the other side of the equation (1 Cor 15:1–12) is provided at the end of this section.

104. The plural ἀπόστολοι here most likely reflects Silvanus's standing as an apostle alongside Paul (Wannamaker, *The Epistles to the Thessalonians*, 99–100). Rigaux adds Timothy to the list (Rigaux, *Les Épîtres aux Thessaloniciens*, 418).

105. The discourse implies that gain in prestige rather than in finances is what Paul has in mind (see BDAG, "βάρος," 167; Rigaux, *Les Épîtres aux Thessaloniciens*, 417; Wannamaker, *The Epistles to the Thessalonians*, 99).

though he could have rightfully resorted to this stance. Paul's language implies that his identity as a minister conformed to the contours of the other apostles of Christ, even though Paul did not always choose to exercise the full rights of his apostleship.

In the next passage of note, 1 Cor 9:1–6, Paul again places his apostleship alongside the ministry of the other apostles. Paul's broader concern is to present his attitude towards service as a model for the Corinthians to imitate (1 Cor 11:1), so that they will learn to give preference to the needs of others over their own needs (1 Cor 8:1b, 13; 10:24, 33).[106] To drive home this principle, Paul describes the way he puts aside his own rights as an apostle for the sake of the people he is serving. The line of thought is an expanded form of what was seen in 1 Thess 2:6–7. First, Paul draws upon his apostleship and his revelation from Christ as potential reasons for exercising his rights in ministry (1 Cor 9:1). Both of these items carry connotations of authority and distinction and help supply Paul a standing equal to that of the other apostles, at least according to a picture of apostleship that is flexible enough to encompass more than just the original twelve apostles. To this list he adds his specific apostolic ministry to the Corinthian church and suggests that the fruitfulness of this ministry confirms Paul's apostolic calling (9:2). The next step in his argument is to show that he sets aside rights that would be expected to accompany the ministry of apostleship (see 9:12, 15, 19–27). These rights include eating and drinking whatever he desires (with reference to his statements about idolatry in 8:13), getting married, and relying on the financial support of others instead of working (9:4–6). Paul even refers specifically to the marriages of other apostles in order to demonstrate that other apostles exercise these rights (9:5). From the structure and wording of Paul's argument, it is clear that he considers himself an apostle on par with others designated with that title, and that there is both common ground and independence in Paul's leadership relationship with the other apostles.

A similar pattern surfaces in 1 Cor 15:1–11. In order to build the doctrine of the believer's resurrection upon truth already accepted by the Corinthian church, Paul draws upon early Christian tradition (15:3). In 15:1 Paul identifies this tradition as being consistent with his gospel. Paul sees no divergence between his gospel and the core teaching of the church as a whole.

---

106. See R. Collins, *First Corinthians*, 328–29; Thiselton, *First Epistle to the Corinthians*, 661–62, 666–67; Garland, *1 Corinthians*, 403. *Pace* Barrett, Bruce, and Fee, who think that Paul's primary purpose is apologetic (Barrett, *First Epistle to the Corinthians*, 200; Bruce, *1 and 2 Corinthians*, 83; Fee, *First Epistle to the Corinthians*, 394–96).

Paul's Identity in the Undisputed Letters

Part of this central teaching Paul had received and proclaimed is a recounting of the resurrection appearances of Christ. The first witnesses listed are Cephas and the other original apostles (15:5), followed by a larger group of disciples, James, and "all of the apostles" (15:6–7).[107] Paul then adds himself to this list, placing his own encounter with the risen Christ at the same level as those of the people mentioned previously.[108] The sense of Paul's self-identification as "one untimely born" (ἔκτρωμα) has been interpreted in various ways.[109] It may refer to the fact that Christ's appearance to Paul and his appointment of Paul as an apostle occurred at an atypical time and in an atypical way, since Paul had not seen nor been commissioned by Christ during his earthly ministry.[110] Or the term may highlight Paul's unworthiness because of his persecution of the church.[111] In either case, Paul's history placed him at a perceived disadvantage compared to the other apostles. Paul expands upon this perceived deficiency (note the use of the explanatory γάρ) by emphasizing his unworthiness to be called an apostle (εἰμὶ ὁ ἐλάχιστος τῶν ἀποστόλων ὅ οὐκ εἰμὶ ἱκανὸς καλεῖσθαι ἀπόστολος). This depiction appears at first glance to elevate the other apostles above Paul, but the characterization has less to do with Paul's current status and more to do with his past actions. Paul confirms this perception by recalling his past as a persecutor of the church and the subsequent grace God bestowed on him in choosing him for apostleship (1 Cor 15:9–10a). The emphasis is on Paul's surprising inclusion among those called to apostleship.[112]

In Paul's present ministry, his pattern of hard and fruitful work, propelled by God's grace, serves to reinforce Paul's standing alongside the other apostles (15:10b). God's surprising choice of Paul as a minister did not bring a deficient outcome (οὐ κενὴ ἐγενήθη), which implies that Paul had enjoyed a fruitful ministry. Paul is thus able to conclude this section of the argument with the assertion that his preaching is equivalent to that

---

107. For a discussion of the options of what is meant by Paul's reference to all of the apostles, see Fee, *First Epistle to the Corinthians*, 731–32; Clark, "Apostleship," 61–62.

108. Kertelge, "Das Apostelamt des Paulus," 165–66; Fee, *First Epistle to the Corinthians*, 732. Paul's apostleship is implied in 15:8 and made explicit in 15:9–11. And from here and elsewhere, Christ's post-resurrection appearance to Paul is seen as part of the basis of his apostleship.

109. For a review of the most likely options, see Nickelsburg, "Απ'Εκτρωμα," 198–200.

110. See the discussion in Barrett, *First Epistle to the Corinthians*, 344; also Kremer, *Der Erste Briefe an die Korinther*, 332.

111. Nickelsburg, "Απ'Εκτρωμα," 204; Lindemann, *Der Erste Korintherbrief*, 334.

112. Kertelge, "Das Apostelamt des Paulus," 165.

Portrait of an Apostle

of the other apostles (15:11). This passage on the whole reveals an attitude of respect and cooperation towards the other apostles. It also numbers Paul among the apostles. Though Paul's past should disqualify him from the honor of apostolic ministry, he is able to vouch for the full legitimacy of his apostleship by virtue of Christ's appearance to him and through appeal to his steadfast and fruitful service enabled by God's gracious work through him.

The pendulum swings back towards an assertion of Paul's authority in 2 Cor 11:5. The issue needing defense in 2 Cor 10–13 is that authentic ministry is founded upon God's powerful work through human weakness, rather than upon the talents of polished and imposing leaders. Paul engages in his opponents' own foolish style of argument (11:1) by building up his own credentials before setting them aside in favor of God's use of his suffering and weakness. As part of the preliminary promotion of his authority, Paul contends for his equality with the other apostles in 2 Cor 11:5. Scholars disagree as to whether the (οἱ ὑπερλίαν ἀπόστολοι) in 11:5 (and 12:11) are the same people as the pseudo-apostles of 11:13 (also implied in 11:4). Some scholars, pointing out that the references occur in the same passage, see the two labels as referring to the same false teachers.[113] Others discern that the two groups are different.[114] The second option is to be preferred, since the two labels are used with different connotations for different purposes. The pseudo-apostles are flatly denounced, while the premier apostles are used in comparison to Paul's own authority.[115] Paul's argument in 2 Cor 11:4–5 is that the Corinthian believers need to accept his teaching in a way that does justice to his authority. If they receive heterodox teaching with such enthusiasm (11:4, with reference to false apostles), they should welcome the teaching of a genuine apostle all the more (11:5, with reference to legitimate apostles).

Paul revisits the same line of thought in 2 Cor 12:11–12, admitting to resort to foolishness again. The wording of 2 Cor 12:11 practically repeats

---

113. See for instance Kertelge, "Das Apostelamt des Paulus," 174; Kruse, *The Second Epistle of Paul to the Corinthians*, 48–50; Barnett, *Second Epistle to the Corinthians*, 507, 522–23.

114. Bruce, *1 and 2 Corinthians*, 239; Harris, *Second Epistle to the Corinthians*, 745, 772. Rudolf Bultmann sees two different groups, neither of which consists of the original apostles (Bultmann, *Der zweite Brief an die Korinther*, 205).

115. In 12:12 the translation of "true apostle" (NAS) for (ἀπόστολος) is misleading since it seems to set up a contrast between Paul and the group described in 12:11, whereas Paul is more likely using the term to place himself in association with the group in 12:11.

the wording of 2 Cor 11:5. Paul's authority should be considered as being on par with the authority of even the most prominent apostles (again most likely corresponding to the leaders of reputation in Gal 2:1–10). Paul supports this position by directing the Corinthians' attention to the signs of an apostle that God displayed in Paul's ministry.[116] The observation from 2 Cor 11:5 and 12:11–12 that is most pertinent to this book is that Paul is willing to highlight and defend his apostleship and equality with other apostles for the sake of ensuring that his gospel receives a proper hearing. The tone is accordingly very similar to the tone in Galatians 1:1—2:10.

Finally, in Rom 11:13 Paul mentions his apostleship to the Gentiles in the midst of a discussion about God's purposes for the Jews in bringing salvation to the Gentiles. This passage aligns well with the delineation of Paul's apostolic ministry in Gal 2:8, where Paul's authority among the Gentiles was equated to Peter's authority among the Jews. Paul shares the name "apostle" with other early apostles and shares their basic message. Where he is distinct, however, is in his commissioning to the Gentiles. This difference is reflected in Paul's gospel as well, since he must highlight and defend the full applicability of Christ's work to Gentiles apart from the Law (see Rom 3:21, 28).

The testimony from the preceding passages produces a coherent composite picture of Paul's apostleship. The emphasis differs somewhat in the various passages, yet these divergences can be explained best by looking at the two passages that are most pronounced in their differences, 1 Cor 15:1–11 and Gal 1:1—2:10. The tone and balance of 1 Cor 15:1–11 as compared to Gal 1:1—2:10 creates no contradiction in Paul's understanding of his apostleship and relationship to tradition.

Both passages uphold both the chronological priority of the earlier apostles and the full membership of Paul in their number. The occasion behind Gal 1:1—2:10 required a stronger emphasis on Paul's independent authority, since the reception of his gospel among the Gentiles was at stake, whereas in 1 Cor 15:1–11, Paul's purposes are better served by accentuating common ground and respect for the first apostles and their teaching.[117]

Both passages also group Paul's revealed gospel with the recognized teaching of the early church. The teaching affirmed in 1 Cor 15:3–7 has been passed down rather than received by divine revelation as in Gal

---

116. Paul's reflection on God's supernatural work in his ministry is recounted using similar language in Rom 15:19a.

117. See Kim, *Origin of Paul's Gospel*, 70; Fung, "Revelation and Tradition," 39–41; Toit, "Encountering Grace," 72–73 for additional discussion of the coherence between the two passages.

1:11–12. But Paul's gospel, with its accent placed on the benefits for Gentiles, is recognized as existing in harmony with the predominant tradition in Gal 2:1–10. This same accord is implied with the inclusion of Paul's witness of Christ in the tradition in 1 Cor 15:8. Therefore, Paul's gospel, while not equivalent to the inherited tradition in either 1 Corinthians 15 or Galatians 1–2, is in both places congruent with that tradition.[118] Other passages fit somewhere on the spectrum between 1 Corinthians 15 and Galatians 1–2. In each case, Paul understands himself as an apostle on the same level as the most eminent apostles and sees his teaching as being in basic harmony with theirs.

Paul's Suffering and Imprisonment

Suffering and imprisonment are prominent themes in Paul's description of his ministry, and these themes are featured as well in the *Epistle to the Laodiceans*, *3 Corinthians*, Colossians, and Ephesians. Among the significant passages on this topic in the undisputed letters are Gal 6:17; 1 Cor 4:8–13; Phil 1:7, 12–26, 29–30; 2:16–18; 3:8–11; 2 Cor 1:5–11; 4:7–12; 6:3–10; Phlm 1, 9–10, 13, 23. Paul's theological appraisal of his suffering and imprisonment as well as his purposes for discussing his hardships will be investigated in this section. It will be argued that Paul understands his suffering as a central aspect of his ministry and as an extension of his theology regarding union with Christ.[119]

Paul shares an enigmatic statement about bearing the marks of Jesus (τὰ στίγματα τοῦ Ἰησοῦ) at the end of his letter to the Galatians (Gal 6:17). The preceding context suggests that Paul is referring to the suffering he has endured because of his association with a crucified Savior (Gal 6:12).[120] Any suffering Paul has endured is consistent with Paul's message of Christ crucified and an outworking of being crucified with Christ (Gal 2:20). Paul may have specific injuries in mind, because he mentions that the marks of Christ are on his body.[121] Paul employs this reminder of his

---

118. See Betz, *Galatians*, 65.

119. Acts 9:15–16 provides further backing for the centrality of this theme to Paul's calling. The believer's union with Christ is unfolded in passages such as Gal 2:20; Phil 3:10–11; Rom 6:3–11; 8:17–18.

120. Leitzmann, *An die Galater*, 264; Ridderbos, *Epistle of Paul to the Churches of Galatia*, 228.

121. Kamlah, "Wie beurteilt Paulus sein Leiden?," 219–20; Fung, *Galatians*, 313; Longenecker, *Galatians*, 300. There is also a possible contrast intended between Paul's scars and the physical marks of circumcision (Schreiner, *Paul, Apostle of God's Glory in Christ*, 96).

afflictions for several possible reasons as part of a warning to those who oppose him. First, as a closing remark, this recollection of Paul's arduous, suffering-laden ministry for the Galatians serves to strengthen the force of Paul's argument in the letter.[122] The sincerity of Paul's devotion to Christ is enhanced by reference to his suffering. Second, Paul's intimate bond with Christ suggests that causing trouble to Paul entails causing trouble to Christ.[123] Third, Paul's brand-marks also function to identify that he belongs to Jesus.[124] So it is possible that the verse serves as a further reminder that Paul answers to God alone and will not succumb to pressure applied by opponents (see the connection between Paul's identity as Christ's servant [δοῦλος] and his resistance to pleasing people in Gal 1:10).

Paul highlights the mistreatments and hardships endured as an apostle in 1 Cor 4:8–13. He does so by placing the position of an apostle in ironic contrast to the supposedly superior status of his readers (4:8). When using the plural ἀποστόλους in 4:9, Paul likely has in mind at least Apollos (mentioned in 4:6), along with other authentic servants of the gospel.[125] These apostles are characterized by the lowly estate they accept for the sake of Christ (4:10). Verse 9 presents the intriguing image of the apostles being displayed (ἀποδείκνυμι) as last in a line of captives who are condemned to death and exposed as a spectacle (θέατρον) to the surrounding world.[126] The reference to a sentence of death need not foresee Paul's eventual martyrdom for the faith but instead metaphorically places his lot in life alongside other undesirables who are en route to death in the public arena.[127] In verse 12, Paul graphically describes his condition with the terms περικάθαρμα and περίψημα. The words in this context carry a derogatory connotation, highlighting the dismissive appraisal the world

---

122. Betz, *Galatians*, 323–25.

123. Ridderbos, *Epistle of Paul to the Churches of Galatia*, 229.

124. See BDAG, "στίγμα," 945; Leitzmann, *An die Galater*, 264; Longenecker, *Galatians*, 300.

125. Fee, *First Epistle to the Corinthians*, 174; Lindemann, *Der Erste Korintherbrief*, 106.

126. For background about the characteristics of Roman public events in which criminals were put to death for show, see Nguyen, "The Identification of Paul's Spectacle of Death Metaphor in 1 Corinthians 4.9," 490–93. The term ἔσχατος in this context contributes to the metaphor by imagining the apostles arriving to the arena at the end of the line, either as conquered war trophies or as condemned criminals, destined for a grisly fate (Fee, *First Epistle to the Corinthians*, 174–75).

127. Barrett, *First Epistle to the Corinthians*, 110; Kremer, *Der Erste Briefe an die Korinther*, 90; Thiselton, *First Epistle to the Corinthians*, 359–60; Lindemann, *Der Erste Korintherbrief*, 107.

has of apostles like Paul. The idea communicated in this passage is that Paul's ministry brings little acclaim but rather opposition, trials, and derision. Paul accepts these features as part of his calling as an apostle.

In Paul's letter to the Philippians, the theme of suffering is traced under the larger topic of participation in the gospel (Phil 1:5, 27; 2:22; 4:3). Paul opens his discussion of suffering by affirming the believers for their willingness to support him in his hardship (1:7).[128] Paul is explicit in this case that his suffering consists of imprisonment (1:7; also 1:13, 14, 17). The Philippians have thrown their lot with Paul in his imprisonment and the ministry resulting from it. According to Paul, when the Philippians share in Paul's suffering in this way, they also share in spiritual benefits.[129] They are συγκοινωνοί with Paul in God's grace. This perspective conforms to Paul's theology of being united with Christ in his suffering and glory (Phil 3:10–11).

In Phil 1:12–26 Paul refers only generally to his circumstances (τὰ κατ' ἐμέ, 1:12), omitting any mention of the physical challenges related to his hardship.[130] His chief interest in the passage is in the positive spiritual effects of his imprisonment in the lives of others. He speaks of the progress of the gospel (1:12) arising from an increased awareness that Paul's profession of Christ is the reason for his incarceration and from a renewed boldness among other preachers of the gospel because of his imprisonment (1:13–14). Opportunities for an expanded ministry influence are never far removed from Paul's thoughts (note especially the language of "open doors" in 1 Cor 16:9; 2 Cor 2:12). The advance of the gospel, consistent with the letter's emphasis on participating in the gospel, takes precedence over Paul's personal comfort (1:17–18).

Paul views prayer from fellow believers as an indispensable resource through the power of God's Spirit (1:19). The prayers are mentioned in connection with Paul's deliverance (σωτηρία). The link to Paul's release in 1:24–26 may imply that Paul's physical deliverance is intended in 1:19, but Paul's fixation on his eschatological hope in 1:21–23 suggests the possibility of a reference to eternal salvation in 1:19 as well.[131] An option that in-

---

128. That the Philippians' financial support is at least partially in view is evident from the similar wording between Phil 1:7 and 4:14.

129. Paul expands on this topic in 2 Cor 1:5–7. The discourse of 2 Cor 1:5–11 as a whole bears a resemblance to Phil 1:7, 12–26.

130. Bloomquist, *The Function of Suffering in Philippians*, 148.

131. Hawthorne and Thurston interpret σωτηρία in terms of physical deliverance (Hawthorne, *Philippians*, 40; Thurston and Ryan, *Philippians and Philemon*, 62). Gnilka contends that eternal salvation is the primary focus (Gnilka, *Der Philipperbrief*, 66).

corporates both meanings is deliverance as Paul's vindication before those who denigrated Paul's apostleship.¹³² Verse 20 is congenial to this position, since the language of not being put to shame envisions public vindication, and Paul himself includes both release from prison and eternal salvation as opportunities for vindication in the verse.¹³³ That Paul is torn between the possibilities of life and death is apparent from his rumination over his possible outcomes in 1:20–24. Suffering reminds him of both his glorious destiny and his commitment to his flock, and these two values lead him in different directions.¹³⁴ In the end, he suspects that God holds a more immediate purpose for Paul's life in the lives of his readers (1:25–26). He is willing to set aside "gain" (1:21) and the "better" (1:23) of being with Christ in deference to the "more necessary" (1:24) task of "fruitful labor" (1:22). In conclusion, Paul adopts a positive attitude towards his suffering and imprisonment. He recognizes the spiritual benefit for others resulting from his ordeal and takes comfort knowing that he will share in the glory of the Christ whom he represents.

Brief mention should be made of a term (ἀγών) Paul uses in connection to suffering (πάσχω) in Phil 1:29–30. The Philippians are encouraged to prepare themselves to suffer and join in Paul's struggle for the gospel.¹³⁵ The past ἀγών that Paul recalls is likely the same one mentioned in 1 Thess 2:2, where Paul also employs ἀγών to depict his struggle to advance the gospel in the midst of conflict throughout Macedonia.¹³⁶ In both cases, Paul uses the imagery of a contest to depict his commitment to the gospel in spite of heated opposition.

Later in Philippians, Paul again accents the centrality of suffering in his ministry, along with his determination to suffer for the sake of those to whom he ministers (Phil 2:16–18). In verse 16, Paul envisions the day in which he will give an account of his ministry to God (2:16). If the Philippians exhibit spiritual maturity, then Paul's labors (κοπιάω), including

---

132. Some scholars suggest that the echo of Job 13:16–18 opens the door to this interpretation (Schenk, *Die Philipperbriefe*, 145; Martin, *Philippians*, 77; Fee, *Philippians*, 130–32. See also Hays, *Echoes*, 21–24; Bockmuehl, *Philippians*, 82–83.

133. The OT, particularly Isa 40–66, sometimes envisions public vindication as not being put to shame before one's enemies (see Ps 25:1–3; Isa 45:16–17; 49:23; 50:5–9).

134. Behind this expectation of future glory undoubtedly lies Paul's understanding of sharing in the suffering and glory of Christ (see Phil 1:29; 3:10–11).

135. See Pfitzner, *Paul and the Agon Motif*, 115–20; Oakes, *Philippians*, 106.

136. See Pfitzner, *Paul and the Agon Motif*, 114; Hawthorne, *Philippians*, 62; Bruce, *Philippians*, 60; **Reumann**, *Philippians*, 294; *contra* Dibelius, *Die Briefe des Apostels Paulus II: Die neun kleinen Briefe*, 6, 52.

his suffering, will not have been in vain (εἰς κενόν).¹³⁷ Paul's suffering, expressed in the sacrificial language of a libation (σπένδω) is best interpreted as figurative language that alludes to death.¹³⁸ The prospect of suffering even death as an offering, in support of the Philippians' own sacrificial service arising from their faith, would bring Paul great joy.¹³⁹ In these three verses, Paul exhibits the value he places on a fruitful ministry among the Philippians, showing that he is willing to labor and even die in order to help the Philippians persevere in their faith.

Philippians 3:8–11 occurs as part of an autobiographical account of Paul's transformation and calling. Paul specifies his goal of gaining Christ and being found in him by means of receiving a righteous standing in God's sight (3:8–9). Gaining Christ is contrasted with losing all else and refers to the privilege of knowing Christ (3:8, 10). The centrality to Paul's thought of union with Christ (εὑρεθῶ ἐν αὐτῷ) as the basis for life and righteousness emerges clearly in these verses.¹⁴⁰ Paul's identification with Christ has entailed enduring the loss of all things. Paul has already indicated twice his willingness to lose his prior advantages for the sake of knowing Christ (3:7–8). The third mention of suffering loss, instead of merely repeating Paul's devaluation of religious or worldly achievement may point to the actual suffering and disadvantage Paul has encountered as a minister of the gospel.¹⁴¹

Paul proceeds in verse 10 by unfolding more of what it means to be found in Christ. Union with Christ consists of knowing Christ, especially

---

137. See also 1 Thess 2:1 for a similar expression.

138. The image carried by σπένδω likely refers at least in part to Paul's death rather than exclusively to his ongoing service (Gnilka, *Der Philipperbrief*, 154–55; Bruce, *Philippians*, 89–90; O'Brien, *Philippians*, 305–6; Silva, *Philippians*, 128; *pace* Fee, *Philippians*, 252–54; Hawthorne, *Philippians*, 105–6). See also 2 Tim 4:6.

139. Paul's sacrifice is perceived as being added to the Philippians own sacrificial service, represented in the phrase ἐπὶ τῇ θυσίᾳ καὶ λειτουργίᾳ τῆς πίστεως ὑμῶν (with the dative nouns forming a hendiadys construction). See Lightfoot, *Philippians*, 118–19; Gnilka, *Der Philipperbrief*, 155; Schenk, *Die Philipperbriefe*, 225; Martin, *Philippians*, 123–24. At the beginning of 2:17, ἀλλά indicates a contrast with Paul's typical labors of 2:16, and the ascensive καί suggests that death is being presented as the most severe case imagined (see also Schenk, *Die Philipperbriefe*, 224–25; O'Brien, *Philippians*, 302–304; Silva, *Philippians*, 132).

140. Ahren, "The Fellowship of His Sufferings," 30–31; Tannehill, *Dying and Rising with Christ*, 118; Polhill, "Twin Obstacles in the Christian Path," 365; Bruce, *Philippians*, 114; Silva, *Philippians*, 162–63.

141. Polhill, "Twin Obstacles in the Christian Path," 364; Hawthorne, *Philippians*, 138; Bruce, *Philippians*, 118.

in the power of his resurrection and the fellowship of his sufferings. This participation in both the power and affliction of Christ is probably understood by Paul as occurring simultaneously in the course of his life and ministry.[142] They are two sides of the implications of being united with Christ. Then, in a chiastic structure Paul discusses life united with Christ as being both "already" and "not yet."[143] First, Paul sees himself being conformed to the pattern of Christ's death (συμμορφιζόμενος τῷ θανάτῳ αὐτοῦ), which is best understood as an expression of the outworkings of the believer's union with Christ.[144] Second, Paul sets his sights on the future resurrection as the end result of his life with Christ (see also Phil 3:21, where Paul speaks of conformity [σύμμορφος] into the glorified body of Christ).[145]

Is Paul speaking of his experience as representative of that of all Christians or is he simply describing his individual calling as a chosen minister? The autobiographical account is enlisted for illustrative purposes, promoting a life with Christ by the Spirit (3:3–4). This suggests some application to a way of life designed for all believers. But we have seen elsewhere (1 Cor 9:1–5) that Paul may use his life as an example even when the particulars do not apply to Christians in general. Such is probably the case here too with respect to the prominent role of suffering. Paul provides the impetus for Christians to seek the righteousness of Christ by describing vividly the account of his own transformation and experience in ministry.[146] Paul's suffering constitutes a central component of his calling as a minister. This is for Paul's life and ministry the tangible outworking of sharing in the sufferings of Christ.

Much of 2 Corinthians as a whole revolves around the topic of suffering. Paul's contention throughout the letter is that true ministry consists in comfort through suffering (2 Cor 1:1–11), comfort through sorrow (1:12—2:13; 6:11—7:16), glory and life through affliction and death (2:14—6:10), riches through poverty (8:1—9:15) and power through weakness (10:1—13:14). Specific passages 2 Cor 1:5–11; 4:7–12; 6:3–10 serve as representative samples of Paul's theology in the letter.

---

142. Tannehill, *Dying and Rising with Christ*, 120; Hawthorne, *Philippians*, 144; O'Brien, *Philippians*, 402; Fee, *Philippians*, 331.

143. Schütz, *Paul and the Anatomy of Apostolic Authority*, 220–21; Hawthorne, *Philippians*, 145–46; Schenk, *Die Philipperbriefe*, 320–21; Fee, *Philippians*, 313, 326, 329.

144. Hawthorne, *Philippians*, 145; O'Brien, *Philippians*, 410.

145. Hawthorne, *Philippians*, 146; O'Brien, *Philippians*, 410; Fee, *Philippians*, 335.

146. Snyman, "A Rhetorical Analysis of Philippians 3:1–11," 278.

Portrait of an Apostle

In 2 Cor 1:5–11, Paul sees the relational significance of his sufferings in terms of two relationships, his relationship to Christ and his relationship to the Corinthians. First, in 1:5 Paul identifies his sufferings as the "sufferings of Christ" (τὰ παθήματα τοῦ Χριστοῦ). This phrasing is best comprehended as the practical experience of Paul's union with Christ.[147] Believers share in the sufferings of Christ and also experience his comfort.[148] Paul thus sees his sufferings as a participation in the sufferings of Christ. Second, Paul views his suffering as endured for the sake of those to whom he ministers. In 1:6 Paul reveals that his suffering is motivated by the goal of the Corinthians' comfort and salvation. Paul expected that his suffering-laden ministry would strengthen the Corinthians through their own trials and would propel them towards the goal of their salvation.[149] Paul hopes that his own experience of comfort through suffering will serve to motivate his readers in their suffering (1:7).[150] Paul then relates a recent trial in his own life as a vivid picture of both the intensity of suffering and the faithfulness of God to sustain and deliver (1:8–10). As was the case with σωτηρία in Phil 1:19, Paul's use of ῥύομαι in 2 Cor 1:10 may point to vindication, whether through release from prison or through death.[151] In

147. This view is preferred by Ahren, "The Fellowship of His Sufferings," 21; Tannehill, *Dying and Rising with Christ*, 91; Furnish, *II Corinthians*, 118–20; Garland, *2 Corinthians*, 66–67; Thrall, *Second Epistle to the Corinthians*, 1:108–10. The backdrop of the concept of Messianic woes, if present, is secondary (see Barnett, *Second Epistle to the Corinthians*, 74).

148. It is difficult to determine the degree of eschatological emphasis in this passage. The repetition of comfort may echo the promise of salvation announced in Isa 40:1–2 and the continued interest in the comfort theme in Isa 49:13; 51:3, 12, 19; 54:11; 61:2; 66:13. Those detecting connotations of salvation in Paul's repeated use of comfort language in 2 Cor 1:3–7 include Tannehill, *Dying and Rising with Christ*, 91–93; Schütz, *Paul and the Anatomy of Apostolic Authority*, 243; Martin, *2 Corinthians*, 9; Barnett, *Second Epistle to the Corinthians*, 69; Garland, *2 Corinthians*, 59–60. In addition, from the ambiguous sense of the language of deliverance (ῥύομαι) in 1:10, it may be inferred that future eschatological deliverance is not far from Paul's mind, especially in view of the connection to Christ's resurrection in 1:9 and the mention of death in 1:10.

149. See Barnett, *Second Epistle to the Corinthians*, 77; Thrall, *Second Epistle to the Corinthians*, 110.

150. It is quite possible that Paul was also attempting to reinforce his relationship with his readers through his recognition of their shared sufferings (Fredrickson, "Paul, Hardships, and Suffering," 182).

151. The possibility that ῥύομαι alternates between vindication through release from prison and vindication at the final judgment is strengthened by the repetition of the verb, the change in tense from past to future, and the reference to God raising Christ from the dead in 1:9 (see Barnett, *Second Epistle to the Corinthians*, 87–88).

the course of his sufferings, Paul once again highlights his reliance on the prayers of his fellow believers and sees potential favorable answers from God in the future as a source of thanksgiving among those who witness God's deliverance (1:11). Paul is keenly aware of both the work of God in the midst of his sufferings and of the potential impact that his sufferings and deliverance may have upon those to whom he ministers.

Paul returns to this dual emphasis in 2 Cor 4:7–12. The greater literary context demonstrates Paul's interest in the juxtaposition of suffering and glory.[152] Paul paints a vivid picture of his sufferings, which are permitted in order to magnify the power of God in him (4:7). Paul's sufferings are severe, but God's sustenance always exceeds the measure of affliction (4:8–9). Paul's sufferings are an extension and illustration of Christ's suffering and death (4:10a).[153] This is confirmed by Paul's use of παραδίδωμι (4:11a) with reference to his experience, echoing the language applied to Christ's suffering and death (Gal 2:20; 1 Cor 11:23).[154] Through the pairing of πάντοτε and ἀεί (both equivalent to "always") in verses 10 and 11 Paul conveys the belief that suffering is an enduring and even a defining part of his identity as an apostle.[155] But suffering and even death do not signify defeat for Christ or for Paul, as demonstrated by Christ's resurrection and the corresponding power that is expressed through Paul in his ministry of suffering (4:10b, 11b). Paul's conclusion then is that the suffering he endures results in life for those to whom he ministers (4:12). In this section as a whole, Paul defines his ministry in terms of intimate participation in the suffering and power of Christ. Paul welcomes this close association with Christ's suffering for the sake of believers such as those in Corinth. He suffers for them so that they will experience the reality of Christ's life in their lives. This concern for the Corinthians is reiterated in 4:15, though in that verse Paul ultimately places the accent of his motivations on pleasing God, returning to his initial theme from 4:7.[156]

As already mentioned earlier 2 Cor 6:3–10 owes some of its direction to the influence of Isaiah 49. Paul draws upon the figure of the servant

---

Multiple textual variants in 1:10 further complicate the matter. See Metzger, *Textual Commentary on the Greek New Testament*, 506–7.

152. Hafemann, *Suffering and Ministry in the Spirit*, 64; Barnett, *Second Epistle to the Corinthians*, 227–28.

153. See Barnett, *Second Epistle to the Corinthians*, 236; Thrall, *Second Epistle to the Corinthians*, 334.

154. Thrall, *Second Epistle to the Corinthians*, 336.

155. Furnish, *II Corinthians*, 283.

156. This also echoes Paul's perspective from 2 Cor 4:5.

of Isaiah 49 as inspiration for how he carries out his ministry. Paul characterizes his ministry as a servant of God in part by the experience of suffering. This suffering ministry goes hand in hand with Paul's obligation to proclaim God's message of reconciliation. Paul suffers not randomly or incidentally, but his suffering constitutes a central aspect of God's communication of salvation through Paul's life.[157] This suffering, which is in keeping with being a servant of God, serves to help commend Paul as an authentic messenger. Specifically, Paul demonstrates the sincerity of his message and his labors by pointing to his resolve in the presence of much suffering (6:3–5). Suffering has often been severe, and yet God has always sustained Paul in the process (6:9–10). Though in a series of surprising contrasts in these two verses Paul underscores God's power in his own life as the main theme, he once again mentions the spiritual benefits that overflow to others in the midst of his hardship (ὡς πτωχοὶ πολλοὺς δὲ πλουτίζοντες). Confirming this ministry concern, Paul reveals that his purpose for highlighting his suffering throughout the passage is to cultivate a stronger relationship with his readers (6:11–13). He desires a more wholehearted reception of his message of reconciliation, which is interwoven with his authority as a minister to them (5:18—6:2). Once again, Paul's sufferings are invoked in relation to both God's ministry to Paul and Paul's ministry to his readers.

The imprisonment reported in Philemon sheds additional light on Paul's perspective toward suffering.[158] Paul's frequent inclusion of his status as a prisoner as part of his address to Philemon (1:1, 9, 10, 13, 23) suggests that his imprisonment shaped significantly his self-perception at the time. Paul identifies himself as a prisoner (δέσμιος) of Christ, thus attributing his imprisonment more than anything to his service of Christ (Phlm 1:1).[159] Paul expresses the same idea in 1:13, where he specifies that his imprisonment is for the gospel, and in 1:23, where he identifies Epaphras as a fellow prisoner (συναιχμάλωτος) in Christ Jesus.[160] For Paul, suffering

---

157. For the inclusion of both the apostle's life and the gospel's content as part of God's ministry through Paul, see Bockmuehl, *Revelation and Mystery*, 142–44.

158. This may or may not reflect the same imprisonment as the one reported in Phil 1. This chapter of the book is written under the assumption that Philippians was written at an earlier date, during a different imprisonment.

159. See Wansink, *Chained in Christ*, 149–56, for a discussion of possibilities for the meaning of the phrase δέσμιος Χριστοῦ Ἰησοῦ.

160. Epaphras was not necessarily an actual chained prisoner in the same way Paul was. He may have earned this title on the basis of his sacrificial assistance to Paul and his ministry (Cassidy, *Paul in Chains*, 74, 250). Wright leans towards the opinion that

is never detached from Christ, who called Paul to ministry and marked the way of suffering in his own ministry.

In Phlm 8–9, Paul's imprisonment, coupled with his advanced age, appears to spotlight Paul's position of weakness in relation to Philemon, so that he must appeal to Philemon on the basis of love rather than an authoritative command.[161] Confinement was often associated with shame in the Roman world, so Paul's status is in one respect lowered because of his incarceration.[162] Paul signals his desire for release from prison by requesting prayer from Philemon (1:22), which resembles the prayers requested in 2 Cor 1:11 and Phil 1:19. But despite the hindrance and shame of imprisonment, Paul's opportunities for fruitful ministry remain, as indicated by the conversion of Onesimus (1:10) and the prospect that Onesimus's service might facilitate Paul's ministry of the gospel. On the whole, Paul's reinterpretation of his confinement according to a Christ-centered and ministry-oriented perspective provides a more positive overall portrait of a condition that would normally be considered a disadvantage or even a stigma.

From these passages, it is evident that Paul viewed his suffering and imprisonment through the lenses of God's will and Christ's suffering, death, and resurrection. The specific outworking of the believer's union with Christ in Paul's life required that he share in Christ's sufferings before sharing in his glory. Paul also evaluated his suffering in terms of how God was using his hardships to promote the advance of the gospel and to foster spiritual life among the people to whom Paul ministered. Paul was able to affirm the role of suffering in his life because it reminded him that he partook in the life of Christ and it resulted in the spiritual benefit of other believers.

Epaphras was indeed in prison with Paul (Wright, *The Epistles of Paul to the Colossians and to Philemon: An Introduction and Commentary*, 191).

161. This interpretation assumes that the participle ὤν has a causal rather than concessive sense and that "old man" (πρεσβύτης) should be read rather than "ambassador" (πρεσβύτης or πρεσβευτής) (see Lohse, *Colossians and to Philemon*, 198–99; Wansink, *Chained in Christ*, 158–64; Moo, *The Letters to the Colossians and to Philemon*, 404–6). Wright opts for the translation "ambassador" while retaining the causal force of ὤν (Wright, *Epistles of Paul to the Colossians and to Philemon*, 180–81).

162. For instance, with respect to the shame of chains, Ulpian labels chains an "affront" (*Dig.* 49.7.1), and in Josephus's work they are called a "disgrace" (Josephus, *J.W.* 4.628).

Portrait of an Apostle

Conclusion

When the different facets of Paul's ministry, including his calling, God's grace towards him, his reception of the revealed mystery, his interpretation of his appointment against the backdrop of OT expectations, his relationship to other apostles, and his understanding of suffering as a means of carrying out his calling, are viewed in concert, certain common features stand out. First, both the OT Scriptures and God's unexpected bestowal of grace and revelation to Paul shaped Paul's basic orientation in ministry. These two components complement each other, since the servant of Isaiah 49 and other prophets who shaped Paul's self understanding engaged in a ministry of suffering and proclamation based on an unmistakable call from God. Likewise, Paul's proclaimed mystery was grounded in the OT yet was brought to new clarity through his encounter with the glorified Lord. Second, Paul's ministry was situated within an already established tradition of faith, but his specific calling to the Gentiles resulted in a message that applied distinct aspects of the church's tradition. Third, Paul's self-awareness as a divinely-called apostle to the Gentiles shaped his resolution both to please the God who called him by grace and to serve the Gentile churches, even to the point of suffering and death, in fellowship with his suffering Savior.

This analysis of the composite portrait of Paul's perception of his ministry helps set the stage for evaluating the portrayal of Paul in Colossians and Ephesians in chapters 4 and 5. But first subsequent imitations (*Epistle to the Laodiceans, Third Corinthians*) of this image will be dissected in chapter 3.

3

Imitation of Paul in the *Epistle to the Laodiceans* and *3 Corinthians*

Leveraging Paul's Authority

In the second century, two works emerged in which authors attempt to speak for Paul in a later setting. The *Epistle to the Laodiceans* and *3 Corinthians* show significant indebtedness to Paul's letters in their portrayals of ministry and suffering. As part of the strategy of creating the impression that their productions originated with Paul, the authors mimic passages in which Paul describes his calling and his hardships.

Only excerpts related to Paul's apostleship will be investigated in this chapter. For these two pseudepigraphal works, constructing a believable portrayal of Paul's apostleship is essential for maintaining the illusion that the works originate with Paul. Both authors resort to a similar strategy. They avoid straying too far from the picture of Paul in the canonical letters by borrowing directly from single passages or combining two passages. Later in this book the pseudepigraphal tactics observed in these letters will be measured against what is found in Colossians and Ephesians.[1]

---

1. Other scholars have compared potential cases of Pauline canonical pseudepigraphy to the certain instances of the practice found in *Ep. Lao.* and *3 Cor.* (Guthrie, "Acts and Epistles in Apocryphal Writings," 338–45; Kiley, *Colossians as Pseudepigraphy*, 27–32 (Laodiceans only); Bauckham, "Pseudo-Apostolic Letters," 475–92; Harding, "Disputed and Undisputed Letters of Paul," 138–43).

Portrait of an Apostle

The Challenge of Creating a Pseudepigraphal Letter

It is generally agreed that creating a pseudepigraphal letter was no easy task. Writers faced unique challenges when they attempted to produce effective pseudepigraphal letters, challenges that were not encountered when authors mimicked authentic works in other genres. Writing texts under the name of a famous religious figure was common in early Christianity, but the use of the genre of the letter was less widespread than the use of other forms. Montague James attributes this lack of popularity to several factors: "the Epistle was on the whole too serious an effort for the forger, more liable to detection, perhaps, as a fraud, and not so likely to gain the desired popularity as a narrative or an Apocalypse."[2] Even short pseudepigraphal documents demonstrate the difficulty of simultaneously saying something meaningful and adhering faithfully to the language and style of the purported author. Richard Bauckham notes that pseudepigraphal letters reveal their true colors in either their lack of a guiding purpose or their inclusion of unnecessary background detail that would have already been known by the implied audience.[3] The high risk of detection coupled with the low potential for influence helps explain why there are relatively few extant examples of undisputed pseudepigraphy, even for a prominent figure such as Paul.

In the face of these challenges, the *Epistle to the Laodiceans* and *3 Corinthians* were written. As a relatively simple imitation of Paul's self-portrayal and the less imaginative of the two works in Paul's name, the *Epistle to the Laodiceans* will be examined first.

The Epistle to the Laodiceans

Scholars are nearly unanimously unimpressed with this short imitation of Paul's non-canonical letters, seeing it as an unimaginative compilation of verses primarily from Philippians. As a result, this document attracts little interest within the academic community, even though its presence in a number of New Testament manuscripts attests to its esteem among certain parts of the church throughout history.[4] Many experts assume that the

---

2. James, *The Apocryphal New Testament*, 476. Donald Guthrie concurs with James' analysis (Guthrie, "Acts and Epistles in Apocryphal Writings," 344–45).

3. Bauckham, "Pseudo-Apostolic Letters," 475–78, 485–87.

4. See Lightfoot, *Epistles to the Colossians and to Philemon*, 294–99. The most significant manuscript containing the epistle is the Latin Vulgate Codex Fuldensis (ibid., 282, 286).

reference to a letter to the Laodiceans in Col 4:16 served as the catalyst for the pseudepigrapher, and that there may have been no other impulse behind his creation.⁵ Pseudepigraphal works commonly arise from similar allusions to lost works in literature.⁶ The author of the *Epistle to the Laodiceans* (*Ep. Lao.*) reveals this intent through the closing line of the letter: "And see that this epistle is read to the Colossians and that of the Colossians among you."

In contrast to the majority position, a few scholars have advanced theories that there was an additional motivation behind the letter. Harnack posited that followers of Marcion were responsible for its composition.⁷ In support of this theory, the Muratorian Canon, which most likely dates to the late second century, mentions the rejection of a Marcionite document called The Epistle to the Laodiceans.⁸ And some of the minor alterations of Paul's letters appearing in *Ep. Lao.* could be explained by the work of a Marcionite redactor.⁹ It is also possible that the extant *Ep. Lao.* incorporates material that originated in the Marcionite community but was written in its final form for orthodox purposes.¹⁰ Still, the letter cannot be considered a major expression of Marcionite theology, since the letter was accepted for a time within segments of orthodox Christianity.¹¹ It has even been suggested that the letter was penned as a response to a heretical Marcionite epistle with the same title, with the hopes that the appearance of an "orthodox" letter to the Laodiceans would discredit

---

5. "[I]ts wooden method of stringing together Pauline texts seems to testify more to a pure literary interest in 'reconstructing' a lost Pauline letter than to a desire to recapture Pauline thought" (Meade, *Pseudonymity and Canon*, 196–97). See also Lightfoot, *Epistles to the Colossians and to Philemon*, 281–82; Guthrie, "Acts and Epistles in Apocryphal Writings," 342–43; Penny, "The Pseudo-Pauline Letters of the First Two Centuries," 325–26; Schneemelcher, "Epistle to the Laodiceans," 43.

6. Bauckham, "Pseudo-Apostolic Letters," 485.

7. Harnack, *Marcion: Das Evangelium vom fremden Gott*, 172–73, 143*–44* (appendix).

8. From the fragment, we read, "There are also in circulation one to the Laodiceans, and another to the Alexandrians, forged under the name of Paul, and addressed against the heresy of Marcion" (*Muratorian Canon* [ANF 5:603]). It is debated whether this letter to the Laodiceans is the same one that was included in later Bibles.

9. See for instance the omission of καὶ θεοῦ πατρός from Gal 1:1 in *Ep. Lao.* 1 or the addition of *perpetuam* to Phil 1:19 in *Ep. Lao.* 7 (Harnack, *Marcion: Das Evangelium vom fremden Gott*, 123, 141,* 143*).

10. This theory is considered briefly by Blackman, *Marcion and His Influence*, 61–62.

11. Schneemelcher, "Epistle to the Laodiceans," 44.

the Marcionite document.¹² A more general purpose of combating heresy has also been posited.¹³ Or perhaps the letter was designed to supply the Laodicean church with a more substantive connection to the beloved apostle.¹⁴ In the end, though, the evidence in support of these theories is not compelling. The best explanation remains that the author of *Ep. Lao.* had no major theological motive in producing the work but simply hoped to supply the church with the "lost" epistle mentioned in Colossians.

Though an original Greek manuscript does not exist, Greek is believed to be the original language of the work: "The Latin reflects Greek idiom, and the Pauline language does not follow the known Latin version of the canonical epistles."¹⁵ Because of the striking similarity between the letter and Paul's letters to the Philippians and the Galatians, the original Greek wording may be postulated by recourse to Paul's letters.¹⁶

The epistle begins with an excerpt from Gal 1:1: "Paul, an apostle not of men and not through man, but through Jesus Christ." The incorporation of Gal 1:1 in *Ep. Lao.* 1 is one of several places in the first few verses in which the author opts for wording from Galatians rather than Philippians. After the first four verses the author draws almost exclusively from Philippians throughout the remainder of the epistle. Galatians 1:1 opens the letter with a more aggressive tone than does Phil 1:1. Harnack promoted the idea that the use of Gal 1:1 in *Ep. Lao.* 1, with the elevation of Paul and the omission of God the Father, signals the Marcionite character of the letter.¹⁷ Schneemelcher argues that this hypothesis gives too much credit

---

12. See for instance Pink, "Die pseudo-paulinischen Briefe II," 192; Ehrman, *Lost Christianities*, 214–15.

13. Donelson, *Pseudepigraphy and Ethical Argument in the Pastoral Epistles*, 43.

14. Burnet, "Pourquoi avoir récrit l'insipide épître aux Laodicéens?," 140–41.

15. Elliott, *Apocryphal New Testament*, 544. See also Lightfoot, *Epistles to the Colossians and to Philemon*, 291–92.

16. Lightfoot took this approach in producing his hypothetical Greek translation of the letter (Lightfoot, *Epistles to the Colossians and to Philemon*, 293–94). Lightfoot's critical edition of the Latin text is used in this section (ibid., 287–89). The English wording discussed in this section is taken from the translation found in Schneemelcher, "Epistle to the Laodiceans," 44–45.

17. Harnack, *Marcion: Das Evangelium vom fremden Gott*, 141,* 144*. According to indirect testimony by Tertullian and direct testimony from Epiphanius, Galatians was the first epistle in Marcion's Pauline canon (J. Knox, *Marcion and the New Testament*, 44–45). Tertullian begins with Galatians in his interaction with Marcion's use of Paul's letters (Tertullian, *Against Marcion* 5.2). Epiphanius observes that Galatians stood at the beginning of Marcion's Pauline canon (Epiphanius, *Pan.* 9.4, 12.2).

to the otherwise pedestrian author of *Ep. Lao.*[18] While it is agreed that the author is not advancing substantive thinking in the letter as a whole, the verse may at least betray a high regard for Paul and his authority.

But does the placement of Gal 1:1 in the new context of *Ep. Lao.* result in a coherent line of discourse? In Galatians, this opening statement anticipates an important theme in the first two chapters of the letter. In Galatians Paul defends a gospel that is tied directly to the revelation and calling he received from God. Paul's fight for the true gospel emerges quickly in Gal 1:6–9, where he condemns a "different" (ἕτερος) gospel (1:6–7), or a gospel that departs from his (1:8–9). He then follows by emphasizing the origin of his gospel as being from Jesus Christ himself (1:11–12). In Gal 2:5, 11–14 Paul recalls his persistence in upholding the gospel in the face of opposition. In the remaining chapters, Paul engages in a vigorous defense of the content of the gospel that had been entrusted to him by God. So, in Galatians, Paul begins in 1:1 with a tone and theme that reflects the content that will follow in the first two chapters of the letter.

Such is not the case with *Ep. Lao.* Apart from some very vague and relatively mild statements about opponents of the gospel in v. 4 ("the vain talk of some people who . . . lead you away from the truth") and v. 13 ("those who are out for sordid gain") there is little evidence that "Paul" is mounting an energetic advance of his teachings in the face of sustained opposition or teetering loyalties. Therefore, there is no need for "Paul" to assert his authority in a forceful way, as was the case in Gal 1:1. The author of *Ep. Lao.* has misappropriated Paul's self-description. In Galatians, Paul must highlight the divine origins of his apostleship and gospel because he fears that the faith of the Galatians is in danger. But in the *Epistle to the Laodiceans* the content of the letter does not call for an elevation of Paul's status. Though such an elevation might be deemed necessary for a group that wanted to insist on Paul's enhanced position after his lifetime, it would not fit Paul's own agenda or pattern in a non-polemic context during his own lifetime and ministry. In Paul's other undisputed letters, his apostleship is stated briefly (1 Cor 1:1; 2 Cor 1:1; Rom 1:1) or omitted altogether (1 Thess 1:1; Phil 1:1; Phlm 1) in the opening greetings.

A high esteem for Paul is further confirmed in *Ep. Lao.* 4, where the author qualifies "the truth of the gospel" with the clause "which is proclaimed by me (Paul)."[19] The wording reflected here may originate from

---

18. Schneemelcher, "Epistle to the Laodiceans," 44.

19. Harnack again sees evidence in these phrases for a Marcionite agenda (Harnack, *Marcion: Das Evangelium vom fremden Gott*, 141*). The verse certainly does

Gal 2:5 or 14 and Gal 1:11. In Gal 1:11 the qualifier τὸ εὐαγγελισθὲν ὑπ' ἐμοῦ functions to help specify the topic that will be under discussion in Gal 1:11b-12. It is *Paul's* gospel that is at issue. In *Ep. Lao.* 4, the addition of the words "which is preached by me" serves no obvious purpose. Following on the heels of a warning against succumbing to false teaching, one might have expected instead "which was preached to you" as a means of redirecting the readers to their original acceptance of the truth. For instance, in 1 Cor 15:1 a construction similar to that of Gal 1:11 places the emphasis more on the readers' reception than on Paul's act of preaching, since this focus is more suited to the context. The combination in *Ep. Lao.* 4 of a reader-oriented concern and a focus on the legitimacy of Paul's gospel is not as coherent as the consistent emphasis on the reader's faith in 1 Corinthians 15 or the consistent defense of Paul's gospel in Galatians 1.

Taken in unison, *Ep. Lao.* 1 and 4 betray influence from Galatians and highlight Paul's apostolic calling and the divine origin of his teaching. What is absent though is a moderating perspective that associates Paul's teaching with the teaching of the other apostles. The unknown compiler's adoption of Gal 2:5/14 and especially Gal 1:1, 11 apart from the rest of the discourse from Galatians 1–2 has the effect of isolating Paul as an independent agent for the truth without the balancing component of situating his apostleship and gospel within a greater landscape. Even in the context of great tension and high stakes in Galatians, Paul's gospel is purposefully located within the larger stream of Christian tradition (Gal 2:1–2; see also 1 Cor 15:3). Thus whereas Paul's intent in Galatians is to maintain that his ministry and apostleship is on equal footing and in essential harmony with that of the other apostles, the writer of the *Epistle to the Laodiceans* appears to incorporate the material in Gal 1:1 and 1:11 without an obvious goal in mind. The combination of fragments from Galatians 1–2 reveals the pseudepigrapher's support for Paul but does not contribute to an overall message that echoes Paul's teachings.

The compiler of the *Epistle to the Laodiceans* makes further reference to Paul's ministry by bringing attention to Paul's imprisonment (v. 6–8). At this point in the letter, the writer is simply following a straight though significantly abbreviated path through the canonical letter to the Philippians. The wording of *Ep. Lao.* 6 ("And now my bonds are manifest, which I suffer in Christ, on account of which I am glad and rejoice") is a conflation

---

betray a high regard for Paul, but the more likely scenario is that the author is trying to imitate Pauline language by drawing upon Gal 1–2 (which is a central passage for depicting Paul's ministry and gospel).

of Phil 1:13 and 1:18. But both Phil 1:13 and 18 lose their original force in the new context of *Ep. Lao.* 6. First, the separation in *Ep. Lao.* 6 of *palam* from *in Christo* in the declaration *palam sunt vincula mea quae patior in Christo* conveys a nuance that is slightly different from that of Phil 1:13, where the connection of φανερούς and ἐν Χριστῷ highlights Paul's public identification with Christ in his imprisonment. This is confirmed by how τοὺς δεσμούς μου φανεροὺς ἐν Χριστῷ γενέσθαι provides the tangible result (ὥστε) of how his circumstances have advanced the gospel (Phil 1:12). This rich theology of suffering for the sake of the church is weakened in *Ep. Lao.* 6, so that there remains only a general statement that Paul's chains are publicly recognized. The second half of *Ep. Lao.* 6, which echoes Phil 1:18, expresses Paul's rejoicing in Christ. In Phil 1:18 the cause for rejoicing is identified as the propagation of the message of Christ. This explicit cause has not been retained in *Ep. Lao.* 6. The picture of Paul rejoicing in publicly suffering for Christ has the effect of presenting suffering as a badge of honor. Thus in *Ep. Lao.* 6 the original evangelistic context has been bypassed in favor of an elevation of the nobility of Paul's suffering.

Far from considering the ministry implications of Paul's sufferings, *Ep. Lao.* 7 moves immediately to the personal spiritual benefits of Paul's hardship, when the author states, "This ministers to me unto eternal salvation." The clause reflects Phil 1:19. The addition of *perpetuam* demonstrates that the author of *Epistle to the Laodiceans* (or perhaps a translator) understood σωτηρία in terms of eschatological deliverance rather than deliverance from prison or vindication.[20] It has been argued in chapter 2 of this book that the ambiguity of the term σωτηρία in Phil 1:19 allows for a rhetorically effective deliberation between the options of life and death. But this weighing of choices never unfolds in *Ep. Lao.* 6–8. The author looks to the Laodiceans' prayers and the support of the Holy Spirit for the attainment of salvation, mirroring the same dual interest in Phil 1:19. But by ignoring some material from Phil 1:20 (especially ὅτι . . . μεγαλυνθήσεται Χριστὸς ἐν τῷ σώματί μου), the author once again reflects a shallow understanding of Paul's central motivation in the original passage. Because of this disregard for Paul's goal to magnify Christ through his trying circumstances, the part of Phil 1:20 that is picked up in *Ep. Lao.* 7 (εἴτε διὰ ζωῆς εἴτε διὰ θανάτου) does not have the same rhetorical impact in its new context. The inclusion of the options of life and death is out of place in *Ep Lao.* 6, since one of the two options (ongoing life for the sake

---

20. Alternatively, the addition reflects Marcionite interests (Harnack, *Marcion: Das Evangelium vom fremden Gott*, 143*).

of ministering to others) is never developed in the passage. In Phil 1:22–26 Paul expands upon the benefits of each option, but these verses are absent in *Ep. Lao.* 6–8. The author merely echoes Phil 1:21 (*Est enim mihi vivere in Christo et mori gaudium* for Ἐμοὶ γὰρ τὸ ζῆν Χριστὸς καὶ τὸ ἀποθανεῖν κέρδος), which apart from a broader ministry concern serves only to reinforce the narrow scope of Paul's interests in *Ep. Lao.* 6–8.

In short, *Ep. Lao.* 6–8 significantly abbreviates the longer discussion in Phil 1:12–26, so that whereas in Philippians Paul's chains are seen both in relation to his own experience (1:19) and in relation to the experience of others (1:12–13, 24–25), in *Ep. Lao.* 6–8 Paul's bonds are viewed only with respect to his own struggle and destiny. This reflects a view of suffering and status that idealizes the sufferer, perhaps conceiving of suffering as the purest expression of discipleship. Paul understood suffering as a necessary corollary to the believer's union with Christ and as a required service for the advance of the gospel. The author of the *Epistle to the Laodiceans* understands suffering more as a journey with Christ towards salvation and appears to have been oblivious to ministry implications of Paul's trials. In other words, the author has borrowed verses from Paul while inadvertently importing ideas of suffering that are foreign to Paul.

The characterization of Paul in the *Epistle to the Laodiceans* reflects direct dependence on Galatians 1 and Philippians 1, without evidence of a fresh expression according to the author's context or according to the creative mind of the original apostle. The resulting portrayal of Paul overstates his apostolic calling and status for such a calm letter and restricts the significance of his suffering to his own experience with Christ. Paul is thus upheld as an approved authority figure and a worthy model for discipleship. That this letter fails to sound the voice of Paul credibly even though it confines itself almost exclusively to the language of Paul suggests that the task of mimicking another writer in a letter is very challenging indeed.[21]

Third Corinthians

Third Corinthians receives a warmer reception in the academic community than does the *Epistle to the Laodiceans*. The letter from Paul is presented as a response to a letter written from the Corinthian community to Paul.[22]

---

21. See Guthrie, "Acts and Epistles in Apocryphal Writings," 344.

22. In this section, *3 Corinthians* refers to both the letter to Paul and the letter from Paul. There is introductory material to both letters, but this was most likely inserted after *3 Corinthians* was written in order to facilitate the incorporation of the letters into

Before analyzing the text itself, a few preliminary remarks need to be made about the relationship of the two letters to the apocryphal Acts of Paul and about the general qualities that mark the work as pseudepigraphal.

Third Corinthians and the Acts of Paul

In departure from the consensus opinion of the past, scholars today typically hold that 3 *Corinthians* was not originally contained in the *Acts of Paul* (AP).[23] Vahan Hovhannessian does a thorough job of unfolding the case for the independence of the two works.[24] On the whole, the evidence suggests that a later editor combined AP and 3 *Corinthians*, adding the brief introductory narratives before each letter in order to fit the letters into the flow of the AP.[25]

Observations on the Pseudepigraphal Character of 3 *Corinthians*

Though 3 *Corinthians* was valued for a time as canonical in segments of the Syrian and Armenian churches, scholars today recognize its pseudepigraphal character. With Lapham, observers readily recognize the "ideas and phrases borrowed from previous Pauline correspondence."[26] Rist adds that 3 *Corinthians* contains a variety of "circumstantial details and incidents in order to prove apostolic authorship."[27] Hovhanessian embarks on

---

the narrative in the *Acts of Paul*. See further explanation in the section that follows and in Hovhanessian, *Third Corinthians*, 47–56.

23. See for instance Testuz, *Papyrus Bodmer X-XII*, 24; Klijn, "The Apocryphal Correspondence between Paul and the Corinthians," 10–16; Schneemelcher, "The Acts of Paul," 2:229; Elliott, *Apocryphal New Testament*, 354; Rodorf, "Hérésie et Orthodoxie," 57–58; Lapham, *An Introduction to the New Testament Apocrypha*, 143. Contra Guthrie, "Acts and Epistles in Apocryphal Writings," 338–39; Bauckham, "Pseudo-Apostolic Letters," 485–86.

24. Hovhanessian, *Third Corinthians*, 48–53.

25. This conclusion reduces the relevance to 3 *Corinthians* of Tertullian's testimony about the writer of the *Acts of Paul* who had admitted to attributing his own work to Paul: "But if the writings which wrongly go under Paul's name, claim Thecla's example as a license for women's teaching and baptizing, let them know that, in Asia, the presbyter who composed that writing, as if he were augmenting Paul's fame from his own store, after being convicted, and confessing that he had done it from love of Paul, was removed from his office" (Tertullian, *Baptism* 17 [*ANF* 3:677]).

26. Lapham, *New Testament Apocrypha*, 144.

27. Rist, "Pseudepigraphy and the Early Christians," 76.

an extensive discussion of the pseudepigraphal markers in *3 Corinthians*. He highlights the discontinuities in style, wording, theology, and historical sequence with the canonical portrayal of Paul that are cues to the pseudepigraphal nature of *3 Corinthians*.[28] He also suspects the author's use of specific techniques of deception: "The pseudo-historical setting of 3 Cor is created by inserting references to events and problems in the history of the Corinthian Church or in the life of Paul known to the reader from other sources," including false teaching, disagreement over the resurrection, Paul's captivity, and prior interaction between Paul and the Corinthians.[29] Hovhanessian also charges that the author betrays his attempts to mimic Paul's habits of communication, though the author fails in some key areas such as in the omission of substantial introductory and concluding prayers for his readers.[30] Most telling is that the major components of the heretical teachings that the letters engage are attested in the second century rather than the first.[31] In *3 Corinthians* the community that pens the letter to Paul describes the errors of their opponents very specifically:

> For such is what they say and teach: We must not, they say, make use of the prophets, and that God is not almighty, and that there is no resurrection for the flesh, and that the creation of man is not by God, and that the Lord did not come in the flesh nor was he born of Mary, and that the world is not of God but of angels.[32]

This description conforms to what we know of the second-century heresies that fall under the broad umbrella of gnosticism.[33]

Now that the broad outlines of pseudepigraphal tendencies have been identified, we may look more closely at the verses in *3 Corinthians* that relate to Paul's ministry.[34]

28. Hovhanessian, *Third Corinthians*, 88.

29. Ibid., 95–96. See also Penny, "The Pseudo-Pauline Letters of the First Two Centuries," 294–95.

30. Hovhanessian, *Third Corinthians*, 97, 100.

31. Ibid., 107–19.

32. All English quotes, unless otherwise indicated, are taken from Hovhanessian's English translation of the Greek manuscript PBodm X. This manuscript is the only extant witness in what was likely the original language of the work, and it is considered relatively reliable in what it has preserved (ibid., 76).

33. Ibid., 107–19; Meade, *Pseudonymity and Canon*, 158; Bauckham, "Pseudo-Apostolic Letters," 486. Most scholars date the letter later in the second century (see for instance Testuz, *Papyrus Bodmer X-XII*, 23).

34. Though in *3 Corinthians* the author does submit content not directly borrowed from Paul's letters, he does so primarily in sections not related to Paul's apostleship and ministry.

Analysis of Paul's Ministry in *3 Corinthians*

The letter from Paul to the Corinthians begins with a standard Pauline self-identification: "Paul, the prisoner for Christ Jesus." This title is very similar to what is used in Phlm 1 and Eph 3:1. In Philemon and Ephesians, the title refers to the actual imprisonment of Paul.[35] The situation in 3 *Cor.* is not as clear. The introductory scene-setting before Paul's letter mentions his imprisonment, but this is likely a later interpretation of the letters when the letters were grafted into the *Acts of Paul*. There are allusions to Paul's hardships in *3 Cor.* 2:2 and 2:34–35,[36] and since nothing in the context suggests a metaphorical understanding of the term δέσμιος, the term should probably be taken literally. Given that this is a pseudepigraphal work, what is the author's motive for including this designation of Paul? It is likely that the image of Paul as a prisoner was employed because of its ready association with Paul, in a move to bolster the authentic feel to the letter.[37] This connotation of Paul as a prisoner suffering for his convictions may also have the added effect of strengthening the force and urgency of his words.[38] The opening phrase thus sets the tone for what will follow in the letter. But in light of this function of an opening verse, a similarity between the *Epistle to the Laodiceans* and *3 Corinthians* is observed. Both begin with a specific image of Paul (Paul as a divinely authorized apostle in *Ep. Lao.* and as a chained prisoner in 3 *Cor.*) that is not explicitly and fully developed throughout the rest of the letter.[39]

The next phrase of interest follows the mention of the Corinthians but modifies Paul: ΕΝ ΠΟΛΛΟΙΣ ΩΝ ΑΣΤΟΧΗΜΑΣΙ. The rendering

---

35. See Phlm 9 (10, 13, 22); Eph 4:1 (6:20).

36. There is no standard verse numbering system for *3 Cor.* This paper follows Hovhanessian, who calls the letter from the Corinthians chapter 1 and the letter to the Corinthians chapter 2 (skipping the intervening material that was included later).

37. Penny, "The Pseudo-Pauline Letters of the First Two Centuries," 303; Hovhanessian, *Third Corinthians*, 95–96.

38. Or, the purpose could have been to garner "a more sympathetic hearing from the reader" (Penny, "The Pseudo-Pauline Letters of the First Two Centuries," 295). If this had been an authentic letter of Paul's we might have expected him to raise his apostleship at the beginning of the letter, since he was preparing to exert his authority to counter false teachings in a decisive way.

39. In the canonical letters, either the actual physical and emotional hardships (2 Tim) or the spiritual and ministry significance (Eph, Phil, Col) of the imprisonment appear as a theme throughout the letters. Some of the spiritual significance of Paul's imprisonment surfaces in *3 Cor.* (2:34–35), but it is relatively undeveloped compared to what is found in the canonical letters.

of the participial phrase should keep the phrase within the greeting itself (ΤΟΙΣ ΕΝ ΚΟΡΙΝΘΩ ΑΔΕΛΦΟΙΣ ΕΝ ΠΟΛΛΟΙΣ ΩΝ ΑΣΤΟΧΗΜΑΣΙ ΧΑΙΡΕΙΝ) and not be carried over to the next sentence.[40] The word ἀστόχημα does not occur in the NT or early Christian works aside from this verse.[41] The cognate verb ἀστοχέω occurs in the Pastoral Epistles in the context of straying from the truth (1 Tim 1:6; 6:21; 2 Tim 2:18).[42] A translation of "failures" appears to be a literal rendering of the word,[43] though in certain contexts, there may be flexibility for a broader meaning of "unexpected troubles." The combination of the participial form of εἰμί and the preposition ΕΝ lends itself naturally to a description of the state or circumstances in which one is found. The content of the letter refutes false teaching, suggesting that the theological errors were on the writer's mind, but Paul's imprisonment is mentioned in the greeting, which supports a meaning of "setback" for ἀστόχημα. Also, a reference to Paul's struggles is probably more suited to a greeting than is a reference to false teaching. All things considered, ΠΟΛΛΟΙΣ ΩΝ ΑΣΤΟΧΗΜΑΣΙ probably pertains to the challenges Paul faced in his imprisonment.[44]

The writer's purpose in alluding to Paul's difficult situation would align well with his decision to set Paul's imprisonment squarely in focus at the beginning of the letter. There could be a vague recollection here of 2 Cor 1:4; 2:4; or 6:4, in which Paul's experience of θλίψις is mentioned.[45]

---

40. Schneemelcher ("The Acts of Paul," 255) places this clause with the next sentence and translates the term as "tribulations" ("Since I am in many tribulations, I do not wonder that the teachings of the evil one are so quickly gaining ground"). Two Latin manuscripts (L, M) also separate the clause from the greetings (see texts in Bratke, "Ein zweiter lateinischer Text des apokryphen Briefwechsels zwischen dem Apostel Paulus und den Korinthern," 586–87; Pink, "Die pseudo-paulinischen Briefe I," 84). This placement is not supported by the Greek word order. A third Latin manuscript (B), a Coptic text, and two Armenian manuscripts follow the Greek by keeping the clause in the greeting (Boese, "Über eine bisher unbekannte Handschrift des Briefwechsels zwischen Paulus und den Korinthern," 70, 73).

41. BDAG, "ἀστόχημα,"146, renders the term as "mistake, error."

42. This verb and the related noun ἀστοχία both denote the idea of "missing the mark" (LSJ, "ἀστόχ-αστος," 262).

43. Ibid.

44. This agrees with Testuz, *Papyrus Bodmer X-XII*, 33–35; Rist "III Corinthians as a Pseudepigraphic Refutation of Marcionism," 51.

45. Guthrie, "Acts and Epistles in Apocryphal Writings," 339–40. See also Schneemelcher, "The Acts of Paul," 268. Hovhanessian points out other examples in which the author of *3 Corinthians* substitutes his own terms for Paul's more typical wording (Hovhanessian, *Third Corinthians*, 92). Perhaps the author has opted for ἀστόχημα as a synonym for θλίψις in this instance.

Imitation of Paul in the Epistle to the Laodiceans and 3 Corinthians

But there is an important contrast between the depiction of Paul in a letter such as 2 Corinthians and in *3 Corinthians*. When Paul stresses his adverse circumstances in his undisputed letters, he often places them within the context of God's redemptive use of them in the lives of others (2 Cor 1:6; 4:7–12; Phil 1:12–18, 22–25; 2:16–17). The inclusion of Paul's difficulties in the greeting of *3 Corinthians* appears to serve no purpose other than to further highlight Paul's challenges. Since in the second century those who were willing to suffer and die for their faith attracted the respect and attention of other believers, the picture of Paul persevering through trials likely reinforces the sincerity and authority of the message in the letter.[46]

In *3 Cor.* 2:4, the status and identity of Paul is developed further, and the question of Paul's relationship to the other apostles surfaces. The writer positions Paul as a recipient and transmitter of Christian teaching: ΕΓΩ ΓΑΡ ΕΝ ΑΡΧΗ ΠΑΡΕΔΩΚΑ ΥΜΙΝ Α ΚΑΙ ΠΑΡΕΛΑΒΟΝ ΥΠΟ ΤΩΝ ΠΡΟ ΕΜΟΥ ΑΠΟΣΤΟΛΩΝ ΓΕΝΟΜΕΝΩΝ ΤΟΝ ΠΑΝΤΑ ΧΡΟΝΟΝ ΜΕΤΑ ΙΗΥ ΧΡΥ. The language of receiving and delivering tradition stems from two passages in 1 Corinthians. First, referring to the Lord's supper, Paul says in 1 Cor 11:23, Ἐγὼ γὰρ παρέλαβον ἀπὸ τοῦ κυρίου, ὃ καὶ παρέδωκα ὑμῖν. Then, introducing the core of Christian doctrine in 1 Cor 15:3, Paul declares, παρέδωκα γὰρ ὑμῖν ἐν πρώτοις, ὃ καὶ παρέλαβον. The order in the sentence in *3 Cor.* 2:4 resembles 1 Cor 15:3 more closely than it does 1 Cor 11:23, but the introductory ΕΓΩ ΓΑΡ mirrors 1 Cor 11:23. It is noted that in *3 Cor.* 2:4, Paul receives the teaching from the apostles who were before him, whereas in 1 Cor 11:23, the teaching is from the Lord, and in 1 Cor 15:3, the source is unspecified. The change is not likely intentional but rather reflects a later time when the apostles were seen as the founding fathers of Christian doctrine.[47] The phrase ΥΠΟ ΤΩΝ ΠΡΟ ΕΜΟΥ ΑΠΟΣΤΟΛΩΝ is probably borrowed from Gal 1:17 (πρὸς τοὺς πρὸ ἐμοῦ ἀποστόλους). This phrase functions as shorthand for Paul's relationship to the other apostles. They precede him chronologically but he is counted in their number.

Schneemelcher's translation of 3 Cor. 2:4 is preferred in this verse: "For I delivered to you in the beginning what I received from the apostles who were before me, who at all times were together with the Lord Jesus

---

46. For the connection between authority or prestige and suffering in early Christianity, see for instance Ign. *Eph.* 3:1; *Trall.* 12:2; *Phild.* 7:2; *Herm.* 9:9—10:1; 69:6–8; 105:5–6; Pol. *Phil.* 1:1; 9:1–2; *Mart. Pol.* 2:1; 14:3.

47. Hovhanessian assumes that there has been an intentional change from 1 Cor 11:23 to *3 Cor.* 2:4 (Hovhanessian, *Third Corinthians*, 63).

Christ."[48] In Schneemelcher's translation the modifier ΠΡΟ ΕΜΟΥ is placed correctly with ἀπόστολος (ΠΑΡΕΛΑΒΟΝ ΥΠΟ ΤΩΝ ΠΡΟ ΕΜΟΥ ΑΠΟΣΤΟΛΩΝ – literally, "the before-me apostles"), rather than with the clause that follows. This is consistent with the meaning of the phrase in Gal 1:17 as well. This translation groups Paul with the apostles but acknowledges their chronological priority and their relatively extensive access to the Lord. There is no trace of the divine source of Paul's teaching and apostleship in the larger context of 3 *Corinthians*. This emphasis was most likely overlooked by the author of 3 *Corinthians*. The writer lived in an era in which Paul was no longer the upstart minister contending for his place at the Christian table but was one of the revered apostles from bygone days. As a result the memory of Paul's own transformative calling and his corresponding authority to deliver God's message has faded from view. Direct and indirect recollections of Paul's Damascus-road encounter are absent. Instead, the writer attaches Paul's teaching to the great tradition of the church, as would be expected in a second-century setting.[49] The energetic, assertive picture of Paul does not shine through in 3 *Corinthians* as it does in the canonical letters of Paul.[50]

After unfolding the content of the letter, in response to the concerns over heresy raised in the letter from the Corinthians, the writer revisits Paul's persona and ministry in 3 *Cor.* 2:34–35: ΕΙ ΔΕ ΤΙ ΑΛΛΟ ΠΑΡΑΔΕΧΕΣΘΕ ΚΟΠΟΥΣ ΜΟΙ ΜΗ ΠΑΡΑΧΕΤΕ. ΕΓΩ ΓΑΡ ΤΑ ΔΕΣΜΑ ΕΙΣ ΤΑΣ ΧΕΙΡΑΣ ΕΧΩ ΕΙΝΑ ΧΡΝ ΚΕΡΔΗΣΩ ΚΑΙ ΤΑ ΣΤΙΓΜΑΤΑ ΕΝ ΤΩ ΣΩΜΑΤΙ ΜΟΥ ΕΙΝΑ ΕΛΘΩ ΕΙΣ ΤΗΝ ΕΚ ΝΕΚΡΩΝ ΑΝΑΣΤΑΣΙΝ.

The writer takes up Gal 6:17 in these verses: (κόπους μοι μηδεὶς παρεχέτω· ἐγὼ γὰρ τὰ στίγματα τοῦ Ἰησοῦ ἐν τῷ σώματί μου βαστάζω). The verse is expanded, however, with the insertion of Paul's chains and with the spiritual outcome of Paul's hardships. References to chains (δεσμός) were common enough in Paul's undisputed letters.[51] The expressions of

---

48. Schneemelcher, "The Acts of Paul," 255.

49. See Rodorf, "Hérésie et Orthodoxie," 45–46. At this point in church history, the church was beginning to emphasize the stability and authenticity of Christian teaching using the concepts of the rule of faith and apostolic succession. The language in 3 *Cor.* 2:4 may betray traces of this mindset.

50. As will be seen in chapter 5 of this book, even when Eph 3:5 situates Paul within the broader Christian tradition, there is still substantial development of Paul's own claim to having received divine revelation (Eph 3:3–4, 7–9).

51. Phil 1:7,13,14,17; Phlm 10, 13.

spiritual result are likely derived from Phil 3:8 (ἵνα Χριστὸν κερδήσω) and 3:11 (εἴ πως καταντήσω εἰς τὴν ἐξανάστασιν τὴν ἐκ νεκρῶν).

Once again, we see that the author of *3 Corinthians* has incorporated material in a way that diverges from the original setting. The combative statement about causing no trouble to Paul fits well within the polemic context of Galatians, but sounds out of place in the relatively measured defense of teaching in *3 Corinthians*. Moreover, the Galatian threats had significantly infiltrated the Christian community, whereas the dangers appear to be from the outside and less immediate in *3 Corinthians*. As a result, the forceful tone seems unnecessary in the Corinthian context.

Some of the same criticisms about the writer's mention of imprisonment in *3 Cor.* 2:1 can be applied to the chains of 2:24. The theme of imprisonment serves no obvious purpose, since Paul does not appeal for prayers for the gospel's penetration or for practical help, and his perspective towards his imprisonment is not put forward as a model to follow. The reference to imprisonment does not appear to have implications beyond Paul's own personal destiny.

The connection between gain and suffering in *3 Cor.* 2:35 comes across as a simplistic cause and effect formula compared to the complex view of the outworkings of the believer's union with Christ in Phil 3. In *3 Cor.* 2:35, the rewards of Christ and the physical resurrection are presented as the motivations for Paul's suffering and imprisonment. Notably absent is any soteriological underpinning to this perspective. The description of how Paul strives towards a glorious goal in Phil 3 occurs within a context of rich reflection on the gracious transformation God produced in his life. Paul observes that his gains in Christ are much more precious than any benefit he possessed beforehand, but he understands his personal gain only within the framework of God's righteousness and the work of Christ. He eschews confidence in his own righteousness in deference to God's gracious provision of righteousness. Paul enters into the saving benefits of Christ's death and resurrection through faith and then gladly participates in Christ's sufferings along the path to sharing in Christ's eternal glory.

Some have supposed that after Paul's defense of the bodily resurrection in *3 Corinthians* he turns to his own expectation of resurrection in 2:34–35.[52] But the proximity of the allusion to Phil 3:11 to the prior defense of the believer's resurrection is probably coincidental. It seems that the writer is employing both familiar wording from Paul and a familiar image of Paul (as a suffering prisoner) in order to strengthen the prospects

---

52. Hovhanessian, *Third Corinthians*, 125.

that the letter will be received as coming from Paul himself. The brief portrait of Paul also helps end the letter on an authoritative note, appealing to Paul's sincere persistence in suffering to the point of death. This theory is supported by the general character of the list of warnings and exhortations that follow in 2:36–39. As part of the overall conclusion to the letter from 2:34–40, verses 34–35 attempts to infuse an authoritative force to the letter without providing any substantive or original teaching. The author has already promoted his primary agenda in the letter's middle section, when he refuted the various errors of the false teaching. The material about Paul's ministry and suffering at the end (as well as at the beginning) of the letter appears to have been included to reinforce the authentic and authoritative feel of the letter and its contents.

Examining the passages in *3 Corinthians* as a group, several trends stand out. First, there is clear imitation of Pauline language in each case, apart from the use of ἀστόχημα in 2:1. Second, the incorporation of Pauline language functions to strengthen the authority behind the writer's arguments. References to imprisonment and suffering serve to heighten the perception of what is at stake. Third, the verses from the canonical letters are adapted in such a way that much of the original context is lost. At times the author even tips his hand by inadvertently reflecting ideas more common to his second-century church setting. Thus, the quotations and allusions depicting Paul's standing as a Christian leader and prisoner are more correctly understood as pseudepigraphal devices.

Conclusion

In this chapter, we have examined two letters written after Paul's time but in his name. In both cases, though descriptions of calling to ministry and endurance of suffering at first bear a close resemblance to Paul's self-portrayals in his undisputed letters, upon closer inspection the passages echoing Pauline material are discovered to be incompatible with Paul's own experiences or perspective. The two pseudepigraphal letters exhibit incomplete or distorted understanding of the original material from Paul's letters. This can be the case even when the writer has quoted an earlier passage verbatim. The letters extract Paul's statements from their original literary and historical contexts and include them in new contexts that do not align with the original force of the words.

These examples provide glimpses of undisputed imitation of Paul by later writers. The pseudepigraphal works represent methodical and deliberate attempts to recreate the voice of Paul in a later generation. Paul's personality is the sole personality intended to be revealed. Accordingly, the authors stay close to Paul's recognized and accepted script when they describe Paul's authority and suffering. Letters such as Colossians and Ephesians, if not originating from Paul, would be expected to exhibit some characteristics found in these other letters written in his name.

4

Paul's Identity in Colossians

Guiding Questions for the Analysis of the Letter

THE FAMILIAR CHARACTERIZATION OF Paul from his early letters has been established. Attempts at mimicry have been analyzed. Now, Colossians takes center stage. In this chapter the key passages under analysis are Col 1:1; 1:23–2:3, 5; 4:4, 10, 18. A careful interpretation of each passage will be presented. The passages will be examined with several questions in mind. First, is the material reflecting Paul's ministry consistent with the broader agenda in the letter in substance and tone? Second, are verbal and conceptual correspondences between these passages and content from undisputed letters of such a nature that those passages in Colossians are best attributed to Paul's own hand (or at least to someone under his direct and active supervision)?[1] Third, are there satisfactory explanations for the absence in Colossians of emphases about Paul's ministry observed in Paul's earlier letters? As seen from the previous chapter of this book, the *Epistle to the Laodiceans* and *3 Corinthians* falter in one or more of these areas. On the other hand, as will be demonstrated by how these same questions are answered, Colossians holds a convincing claim to having originated with Paul.

---

1. This is a difficult question to answer, since the criteria for discerning literary dependence, whether in the form of direct consultation with earlier works or as a product of memory and familiarity, are notoriously subjective, yielding varying opinions even among those who do not hold to Pauline authorship of Colossians. As a result, each alleged occasion of literary borrowing will be handled according to its own characteristics. For a brief overview of the recent investigation into literary dependence and Colossians, see Leppä, *The Making of Colossians*, 15–21.

Paul's Greeting—Colossians 1:1

In Col 1:1, Paul identifies himself as an apostle of Christ Jesus, through the will of God.[2] This conforms to a similar opening in 1 Cor 1:1 and an identical one in 2 Cor 1:1. The introduction puts forward Paul's apostleship and indicates the divine origin of Paul's calling (διὰ θελήματος θεοῦ). It is less forceful than Gal 1:1, where Paul's apostleship is defended, but it is more assertive than 1 Thess 1:1 (where no title is used), Phil 1:1 (δοῦλος) or Phlm 1 (δέσμιος). As mentioned in chapter 2 of this book, Paul introduces himself as an apostle at the beginning of the letter because this role shapes his sense of identity, supports his platform for exhorting his readers, and provides further assurance that the gospel he is proclaiming bears God's authority.

It has been alleged that the resemblance of the Colossian identification of Paul to those in the Corinthian letters confirms a pseudepigraphal undertaking and that no other reason can be posited for having the letter open in this way.[3] But the opening in Col 1:1 both accords with the practice of Paul's earlier letters and fits well into the context of Colossians. Though Paul's apostleship is not under examination in Colossians, as is the case in 1 Corinthians and especially in Galatians and 2 Corinthians, the general wording of Paul's apostleship in Col 1:1 is suited well enough to a letter delivering authoritative teaching. The introduction establishes the grounds upon which Paul instructs his readers in matters of faith and practice. Similar to Romans, where Paul's apostleship is announced at the start but not defended subsequently, the moderately authoritative opening in Colossians is appropriate for a letter addressed to people Paul has not met in person (2:1).[4]

---

2. The author of Colossians will be referred to as Paul in this chapter, for the sake of convenience and in expectation of the conclusions that are being drawn.

3. Wolter, *Der Brief an die Kolosser*, 47. Leppä, beginning with the presupposition of pseudepigraphy, argues for the literary dependence of Col 1:1 upon 2 Cor 1:1, after discounting the potentially significant fact that 2 Cor 1:1 is very similar to 1 Cor 1:1 on the basis that the two were written to the same church and thus would be expected to resemble each other (Leppä, *The Making of Colossians*, 59–63).

4. See Ernst, *Die Briefe an die Kolosser*, 153; Houlden, *Paul's Letters from Prison: Philippians, Colossians, Philemon, and Ephesians*, 145–46; *contra* Collins, who sees "an uncalled for solemnity, especially in an epistle addressed to a community in which Paul's authority had not been opposed" (R. Collins, *Letters That Paul Did Not Write*, 203). Dunn posits that Colossians might lack the hesitancy communicated in Rom 1:11–12 because Paul's associates had been responsible for founding the church at Colossae, as was not the case in Rome (Dunn, *The Epistles to the Colossians and to Philemon*, 45).

An Introduction to Paul's Ministry—Colossians 1:23–2:5

A portrait of Paul as a suffering minister, called by God to advance the gospel and transmit the mystery of Christ, surfaces in Col 1:23—2:5. In this section, the passage will be examined verse by verse, with a particular emphasis on material that relates to the image of Paul as a minister. Verbal and conceptual affinities to Paul's earlier letters will be identified and comparisons with the prior material will be made.

The Transition to the Topic of Paul's Ministry in Colossians 1:23

Paul initiates a change of topic in Col 1:23, signaling at the end of the verse that he will begin to explain his own relationship to the saving gospel. The passage likely functions to foster a connection between Paul and his readers. Several undisputed letters have what is known as an "apostolic apology" (Gal 1:10—2:21; 1 Thess 2:1-12; Phil 1:12-26; 2 Cor 1:12-17) that resembles the discourse of Col 1:23—2:5.[5] As a result, the appearance of a section that sets forth Paul's ministry and self-understanding at this point in Colossians should not be viewed as unexpected.[6] These apostolic apologies serve to remind the readers of the basis for and characteristics of Paul's responsibilities to them.[7] In the apostolic apology of Col 1:24-2:5, Paul does this very thing, by describing the divine calling to suffer for and proclaim God's message and by emphasizing that the scope of his calling includes believers such as the Colossians and others in that area (Col 2:1; cf. 4:13).

The clause οὗ ἐγενόμην ἐγὼ Παῦλος διάκονος has τὸ εὐαγγέλιον as its antecedent. The gospel is the focus and the main topic of 1:23, and Paul is reintroduced with reference to this topic at the end of the verse. Two other descriptions of the gospel precede the mention of Paul. First, Paul specifies that this is gospel that the readers heard, because the readers' response to the gospel is at issue (Col 1:23a). Second, Paul specifies that this gospel is

---

5. Boers says that in the apostolic apology "the apostle speaks of himself and the gospel he proclaims, evidently to establish or reaffirm himself and his proclamation with his readers" (Boers, "The Form Critical Study of Paul's Letters," 153; The term "apostolic" is used in "apostolic apology" to represent Paul's ministry in general and does not indicate that Paul is defending specifically his apostolic standing in this section.

6. *Contra* Betz, "Paul's 'Second Presence' in Colossians," 515.

7. Boers, "Form Critical Study of Paul's Letters," 153.

the one preached everywhere. The wording of Col 1:23b suggests that Paul sees himself as one participant in the larger drama of the gospel's spread.[8] After these two modifiers of the gospel, Paul introduces his connection to the gospel with the clause οὗ ἐγενόμην ἐγὼ Παῦλος διάκονος.

Paul's propensity to define his ministry under the umbrella of the church's wider authentic ministry of the gospel is attested in the undisputed letters. The greeting in Rom 1:1 demonstrates that Paul's ministry is dedicated to the cause of the gospel (ἀφωρισμένος εἰς εὐαγγέλιον θεοῦ).[9] Similarly, Paul speaks of being entrusted with the gospel in 1 Thess 2:4 (δεδοκιμάσμεθα ὑπὸ τοῦ θεοῦ πιστευθῆναι τὸ εὐαγγέλιον). In addition, Paul never envisions himself as the sole bearer of the gospel, apart from the work of the broader church. For example, in Gal 2:7, Paul's and Peter's outreaches are both seen as legitimate vehicles for the gospel message. Paul's ultimate concern according to 1 Cor 15:11 and Phil 1:15–18 is that the true message of the gospel is being proclaimed, regardless of the source or the motive. Though the absence of discussion about the standing of Paul relative to other apostles is noted (and will be explored at the end of this chapter), Col 1:23 nonetheless attaches Paul's ministry to the all-encompassing ministry of the gospel. It is noteworthy, then, that Col 1:23 conveys a concept of Paul's relationship to the gospel that is consistent with the portrayal in the undisputed letters without using the same wording to express the idea.

The subjugation of Paul's ministry to the greater gospel expansion in Col 1:23 rings true to Paul because it locates Paul within the broader stream of early Christian preaching rather than elevating or isolating him.[10] In other words, Col 1:23 does not go the route of unduly accentuating Paul's authority (as with the *Epistle to the Laodiceans*). At the same time, Paul's individual calling is not forgotten (as was the case in 3 *Cor.* 2:4). Paul became a minister of this gospel, presumably by means of God's appointment (see also the reference to the will of God in Col 1:1).

8. This was the case with Epaphras's role in Col 1:7 as well. O'Brien notes: "It is the gospel that gives the validity to Paul's commission: he is to serve that gospel and to proclaim it fully and effectively throughout the world" (O'Brien, *Colossians, Philemon*, xlviii). In contrast, Lohse believes that the author employs Paul's ministry as a means of authenticating the gospel message (Lohse, *Colossians and Philemon*, 67; cf. Gnilka, *Der Kolosserbrief*, 92; Penny, "The Pseudo-Pauline Letters of the First Two Centuries," 347).

9. Cf. Rom 15:16.

10. See Abbott, *Epistles to the Ephesians and to the Colossians*, 228. *Contra* de Boer, "Images of Paul in the Post-Apostolic Period," 364; Nielsen, "The Status of Paul and His Letters in Colossians," 109.

Portrait of an Apostle

While Paul is not isolated as a minister without peer, he still associates himself overtly with an authorized gospel ministry. The inclusion of the emphatic personal pronoun ἐγώ as part of the shift in topic to Paul's ministry helps achieve a clear connection between Paul and the work of the gospel. The use of this pronoun has been seen by some as one indication of the hand of a later imitator.[11] Similarly, a conscious attempt to underscore Paul's authority as an apostle has been detected.[12] But it is not likely that this rhetorical feature elevates Paul in a way that would be foreign to the true Paul. Paul enlists ἐγώ Παῦλος in Gal 5:2, 1 Thess 2:18, 2 Cor 10:1, and Phlm 19. On two of these occasions, Paul supplements the expression ἐγώ Παῦλος with additional wording intended to spotlight him.[13] The expression is used in Gal 5:2 and 2 Cor 10:1 to summon the readers' attention to Paul's admonitions, while Phlm 19 adds force to an assertion made by Paul. In 1 Thess 2:18, the wording serves to identify Paul in distinction from his coworkers. The latter use may be in operation in Col 1:23.[14] Or, the emphatic identification may support the topic switching that is occurring at the end of the verse. This latter use accords well with the likelihood that Paul is beginning his apostolic apology in the verses that follow.

There is textual discrepancy about whether διάκονος ("minister") is the earliest reading in Col 1:23, but the superior external support for the reading in the text suggests that it is the original. The term signifies someone who is engaged in furthering the interests of someone else, and in many contexts the word designates someone "who serves as an intermediary in a transaction."[15] Paul incorporates this term to describe his role in facilitating the advance of the gospel, a role that he unfolds in the verses that follow 1:23. The term chosen is not meant to grant exclusive

---

11. De Boer, "Images of Paul in the Post-Apostolic Period," 365; Nielsen, "The Status of Paul and His Letters in Colossians," 110; R. Collins, *Letters That Paul Did Not Write*, 204.

12. MacDonald, *Colossians and Ephesians*, 74; Leppä, *The Making of Colossians*, 103.

13. 2 Corinthians 10:1 reads Αὐτὸς δὲ ἐγώ Παῦλος and 1 Thess 2:18 ἐγώ μὲν Παῦλος.

14. O'Brien, *Colossians, Philemon*, 71; Moo, *Letters to the Colossians and to Philemon*, 147.

15. BDAG, "διάκονος," 230; cf. J. Collins, "The Mediatorial Aspect of Paul's Role as Diakonos," 42–43. This intermediary role, especially when not exclusive to one person (see Epaphras in 1:7 and Tychicus in 4:7), should probably retain humble connotations rather than acquiring a sense of elevated importance (*contra* MacDonald, *Colossians and Ephesians*, 74).

prestige to Paul, since Epaphras (1:7) and Tychicus (4:7) are also given the appellation διάκονος.[16]

Paul adopts for himself the title διάκονος several times in the undisputed letters (1 Cor 3:5; 2 Cor 3:6; 6:4; 11:23). Conceptually, in 1 Cor 3:5, an intermediary role for Paul and Apollos, the servants, is explicit (Τί οὖν ἐστιν Ἀπολλῶς; Τί δέ ἐστιν Παῦλος; Διάκονοι δι' ὧν ἐπιστεύσατε). Grammatically, there is no qualification added to the title in 1 Cor 3:5, whereas in 2 Cor 3:6, Paul is grouped among the διάκονοι καινῆς διαθήκης ("ministers of a new covenant"), and in 2 Cor 6:4 and 11:23 Paul is a servant of God and Christ, respectively. The term is used in the plural in all cases, though Paul focuses on his own ministry in 2 Cor 11:23 (διάκονοι Χριστοῦ εἰσιν; . . . ὑπὲρ ἐγώ). The parallel to Col 1:23 may be closest linguistically in 2 Cor 3:6, since in both cases the duty of the διάκονος is attached to an impersonal concept (the gospel and the new covenant respectively). But a broader resemblance in thought may be detected between Col 1:23–29 and 2 Cor 5:18—6:10, which both contain the label διάκονος as a description of Paul's ministry (Col 1:23, 25; 2 Cor 6:4). In both passages Paul projects himself as one who gives witness to the gospel through both proclamation (2 Cor 5:18—6:2; Col 1:25-28) and suffering (2 Cor 6:3-10; Col 1:24; 1:29). A διάκονος in both contexts has the mandate of "making revelation real," through this preaching and sacrifice.[17] This is done in the service of the divine message of reconciliation (2 Cor 5:18-20—καταλλάσσω; Col 1:20, 22—ἀποκαταλλάσσω).[18] The purpose in both passages is similar: Paul establishes his calling and sincerity in ministry as a way of promoting a receptive hearing for his exhortation (2 Cor 6:11-13; Col 2:6ff.). The Paul of Col 1:23-29 communicates with a voice that is consistent with the voice heard in 2 Cor 5:18—6:10. Paul's adoption of διάκονος as a title is part of his larger endeavor to shape his readers' perception of him and his motives.

16. Wilson explains as follows: "What is striking here is that no claim is made for any special status or authority: Paul has become a διάκονος of the gospel, a word applied in v. 7 to Epaphras" (R. Wilson, *Colossians and Philemon*, 167). There has been speculation that grouping Epaphras (1:7) and Tychicus (4:7) with Paul was deemed useful for the sake of reinforcing the authority of these men in the wake of Paul's death (MacDonald, *Colossians and Ephesians*, 74). But since Paul's coworkers carry a variety of titles in this letter (1:1, 7, 4:7, 9, 10, 11, 12) there appears to be no intentional effort to influence perceptions with the particular label διάκονος.

17. J. Collins, "The Mediatorial Aspect of Paul's Role as *Diakonos*," 44, in reference to 2 Cor 5:18—6:10.

18. Similar connections will be observed between 2 Cor 5:18—6:10 and Eph 2:11—3:13 (see Beale, "The Old Testament Background of Reconciliation in 2 Corinthians 5–7," 578–81).

Paul's Ministry of Suffering and Proclamation—Colossians 1:24–29

In Paul's self-perception in Col 1:24–29, being a minister (διάκονος) of the gospel involves both suffering (1:24) and proclamation (1:27–29). Paul exhibits an awareness of his suffering's significance, especially in his responsibility to the church (1:24). A number of scholars protest that the language in 1:24 is too strong for Paul.[19] A careful study of this verse follows.

Rejoicing in Suffering—Colossians 1:24a

Paul begins the verse by affirming his joy in the midst of suffering (Νῦν χαίρω ἐν τοῖς παθήμασιν). It is difficult to determine whether a contrast with Paul's past circumstances or attitudes is intended with the adverb νῦν ("now").[20] Paul's reference to his calling as a minister in Col 1:23 might suggest that he is speaking from the perspective of his dramatic conversion of values, though this pattern of thinking is certainly not as explicit as it is elsewhere (see especially Phil 3:4–8). More probably, the adverb functions with a diluted sense, introducing Paul's present mindset without requiring any distinction from prior thinking.[21]

Even though it is unlikely Paul is making a point about a change in his own perspective with νῦν, the insistence on rejoicing in suffering does

---

19. For example, see Hobson, "The Authorship of Colossians," 156; Löwe, "Bekenntnis, Apostelamt und Kirche im Kolosserbrief," 313; Penny, "The Pseudo-Pauline Letters of the First Two Centuries," 346; Schweizer, "The Letter to the Colossians: Neither Pauline nor Post-Pauline?," 5; Kiley, *Colossians as Pseudepigraphy*, 59–60; R. Collins, *Letters That Paul Did Not Write*, 205–6; Müller, *Anfänge der Paulusschule*, 229; Meeks, "To Walk Worthily of the Lord," 41; Hultgren, "Colossians," 35; Hay, *Colossians*, 74; Standhartinger, "Colossians and the Pauline School," 580.

20. This possibility is considered in reference to Paul's imprisonment by Abbott, *Epistles to the Ephesians and to the Colossians*, 228; Houlden, *Paul's Letters from Prison*, 180; Harris, *Colossians and Philemon*, 65; MacDonald, *Colossians and Ephesians*, 78; or in reference to the current age of salvation in Christ and ministry situated in it by Lightfoot, *Epistles to the Colossians and to Philemon*, 164; O'Brien, *Colossians, Philemon*, 75; Harris, *Colossians and Philemon*, 65; Kremer, "Was an den Bedrängnissen des Christus mangelt," 135.

21. With this use νῦν does not quite approach the function of a mere transitional word that keeps the discourse moving. Instead, it denotes a current state of affairs without emphasizing a temporal distinction (see option 2 and the accompanying verses 1 Thess 3:8; 1 Cor 5:11; 7:14; 12:20 under BDAG, "νῦν," 681; cf. Wright, *The Epistles of Paul to the Colossians and to Philemon*, 89–90).

indicate of a reversal of prevailing cultural attitudes, so that what would normally bring sorrow or shame yields joy instead. Specifically, Paul is able to reinterpret his suffering as an occasion for joy because it benefits believers such as those in Colossae. Paul uses the preposition ὑπέρ to indicate that his suffering is endured for the benefit of the Colossians (ὑπὲρ ὑμῶν).[22] The perspective in Col 1:24a is not foreign to Paul's undisputed letters.[23] The general spiritual welfare of believers under his care is a source of joy for Paul in a number of places (1 Thess 2:19–20; Phil 2:2; 4:1; Rom 16:19). Sometimes a good report about believers' status elicits joy for Paul even in spite of his suffering (1 Thess 3:6–10; 2 Cor 7:4–7). Paul in Phil 2:17 speaks about rejoicing even if his death should be required in support of the Philippians' growth. Likewise, in Phil 1:18, Paul rejoices in the spread of the gospel, even though it has come at the expense of his freedom. In 2 Cor 1:6, Paul also speaks of suffering on behalf of (ὑπέρ) believers' salvation. While rejoicing in suffering for others echoes the theology from the earlier Pauline letters, it also accords well with the emphasis on joy elsewhere in Colossians (1:11 and 2:5).[24] So when Col 1:24 says that Paul rejoices in suffering that benefits believers, this is surprising neither in relation to Paul's earlier works nor in relation to the content of Colossians.

Paul enlists the term πάθημα to describe his sufferings in this first clause of Col 1:24. Though in many instances Paul employs θλῖψις to describe his hardships (1 Thess 3:3–7; Phil 1:17; 2 Cor 1:4–8; 4:17; 6:4; 7:4), πάθημα and the cognate verb πάσχω do surface in his undisputed letters.[25] It is noteworthy that when using these terms, Paul connects the sufferings to Christ in each case. In Phil 1:29 (ὑμῖν ἐχαρίσθη . . . τὸ ὑπὲρ αὐτοῦ πάσχειν) and Rom 8:17–18 (συμπάσχομεν), Paul discusses the sufferings that all Christians should expect to encounter in allegiance to Christ. In relation to his own experience, 2 Cor 1:5 (περισσεύει τὰ παθήματα τοῦ

---

22. The theme of undertaking every challenge in ministry for the sake of believers under his care is a major theme throughout the whole section Col 1:24—2:5 (Lähnemann, *Der Kolosserbrief*, 45). See also BDAG, "ὑπέρ," 1030; Sumney, "I Fill Up What Is Lacking in the Afflictions of Christ," 677–78. The similar use in Col 2:1 is also to be noted.

23. See Ahren, "The Fellowship of His Sufferings (Phil 3,10)," 26; Leppä, *The Making of Colossians*, 104.

24. This connection within Colossians is noted by Kremer, "Was an den Bedrängnissen des Christus mangelt," 135.

25. The alternation between θλῖψις and πάθημα in 2 Cor 1:4–8 indicates that Paul is apt to use these terms interchangeably (Barth and Blanke, *Colossians*, 290; Kremer, "Was an den Bedrängnissen des Christus mangelt," 135, 137; see also Ahren, "The Fellowship of His Sufferings," 27; O'Brien, *Colossians, Philemon*, 76).

Χριστοῦ εἰς ἡμᾶς) and Phil 3:10 (τοῦ γνῶναι . . . κοινωνίαν παθημάτων αὐτοῦ) depict suffering as a participation in the sufferings of Christ. In Col 1:24 Paul proceeds to develop the topic of suffering along these same lines.

Approaches to Interpreting a Difficult Clause—Colossians 1:24b

Though the conjunction καί following the first clause offers no explicit logical connection to the clause that follows, with the clause ἀνταναπληρῶ τὰ ὑστερήματα τῶν θλίψεων τοῦ Χριστοῦ ἐν τῇ σαρκί μου ὑπὲρ τοῦ σώματος αὐτοῦ (literally, "I fill up what is lacking of the sufferings of Christ, in my flesh, on behalf of his body") Paul continues to expound upon the nature of his suffering ministry. This is the part of verse 24 that provokes so much skepticism, not to mention disagreement, among interpreters. Viewed from one perspective, the verse seems to imply that Christ's sacrificial work on the cross was insufficient to save believers.[26] But this reading is rightly rejected by most scholars. Instead, interpreters have proposed other hermeneutical keys for unlocking the meaning of the verse.[27] First, Paul's claim to supplement the sufferings of Christ may be understood by distinguishing between suffering that serves as a catalyst for the expansion and strengthening of the church and suffering that is laden with expiatory significance.[28] Second, the passage may be understood so that it is not in any way Christ's afflictions that are insufficient but Christ's afflictions only as experienced by Paul, as part of his formation and calling.[29] Third, the apocalyptic notion of the Messianic woes that have been ordained for believers before Christ's return may inform Paul's language in the verse.[30]

---

26. Windisch, *Paulus und Christus*, 244–50; Nielsen, "The Status of Paul and His Letters in Colossians," 111–13.

27. These are in some ways overlapping categories because they are not always mutually exclusive.

28. Lightfoot, *Epistles to the Colossians and to Philemon*, 166; Percy, *Die Probleme der Kolosser- und Epheserbriefe*, 131–32. This position aligns easily with the sixth position, mentioned below.

29. In this view, ἐν τῇ σαρκί μου modifies the object of the verb ἀνταναπληρῶ rather than the verb itself (Abbott, *Epistles to the Ephesians and to the Colossians*, 232; Trudinger, "A Further Brief Note on Colossians 1:24," 37–38; Aletti, *Saint Paul, Épitre aux Colossiens*, 134–35; Perriman, "The Pattern of Christ's Sufferings," 62–63; Marguerat, "Paul après Paul," 332).

30. Best, *One Body in Christ*, 136; Lohse, *Colossians and Philemon*, 69–71; Houlden, *Paul's Letters from Prison*, 177–78; Löwe, "Bekenntnis, Apostelamt und Kirche im Kolosserbrief," 313; O'Brien, *Colossians, Philemon*, 78–79; Cannon, *The Use of Traditional Materials in Colossians*, 210; Reumann, "Col 1:24," 461; Harris, *Colossians and*

Fourth, Paul might equate the church's sufferings with Christ's on the basis of the believer's corporate identification with Christ, so that what is lacking in Christ's sufferings becomes a roundabout way of referring to the suffering yet to be experienced by the church.[31] Fifth, the language of Col 1:24 may reflect the Jewish and Greco-Roman ideal of the noble martyr whose suffering and death provide an impetus for others to choose the right course of action.[32] Sixth, Paul might see his own apostolic sufferings as an outworking of his commission to proclaim and embody the gospel to the Gentiles as a servant of Christ.[33] There are other views that combine and adapt these positions.[34] A succinct and fairly influential example of one of these hybrid proposals is Bauckham's, which recognizes the missionary expansion of the church as continuing the work of Christ. Extensive suffering is central to this missionary enterprise and, in a Christian reformulation of the idea of the Messianic woes, a precursor to the return

Philemon, 66; Hultgren, "Colossians," 35.

31. Proudfoot, "Imitation or Realistic Participation?, 157–58; Yates, "A Note on Colossians 1:24," 91–92; Bruce, *The Epistles to the Colossians, to Philemon, and to the Ephesians*, 82; Garland, *Colossians and Philemon*, 121; MacDonald, *Colossians and Ephesians*, 79.

32. Sumney, "I Fill Up What Is Lacking in the Afflictions of Christ," 669–73. Sumney acknowledges that this view corresponds well with Lightfoot's distinction between the suffering of Christ and of his church (ibid., 680). Walter Wilson also enlists the theme of martyrdom as part of his explanation of Col 1:24 (W. Wilson, *The Hope of Glory*, 75).

33. Masson, *L'épître de Saint Paul aux Colossiens*, 111; Ahren, "The Fellowship of His Sufferings," 28; Schweizer, *Colossians*, 105–6; Gnilka, *Der Kolosserbrief*, 97–98; Cahill, "The Neglected Parallelism in Col 1,24–25," 143–47; Barth and Blanke, *Colossians*, 295; Hübner, *An die Kolosser*, 69; Hafemann, "The Role of Suffering in the Mission of Paul," 181; Schreiner, *Paul, Apostle of God's Glory in Christ*, 101–2; Moo, *Letters to the Colossians and to Philemon*, 152–53.

34. Some scholars combine elements of Messianic woes and corporate identification (Moule, *Epistles to the Colossians and to Philemon*, 76–77; Wright, *The Epistles of Paul to the Colossians and to Philemon*, 87–88; R. Wilson, *Colossians and Philemon*, 171–72). Dunn identifies the contribution of both the idea of the Messianic woes and the idea of Paul's calling as shaped by the Isaianic servant (Dunn, *Epistles to the Colossians and to Philemon*, 116). Barth and Blanke perceive a reference to Paul's ministry along with Paul's awareness of not having completed the suffering ordained for him (Barth and Blanke, *Colossians*, 295). Kremer draws together the idea of a set measure of apocalyptic trials and the notion of the risen Christ suffering through ministers of salvation (Kremer, "Was an den Bedrängnissen des Christus mangelt," 137–40). Martin and Stettler believe that Paul is standing in for the church in enduring the Messianic woes appointed for the church (Martin, *Colossians and Philemon*, 70; Stettler, "An Interpretation of Colossians 1:24 in the Framework of Paul's Mission Theology," 187–91).

Completing What Is Lacking in Christ's Afflictions

Now that some of the options for interpreting the clause as a whole have been surveyed, we may take a closer look at some of component parts of the clause (along with the relative clause that follows), with particular reference to possible Pauline parallels. First, wording similar to ἀνταναπληρῶ τὰ ὑστερήματα ("I fill up what is lacking") appears in some of Paul's earlier letters, but not in the same kind of context. While ἀνταναπληρόω is unique to Col 1:24 in the Pauline corpus, the related verbs ἀναπληρόω (particularly 1 Cor 16:17 and Phil 2:30) and προσαναπληρόω (2 Cor 9:12; 11:9) surface in coordination with ὑστέρημα in the undisputed letters. The combination of ἀναπληρόω or προσαναπληρόω with ὑστέρημα refers to fulfilling a financial or practical need in these verses. In at least two of these instances (1 Cor 16:17 and Phil 2:30) those doing the supplying are making up the lack coming from another party. Finally, an example of resolving an abstract deficiency occurs in 1 Thess 3:10, where Paul identifies, with a term roughly synonymous with ἀναπληρόω, his desire to complete what is deficient in the faith of the Thessalonians (καταρτίσαι τὰ ὑστερήματα τῆς πίστεως ὑμῶν).[36] Upon surveying these precedents, it can be concluded that ἀνταναπληρῶ τὰ ὑστερήματα accurately but not woodenly expresses a pattern of speech quite familiar to Paul.[37]

---

35. Bauckham, "Colossians 1:24 Again," 169-70.

36. To be noted is that this goal is expressed within the context of Paul's discussion of afflictions (1 Thess 3:7). Throughout the chapter Paul speaks about suffering in the first person plural, suggesting that he is considering both his and the Thessalonians' suffering in his comments.

37. One explanation for Col 1:24 is that a later author adapts the description of Epaphroditus in Phil 2:30 (Kiley, *Colossians as Pseudepigraphy*, 95; Leppä, *The Making of Colossians*, 104-5), though upon examination the dependence is far from convincing. The additional prefix for the verb ἀναπληρόω differs in each case, the object ὑστέρημα is in the singular in Phil 2:30 and plural in Col 1:24. Since forms of these two words appear in combination in 1 Cor 16:17, 2 Cor 9:12, and 2 Cor 11:9 as well, the pairing of the words is not unusual. Verbally, apart from the incidental similarities of Χριστοῦ and ὑμῶν, there are no other shared words. Conceptually, while the theme of hardship appears in both instances, it is service (λειτουργία) not affliction that is completed in Phil 2:30, and the actors and circumstances are otherwise different. Since λειτουργία is found in 2 Cor 9:12, the parallel between 2 Cor 9:12 and Phil 2:30 is arguably at least as strong as that between Phil 2:30 and Col 1:24.

The sense of the prefix ἀντι- in ἀνταναπληρῶ has been variously interpreted. The prefix might simply intensify the verb, which is not uncommon with Paul.[38] Or, a more precise meaning denoting substitution or correspondence might be present. The prefix may tie either Paul to Christ or Paul's fulfillment to what is lacking. The notion of correspondence between Paul and Christ, which yields a translation of "in my turn" or "for my part" fits best contextually and is appropriate lexically as well.[39] This explanation results in a pattern that approximates the relational dynamics of 1 Cor 16:17 and Phil 2:30, since in those instances the subjects doing the completing compensate for the incomplete service of another entity, whom the subject represents. In Col 1:24 Paul sees himself as carrying on God's work in Christ's stead, now that Christ has ascended to God's right hand.[40]

The phrase τὰ ὑστερήματα τῶν θλίψεων τοῦ Χριστοῦ ("that which is lacking of the sufferings of Christ") is best treated as a unit, since options for the meaning of the afflictions of Christ are narrowed down by the phrase's association with an idea of lack.[41] The theology of Colossians as a whole precludes a meaning that views Christ's atoning death as insufficient (see Col 1:14, 20, 22; 2:13–14). Paul's association with the afflictions of Christ (the fact that he is taking his turn in filling them) suggests that Christ's afflictions are in some sense transferable. At the same time, equating the church with Christ at this juncture, so that the afflictions of Christ are equivalent to the afflictions of the church in simple one-to-one correspondence, is not wholly satisfying, since later in the verse the church as Christ's body is designated as a separate party - the beneficiary of Paul's suffering.[42] More likely the afflictions of Christ represent actual

38. Perriman, "The Pattern of Christ's Sufferings," 67; Barth and Blanke, *Colossians*, 256; Garland, *Colossians and Philemon*, 119.

39. The verb ἀναπληρόω without the prefix already relates the action of filling to the deficiency, so it is proposed here that the additional prefix envisions Paul engaging in an action that corresponds to Christ's (Lightfoot, *Epistles to the Colossians and Philemon*, 165). Others supporting a correspondence view that relates Paul to Christ include BDAG, "ἀνταναπληρόω," 87; Kremer, "Was an den Bedrängnissen des Christus mangelt," 136; Cahill, "The Neglected Parallelism in Col 1,24–25," 146; Harris, *Colossians and Philemon*, 66.

40. Hafemann, "The Role of Suffering in the Mission of Paul," 181.

41. Possible background influences on the thought of this phrase were examined earlier in this section. For a discussion of options for the genitive relationship between the afflictions and Christ, see Kremer, *Was an den Leiden Christi noch mangelt*, 174–95.

42. Those opting for a straightforward correlation between the church's sufferings and Christ's for this verse include Moule, *Epistles to the Colossians and to Philemon*,

divinely ordained sufferings sustained by Christ but now carried out by proxy through chosen ministers such as Paul. These afflictions are yet to be exhausted because the mission to reach the whole world, and especially the Gentiles, with the saving gospel has yet not been accomplished.[43]

Bodily Suffering in Colossians 1:24 and 2 Corinthians 4:10-11

Grammatically, the prepositional phrase ἐν τῇ σαρκί μου ("in my flesh") is parallel to ὑπὲρ τοῦ σώματος αὐτοῦ ("on behalf of his body") and modifies ἀνταναπληρῶ ("fill up") rather than τὰ ὑστερήματα ("what is lacking") or τῶν θλίψεων τοῦ Χριστοῦ ("of the afflictions of Christ").[44] Paul's specification that in his turn he undergoes these afflictions in his body resembles the twofold emphasis on bodily suffering in 2 Cor 4:10-11, which alternates between σῶμα and σάρξ.[45] That passage sheds further light on Col 1:24b. Colossians 1:24 highlights the bodily ordeal of the afflictions of Christ while 2 Cor 4:10 speaks of the dying of Jesus (ἡ νέκρωσις τοῦ Ἰησοῦ). Paul clarifies what is meant by carrying around the dying of Jesus in 2 Cor 4:11, when he restates the idea as being delivered over to death on

---

76-77; Garland, *Colossians and Philemon*, 121; R. Wilson, *Colossians and Philemon*, 171.

43. See especially Bauckham, "Colossians 1:24 Again," 170; Hafemann, "The Role of Suffering in the Mission of Paul," 181. Percy clarifies that "lack" in this context picks up on the reality that the mission shared by Jesus and Paul (that of the growth of the church) has not yet been completed (Percy, *Die Probleme der Kolosser- und Epheserbriefe*, 129-32; cf. Gnilka, *Der Kolosserbrief*, 97-98). Pinpointing the specific concept of the messianic woes may be reading more into the expression than the grammar explicitly indicates. The article likely says nothing more than the fact that the sufferings were a concrete idea in Paul's mind (for further discussion on the "conceptualizing" feature of the article, see Wallace, *Greek Grammar beyond the Basics*, 209).

44. With Proudfoot, "Imitation or Realistic Participation?," 157; Harris, *Colossians and Philemon*, 66; Hafemann, "The Role of Suffering in the Mission of Paul," 181; Kremer, "Was an den Bedrängnissen des Christus mangelt," 139. *Contra* Abbott, *Epistles to the Ephesians and to the Colossians*, 232; Houlden, *Paul's Letters from Prison*, 180; Aletti, *Colossiens*, 134-35; Perriman, "The Pattern of Christ's Sufferings," 62-63; Wolter, *Der Brief an die Kolosser*, 102; Garland, *Colossians and Philemon*, 121; Marguerat, "Paul après Paul," 332.

45. Paul also sees the significance of suffering in his physical body (σῶμα) in Phil 1:20. In both Phil 1:12-26 and Colossians 1:24-25 Paul exhibits an awareness of his suffering's greater significance, especially in his responsibility to the church. O'Brien also notes the mention of bodily suffering (ἐν τῷ σώματί μου) in Gal 6:17 (O'Brien, *Colossians, Philemon*, 80).

account of Jesus (εἰς θάνατον παραδιδόμεθα διὰ Ἰησοῦν).⁴⁶ If this meaning is imported into Col 1:24, then the afflictions of Christ are readily understood as suffering required as part of the propagation of the gospel. The overall conceptual parallel between 2 Cor 4:10–11 and Col 1:24 is that Paul's physical sufferings are an outgrowth of his allegiance to Christ and his mission, resulting in spiritual benefit for others.

Suffering for the Sake of the Church

As was the case in the first clause of Col 1:24, Paul uses ὑπέρ again in relation to the people he serves (ὑπὲρ τοῦ σώματος αὐτοῦ ὅ ἐστιν ἡ ἐκκλησία). The preposition might carry a sense of an advantage bestowed ("for the sake of") or there may be a substitutionary meaning intended.⁴⁷ In the latter scheme, a substitutionary force to the prefix ἀντι- in ἀνταναπληρῶ or an underlying thought of the Messianic woes would be compatible with a substitutionary sense to ὑπέρ.⁴⁸ The former idea is supported by the use of the preposition in Col 1:24a (ὑπὲρ ὑμῶν) and Paul's self-perception of being a minister of the church in Col 1:25 and is thus the preferred understanding. The dual use of the preposition with the Colossians and the church as corresponding objects of the preposition implies that when ministry to the Colossians is mentioned it is representative of Paul's ministry to the church at large.⁴⁹

---

46. The likelihood of a parallel between 2 Cor 4:10 and 11 is increased when the very similar second halves of the verses are noted. For additional discussion on the relevance of 2 Cor 4:7–11, see Hübner, *An die Kolosser*, 68.

47. A substitutionary sense for the preposition in Col 1:24b is advocated by Stettler, "Colossians 1:24 in the Framework of Paul's Mission Theology," 188, 191. The resulting meaning would be that Paul takes on his own shoulders the suffering due to the church (ibid.). For the possibility of a substitutionary meaning, see BDAG, "ὑπέρ," 1030–31; Wallace, *Greek Grammar beyond the Basics*, 383–87. Opting for a non-substitutionary sense are Barth and Blanke, *Colossians*, 295.

48. See for instance O'Brien, *Colossians, Philemon*, 80.

49. The charge that the pseudonymous author has changed the beneficiary of Paul's suffering from a concrete, specific church to an abstract, universal church (Marguerat, "Paul après Paul," 332) misses the mark, since the more likely explanation is that Paul adapts his language in a way that is fitting to his relationship to them. He has not actually suffered for them specifically or directly and does not anticipate doing so, but he does recognize that his struggles are endured for their sake and for the sake of others like them in a more general and indirect sense.

Portrait of an Apostle

Paul's Suffering for the Benefit of Others in the Undisputed Letters

The picture of Paul suffering on behalf of (ὑπέρ) the church corresponds to portraits of Paul seen in the undisputed letters. Paul explains in 2 Cor 1:6 that his affliction is endured with a view to the spiritual life and health of the Corinthians (ὑπὲρ τῆς ὑμῶν παρακλήσεως καὶ σωτηρίας). Elsewhere, without using the same preposition, Paul communicates the same idea. In Phil 1:12-13 Paul welcomes the strain of his imprisonment because he knows that the gospel is being advanced as a result of it. He also accepts the prospect of a prolonged life and ministry because he knows that this will benefit the Philippian believers (Phil 1:24-25). Paul believes that his suffering brings life for the Corinthian believers (2 Cor 4:12), and so he recognizes that his arduous ministry is offered for the sake of (διά, with the accusative) these believers (2 Cor 4:15). Colossians 1:24, with an emphasis on Paul's joyful acceptance of sharing in Christ's sufferings for the benefit of other believers, expresses a familiar idea without any hint of literary dependence on earlier letters.[50]

Paul's Ministry to the Church—Colossians 1:25

In Col 1:25 Paul once again describes his responsibilities using the term διάκονος ("minister"), again as part of a clause that subordinates him to a greater idea (ἧς ἐγενόμην ἐγω διάκονος). This time, Paul is placed in service of the church (Col 1:24b) instead of the gospel. Some scholars have objected that the use of διάκονος with the church is not completely consonant with Paul's perspective.[51] But the sample size of the occurrences in the undisputed Pauline letters is just too small to make this argument, and 2 Cor 4:5 labels Paul and his associates as slaves (δοῦλοι) of the Corinthian readers. Nothing about being a servant of the church contradicts the theology reflected in those letters.

Paul speaks of his ministry as being κατὰ τὴν οἰκονομίαν τοῦ θεοῦ ("according to the administration of God"). The close proximity of terms or cognates of οἰκονομία and μυστήριον (see Col 1:26-27) is observed in 1 Cor 4:1 as well, where οἰκονόμος identifies Paul as a privileged recipient

---

50. Apart from verbal affinity to Phil 2:30 (see footnote 53), Leppä lists a number of other possible sources that were conflated in Col 1:24 (Leppä, *The Making of Colossians*, 104-6). Her argument is not very convincing, since the verbal overlap is relatively slight, and additional connections between the passages that would have led the author to associate these apparently unrelated verses together are not evident.

51. Kiley, *Colossians as Pseudepigraphy*, 60; Wolter, *Der Brief an die Kolosser*, 102.

Paul's Identity in Colossians

of sacred truth from God.⁵² The meaning of οἰκονομία in Col 1:25 is less clear. The genitive modifier τοῦ θεοῦ points to a divine administration or plan, while the relative clause τὴν δοθεῖσάν μοι suggests more of a human stewardship received. Reumann believes that while the human aspect of Paul's commission is required by the relative clause, factors including the Hellenistic connotations of τὴν οἰκονομίαν τοῦ θεοῦ, the likely subjective sense of the genitive modifier τοῦ θεοῦ, and the typical nuance of κατά (in which the material preceding the prepositional phrase is shown to be in alignment with the object of the preposition) root the whole phrase in the overarching plans of God.⁵³ This also accords well with Paul's focus on the nature of his ministry in this section, in which Paul is seen as a human agent carrying out God's eternal plans.

The modifying clause τὴν δοθεῖσάν μοι is familiar from Paul's undisputed letters, but in those instances rather than οἰκονομία it is grace that is given to Paul, (Gal 2:9; 1 Cor 3:10, which is also introduced by κατά; Rom 12:3; 15:15).⁵⁴ Grace and stewardship are complementary ideas with respect to Paul's ministry, since the stewardship is received by grace, and the grace comes with the responsibility of diligent service. The appearance then of an idea of a divine stewardship entrusted to Paul conforms comfortably with the descriptions of Paul's ministry in the earlier letters.

The brief prepositional phrase εἰς ὑμᾶς ("unto you") emphasizes that the bestowal of Paul's ministry is for the benefit of the Colossian believers, who once again stand in for the other churches under Paul's realm of responsibility. Though grammatically the two words could constitute the beginning of the infinitive clause that follows, the parallel use occurring

---

52. Leppä speculates about literary dependence between 1 Cor 4:1 and Col 1:25–27 based on the close proximity of μυστήριον, οἰκονομία/οἰκονόμος, and θεός (Leppä, *The Making of Colossians*, 107). It should be noted, however, that θεός modifies μυστήριον in 1 Cor 4:1 and οἰκονομία in Col 1:25, and the wider word separation between οἰκονομία and μυστήριον in Col 1:25–26 (compared to 1 Cor 4:1, where one word follows the other) supports a shared conceptual association in the passages more than literary borrowing.

53. Reumann, "Οἰκονομία," 162–63. Also highlighting both connotations of the term are Masson, *L'épître de Saint Paul aux Colossiens*, 111; Moule, *Epistles to the Colossians and to Philemon*, 80; O'Brien, *Colossians, Philemon*, 81–82; R. Wilson, *Colossians and Philemon*, 173.

54. See Lohse, *Colossians and Philemon*, 72; Aletti, *Colossiens*, 138. Leppä surmises that Col 1:25 is dependent upon 1 Cor 3:10 (Leppä, *The Making of Colossians*, 107), but the existence of the other similar passages (mentioned in the text above and discussed more extensively in chapter 2 of this book) makes literary dependence much less likely (and would leave open the charge that a passage such as Rom 12:3 was dependent upon Gal 2:9 and/or 1 Cor 3:10).

in Eph 3:2 (εἴ γε ἠκούσατε τὴν οἰκονομίαν τῆς χάριτος τοῦ θεοῦ τῆς δοθείσης μοι εἰς ὑμᾶς) suggests grouping εἰς ὑμᾶς with what precedes rather than what follows in Col 1:25. In any case εἰς ὑμᾶς refers to the Colossian believers and other Gentiles as the object of Paul's ministry rather than as the ones doing the fulfilling of the word. This image of Paul having received a divine commission that promotes the welfare of recipients of his letter conforms both to previous portraits of Paul (1 Cor 3:5; Phil 1:24-25; 2 Cor 4:15; Rom 1:5; 15:15-18) and to the presentation in Colossians as a whole.

The expectations for Paul's service to Gentile believers are specified with a purpose infinitive clause (πληρῶσαι τὸν λόγον τοῦ θεοῦ—"to fulfill the word of God"). Paul declares that his mandate consists of fulfilling the word of God on behalf of the Colossians and other believers.[55] Some scholars have noted the parallel ideas in Col 1:24b and 1:25, since similar verbs are employed.[56] Whereas Paul fulfills God's calling through suffering in Col 1:24, he carries out the same calling by proclamation in Col 1:25-27. This structure suggests that suffering and proclamation go hand in hand in Paul's execution of his ministry, as is the case in 2 Cor 5:18-6:10, where Paul's role as an ambassador who relays the message of reconciliation precedes a description of the manner in which he resolutely faces challenges when carrying out his ministry.

The use of πληρόω in Col 1:25, though, recalls another passage that bears an even closer resemblance to Col 1:25 than 2 Cor 5:18—6:10 does. In Rom 15:19 Paul announces that as a result of his calling (Rom 15:16) he has fulfilled the gospel of Christ (ὥστε με πεπληρωκέναι τὸ εὐαγγέλιον τοῦ Χριστοῦ) throughout the Gentile world.[57] Both Col 1:25-29 and Rom 15:15-19 portray Paul's call to ministry (in terms of χάρις in Romans and οἰκονομία in Colossians), his identification as a minister (λειτουργός in Romans and διάκονος in Colossians), his ministry to the Gentiles (Rom 15:16, 18; Col 1:27), the picture of Paul presenting (παρίστημι-Col 1:28)

---

55. The word of God is a synonym for the gospel in this context (Wolter, *Der Brief an die Kolosser*, 103; Hübner, *An die Kolosser*, 69). See 1 Thess 2:13; 1Cor 14:36; 2 Cor 2:17; 4:2; Col 1:5.

56. Ahren, "The Fellowship of His Sufferings," 28; O'Brien, *Colossians, Philemon*, 82; Pokorný, *Colossians*, 99; Cahill, "The Neglected Parallelism in Col 1,24-25," 142-46; W. Wilson, *The Hope of Glory*," 75; Stettler, "Colossians 1:24 in the Framework of Paul's Mission Theology," 190; Schreiner, *Paul, Apostle of God's Glory in Christ*, 101.

57. It is puzzling as to why Marguerat contends that Paul is portrayed as "le proclamateur par excellence" in this verse (Marguerat, "Paul après Paul," 327), since affirmations of Paul's divine calling to preach are typical in the undisputed letters, and the use of πληρόω in relation to Paul's commission is not unexpected, as seen from the parallel wording in Rom 15.

believers under his care as an offering (προσφορά–Rom 15:16) to God; Christ's empowerment of Paul's ministry (κατεργάζομαι in Rom 15:18; ἐνεργέω in Col 1:29), and Paul's commission to fulfill (πληρόω) the gospel or word of God. Dunn also notes that "an eschatological overtone" is present in both passages.[58] The wording in the two passages rarely overlaps, as the vocabulary and the forms differ, but there is significant conceptual similarity between the two instances.[59] Once more, this combination of conceptual affinity and verbal variance points away from the likelihood of a later author imitating Paul.

A Mystery Revealed in Time—Colossians 1:26

As the proclamation component of Paul's ministry moves to the forefront in Col 1:26, Paul describes the word of God as τὸ μυστήριον ("the mystery"). The general phrase for the gospel message in 1:25 (τὸν λόγον τοῦ θεοῦ - "the word of God") is here further clarified by describing the message in terms of mystery.[60] In other words the word of God serves as a launching point from which Paul begins to discuss the characteristics of the mystery.[61] The term μυστήριον, understood with its Jewish connotations, refers to "secrets of the divine purpose now revealed by divine agency."[62] Paul uses a "once hidden–now revealed" formula (τὸ ἀποκεκρυμμένον . . . νῦν δὲ ἐφανερώθη) most familiar from the textually uncertain Rom 16:25–26 (σεσιγημένου, φανερωθέντος δὲ νῦν).[63] According to Rom 16:25–26 and Col 1:26, people

---

58. Dunn, *Epistles to the Colossians and to Philemon*, 119.

59. It has been put forward that the predominant idea of πληρόω in Rom 15:19 is the fulfillment of OT expectations (Barth and Blanke, *Colossians*, 260). But though interest in OT fulfillment is evident in the broader argument of Rom 15, the immediate context does not require OT Scripture as the object of fulfillment in verse 19. More likely, Paul understands fulfillment there as he does in Col 1:25: that he is carrying out the work assigned to him by God.

60. Kiley finds it significant that λόγος is a common term in Col 1:25 and Phil 1:14 but that the subjects proclaiming the word are different in the two instances. This observation is interpreted as one more reason for suspecting that Colossians is dependent upon Philippians (Kiley, *Colossians as Pseudepigraphy*, 90). Even as one of many examples enlisted in support of his hypothesis, the point is utterly unpersuasive because the shared term is so common and the assumption of having differing preachers of the gospel so unspectacular.

61. The term μυστήριον is linked to other terms describing the gospel in Rom 16:25 (εὐαγγέλιον, κήρυγμα).

62. Dunn, *Epistles to the Colossians and to Philemon*, 120.

63. The emphatic νῦν in both cases highlights a decisive turning point in salvation

Revelation in Colossians 1:26-27 and 2 Corinthians 2:6-16

Given the doubts about the provenance of Rom 16:25-26, the hiding and revealing of the mystery in 1 Cor 2:6-16 as compared to Col 1:26-27 merits examination as well. To portray revelation 1 Cor 2:10 employs ἀποκαλύπτω while Col 1:26b incorporates the similar term φανερόω. Both 1 Cor 2:7 and Col 1:26 enlist ἀποκρύπτω to designate God's act of concealing the truth of his plans. It has been argued in chapter 2 of this book that τὴν ἀποκεκρυμμένην in 1 Cor 2:7 is used primarily to designate concealment from people, whereas the broader context communicates an emphasis on concealment in time. In Col 1:26-27 τὸ ἀποκεκρυμμένον envisions a temporal concealment, which accords with the wider context of 1 Cor 2:6-16 but not the actual usage of the same term.

Colossians 1:26-27 does, however, reveal the assumption that the significance of God's mystery is apprehended only by certain people (with the specification of the ἅγιοι, or "saints," as the recipients of the mystery), which is comparable to the use of first personal plural pronouns to mark insiders from outsiders in 1 Cor 2:6-16. There are two credible options for the referent of the saints in verse 26.[64] It has been contended that ἅγιοι often refers to a narrower group of Christians in other New Testament passages, as when in passages referring to financial contributions to the Jerusalem church (Rom 15:25, 31; 1 Cor 16:1; 2 Cor 8:4; 9:1, 12) ἅγιοι

---

history, suggesting that Paul intends a temporal sense for the preceding ἀπό prepositions in Col 1:26. Though ἀπό can also communicate a spatial notion, so that the mystery is hidden from something or someone (BDAG, "αἰών," 33; Dibelius, *Die Briefe des Apostels Paulus II*, 76; Kiley, *Colossians as Pseudepigraphy*, 90; Houlden, *Paul's Letters from Prison*, 182; Hanson, *The Paradox of the Cross in the Thought of Paul*, 165-68), the temporal sense fits more naturally into the immediate context and the typical revelation pattern in Paul's writings. It is noted that concealment in time also implies concealment from the people of that time period (Aletti, *Colossiens*, 139; R. Wilson, *Colossians and Philemon*, 177). Ernst similarly states that the two concepts have significant overlap (Ernst, *Die Briefe an die Kolosser*, 187).

64. Though ἅγιοι may refer to angels elsewhere (perhaps even in Col 1:12, as BDAG, "ἅγιοι," 11, suggests and Lohse, *Colossians and Philemon*, 36, defends, based on similar statements in Qumran literature), nothing in the context of 1:26 allows for this option in this verse (*contra* Lohmeyer, *Die Briefe an die Kolosser*, 82-83; J. T. Sanders, "Hymnic Elements in Ephesians 1-3," 232).

pinpoints the Christians in Jerusalem.[65] But most scholars adopt a referent of "all Christians" for the saints in verse 26.[66] The term often has this referent in Paul's writings (cf. Rom 8:27, 1 Cor 1:1) and it even appears with this meaning earlier in Colossians itself (1:2, 4). If this understanding of ἅγιοι in Col 1:26 is correct, then there is further agreement with 1 Cor 2:10, where ὑμῖν most likely refers to all believers (as noted in chapter 2 of this book).

Finally, while Col 1:26–27 uses μυστήριον as the primary object of concealment and revelation, in 1 Cor 2:7 it appears as a modifier of σοφία ("wisdom"). Sanders sees this fact as sufficient basis for his insinuation that mystery is understood incompatibly in the two passages.[67] More likely, the strong discourse focus on wisdom led to the secondary position of mystery in 1 Cor 2:7, while in Col 1:26–27 Paul found μυστήριον to be a useful term in its own right for expressing the divine origins and dramatic unveiling of the gospel.

In short, the two passages are oriented slightly differently in their view of concealment and revelation, with a stronger emphasis on wisdom and the division between insiders and outsiders in 1 Cor 2. Nonetheless, comparable revelatory language and the dual emphasis on concealment from people and concealment in time surface in both passages. Beyond these initial similarities, additional connections will be observed later in this section.

Recipients and Beneficiaries of the Mystery—Colossians 1:27

Returning to the flow of argument in Col 1:26–27, there are several grammatical possibilities for how the relative pronoun οἷς and prepositional phrase ἐν τοῖς ἔθνεσιν relate to one another and to the sentence as a whole. For each possibility, "Gentiles" rather than "nations" is the preferred translation of ἔθνη. While the universal scope detected in other parts of the

---

65. Cerfaux, *The Church in the Theology of St. Paul*, 130; D. Robinson, "Who Were 'The Saints'?," 47. Brown appears to narrow the scope of the saints by equating them with the mature believers of 1 Cor 2:6 (Brown, *The Semitic Background of the Term "Mystery" in the New Testament*, 53).

66. See Lohse, *Colossians and Philemon*, 75; Gnilka, *Der Kolosserbrief*, 101; O' Brien, *Colossians, Philemon*, 84–85; Best, "The Revelation to Evangelize the Gentiles," 23; Barth and Blanke, *Colossians*, 98, 186; Dunn, *Epistle to the Colossians and to Philemon*, 120; Hübner, *An die Kolosser*, 70.

67. E. P. Sanders, "Literary Dependence in Colossians," 40.

letters has been enlisted in support of "nations" rather than "Gentiles,"[68] the phrase ἐν τοῖς ἔθνεσιν in reference to the Gentiles is familiar from Paul's earlier letters (Gal 1:16; Gal 2:2; Rom 2:24; cf., 1 Thess 2:16; Rom 1:13; 11:13; 15:9, 16). Furthermore, all three options below make more sense if the reference is to the Gentiles. With that said, the most plausible options for the relationship between οἷς and ἐν τοῖς ἔθνεσιν are as follows.

A first proposal is that οἷς agrees with the case of its antecedent τοῖς ἁγίοις αὐτοῦ but functions as the accusative subject of the infinitive γνωρίσαι in the relative clause, while ἐν τοῖς ἔθνεσιν modifies the infinitive γνωρίσαι and specifies the recipients of what is made known. In this option, God determines that certain saints make known the riches of the mystery to the Gentiles.[69] The fairly common phenomenon of the attraction of the case of the relative pronoun to its antecedent would explain the dative form of οἷς.[70] Such an understanding, however, would detract from Paul's main agenda in Col 1:26–27. He is less concerned with specifying the identity of the heralds of God's mystery's and more interested in noting the dramatic turning point in history seen in the Christ event.

Second, οἷς could function as a dative direct object of γνωρίσαι in the relative clause οἷς ἠθέλσεν ὁ θεὸς γνωρίσαι τί τὸ πλοῦτος τῆς δόξης τοῦ μυστηρίου τούτου ἐν τοῖς ἔθνεσιν. In addition ἐν τοῖς ἔθνεσιν, also modifying the infinitive γνωρίσαι, would describe the direct object recipients more specifically.[71] One weakness here is that ἐν τοῖς ἔθνεσιν seems to restate the object of γνωρίσαι in a way that is oblivious to the previous object mentioned in the form of οἷς. Thus, Wright correctly notes that such a reading would be "redundant."[72]

---

68. Hay, *Colossians*, 76.

69. Bowers, "A Note on Colossians 1:27a," 111–14. Since then, O'Brien and Bockmuehl have both been intrigued by Bowers' proposal on logical grounds but have ultimately bypassed it out of concerns over the absence of parallel grammatical constructions elsewhere in support of this reading (O'Brien, *Colossians, Philemon*, 85; Bockmuehl, *Revelation and Mystery*, 185).

70. This grammatical pattern is described and supported with New Testament references in a number of Greek grammars (Robertson, *A Grammar of the Greek New Testament in Light of Historical Research*, 715; Smyth, *Greek Grammar*, §2524; Moule, *An Idiom Book of New Testament Greek*, 130; BDF §294.1; Wallace, *Greek Grammar beyond the Basics*, 339).

71. NIV; TNIV; HCSB; O'Brien, *Colossians, Philemon*, 85–86; Pokorný, *Colossians*, 103; Sappington, *Revelation and Redemption at Colossae*, 185; Moo, *Letters to the Colossians and to Philemon*, 158.

72. Wright, *Colossians*, 91–92; cf. Aletti, *Colossiens*, 142–43.

Third, οἷς could function as a dative direct object of γνωρίσαι in the relative clause, and ἐν τοῖς ἔθνεσιν could modify the noun τοῦ μυστηρίου or the noun phrase τὸ πλοῦτος τῆς δόξης τοῦ μυστηρίου τούτου, with the Gentiles being accentuated as beneficiaries of the mystery or the riches of the mystery.[73] Is the revealed mystery in this passage then seen as pertaining only to the Gentiles? Paul does not so much confine the blessings to the Gentiles as he does highlight this aspect of the mystery because of his calling to the Gentiles and the relevance to his Gentile readers. This is the most likely understanding for the relationship between οἷς and ἐν τοῖς ἔθνεσιν.

Unless the first interpretation above is correct, which is unlikely, then in the actual formulation of the mystery in 1:26–27, Paul does not overtly discuss the role of human agents of revelation, opting instead to focus on the divine originator (God) and ultimate recipients (the saints). While Paul sees himself elsewhere as a revealer of the mystery (1 Cor 15:51; Rom 11:25) or a steward of the mysteries (1 Cor 4:1), 1 Cor 2:8–10 parallels Col 1:26–27 in temporarily setting aside Paul's intermediary role when the mystery is actually described. In the broader contexts, however, of both 1 Corinthians 2 and Colossians 1, Paul's participation in the mystery's disclosure is obvious. Paul highlights his individual calling to proclaim God's message (1 Cor 2:1–5; Col 1:23–25) and affiliates himself with his coworkers in the discharge of the responsibility to proclaim God's truth (1 Cor 2:6–7 and Col 1:28–29). In both 1 Corinthians 2 and Colossians 1, Paul identifies his special calling in relation to the mystery, but recognizes that a similar calling is possessed by others as well. These intermediaries serve to announce and clarify the blessings God has designed and delivered for privileged beneficiaries.

Eschatological Blessings for the Gentiles—Colossians 1:27

The blessings entailed in the mystery and made known by God are depicted using lofty language (τί τὸ πλοῦτος τῆς δόξης τοῦ μυστηρίου τούτου ἐν τοῖς ἔθνεσιν—"what are the riches of the glory of this mystery"). The first two nouns of the genitive chain have the combined effect of ascribing great eternal value to the mystery.[74] This part of the verse bears a strong

---

73. NRSV; Lightfoot, *Epistles to the Colossians and to Philemon*, 169; Masson, *L'épître de Saint Paul aux Colossiens*, 112–13; Wright, *Colossians*, 91–92; Harris, *Colossians and Philemon*, 71; Bockmuehl, *Revelation and Mystery*, 82.

74. The words "riches" and "glory" constitute a common word association found

resemblance to Rom 9:23 (ἵνα γνωρίσῃ τὸν πλοῦτον τῆς δόξης αὐτοῦ), with the close proximity of γνωρίζω, πλοῦτος, and δόξα in both verses and the shared meaning of God making known the wonderful blessings of salvation. Furthermore, Gentile inclusion in these benefits moves to the forefront in the material that follows in both cases. Despite the claim of Sanders, there is no apparent reason that a pseudonymous author would have chosen wording from Rom 9:23 to augment the description of the mystery, since Rom 9:23 has no immediate connection to mystery.[75] The common language and thought is better explained as Paul's own creation in Col 1:27, since the concepts and wording faithfully preserve Paul's theology from Rom 9:23-24 and conform well to the discourse and unique emphases of Colossians as well (see πλοῦτος in 2:2; cf. 3:16, δόξα in 1:11, 27b; 3:4, γνωρίζω in 4:7).

---

in OT passages (O'Brien, *Colossians, Philemon*, 86). For an extended discussion about the background and significance of δόξα in Col 1:27, see Moule, *Epistles to the Colossians and to Philemon*, 83-84.

75. Sanders asserts, "This passage very clearly shows evidence of literary conflation," with 1 Cor 2:7, Rom 16:25-26, and Rom 9:23-24 identified as the alleged sources (E. P. Sanders, "Literary Dependence in Colossians," 39; see also additional modification and comment in Leppä, *The Making of Colossians*, 109-10). But the instances of similar wording pointed out by Sanders are by no means frequent, seeing that three passages with five verses are targeted as possible sources. Furthermore, the overlap among the three original passages (which is needed according to Sanders's definition of conflation, "Literary Dependence in Colossians," 32) amounts to the appearance of the standard words ἔθνη and γνωρίζω in Rom 9:23-24 and Rom 16:25-26 and the use of μυστήριον in 1 Cor 2:7 and Rom 16:25-26 (Sanders could have added the occurrence of δόξα in 1 Cor 2:7 and Rom 9:23). While the phrase τὸ(ν) πλοῦτος τῆς δόξης surfaces in both Rom 9:23 and Col 1:27, Sanders's logic that the proximity of γνωρίζω and ἔθνη in both Rom 9:23-24 and Rom 16:25-26 brought Rom 9:23-24 to the attention of the author of Colossians (and thus put the phrase τὸ(ν) πλοῦτος τῆς δόξης into play) falls well short of persuading, since the words are common and are actually quite far removed from one another in Rom 9:23-24 (separated by 23 words!) and not even in the same sentence. Moreover, there is no explanation for why the author of Colossians would have altered the gender of πλοῦτος from neuter to masculine, if Rom 9:23 were being mined. One other criteria put forward for Sanders's detection of conflation is that the later author uses the same words dissimilarly (page 33). For Col 1:26-27 Sanders pinpoints the different nouns (σοφία in 1 Cor 2:7 and μυστήριον in Col 1:26) being modified by the participial form of ἀποκρύπτω as evidence of conflation (page 40). But σοφία is so closely related to μυστήριον in 1 Cor 2:7 that the resulting difference in meaning is negligible. Finally, many of the words targeted by Sanders (terms of revelation, riches, and glory) tie into repeated themes in Colossians, so their inclusion in these verses should not be deemed as unusual. Sanders has simply failed to support his confident accusation of conflation in a convincing way. Also dubious of Sanders's argument is Kiley, *Colossians as Pseudepigraphy*, 71-72.

"Glory" surfaces again later in the Col 1:27 when Paul insists that the mystery of "Christ in you" (Χριστὸς ἐν ὑμῖν) is the grounds for the believer's hope of glory (ἡ ἐλπὶς τῆς δόξης). The terms "hope" and "glory" in Colossians both point to the eschatological hope of eternal life in God's presence. The term "hope" appears elsewhere in the letter with an eschatological sense (Col 1:5, 23), and the use of "glory" in 3:4 depicts the future return of Christ and its effects on believers.[76] So Paul enlists the eschatological term δόξα two times in close association with μυστήριον in Col 1:27.

Two other mystery passages display an eschatological concern. Though 1 Cor 15:51 does not enlist δόξα as part of the discussion, the eschatological direction of the mystery is in the foreground there as well. More significantly, 1 Cor 2:7–8 repeats δόξα in connection with the mystery's benefits. In Cor 2:7 God's wisdom is identified as resulting in the believer's glory (εἰς δόξαν ἡμῶν), which directs the reader's attention to the future blessings entailed in the revealed mystery. A verse later, Christ is called the Lord of glory (τὸν κύριον τῆς δόξης), which reminds Paul's audience of the destiny of Christ and by implication the destiny of all believers as well. Both 1 Cor 2:7–8 and Col 1:27 exhibit a marked interest in the eschatological component of the mystery.

When Paul ponders the marvelous eschatological riches of the mystery in Col 1:27, he stresses in particular the appropriation of those benefits among the Gentiles (ἐν τοῖς ἔθνεσιν). Some scholars have noted that this introduces an ecclesiological component into the passage alongside the eschatological component. An ecclesiological interest is not completely foreign to Paul's earlier discussions about God's mystery. The highlighting of the Gentiles' participation in the saving benefits of the mystery brings to mind Rom 11:25. Though in Rom 11:25 the Gentile inclusion is assumed for the sake of argument in order to make a point about the future of the Jewish people, it demonstrates that the universal application of the gospel is considered by Paul as part of the field of ideas relevant to the term μυστήριον. In Col 1:26–27, apart from advancing Paul's rhetorical aims with his Gentile audience, the mention of the Gentiles as beneficiaries of the mystery similarly highlights the far-reaching impact of the gospel.

While ecclesiology is not far from Paul's mind in Col 1:27, the passage resumes a soteriological/eschatological direction at the end of the verse. The relative clause ὅ ἐστιν Χριστὸς ἐν ὑμῖν functions to modify the

---

76. The terms are used together with a probable eschatological meaning in Rom 5:2 as well.

preceding material about the riches of the glory of mystery among the Gentiles. The addition of the clause provides the focal point of the riches of the mystery, but it remains to be decided whether the phrase has the nuance of "Christ in (within) you" or "Christ among you." Though the difference is subtle and both ideas can be found elsewhere in Paul's writings, the first option holds a stronger case for supremacy. While the latter possibility brings out the truth that Christ is present in the Gentiles in the same way he is among the Jews, unlike in Ephesians, discussion of the relative status of Jews and Gentiles in the family of God is fairly subdued in Colossians. Gentile inclusion in divine blessings is pronounced, but the topic of the shared standing of Jew and Gentile remains largely untouched.[77] On the other hand, the former nuance ("Christ in/within you") places the emphasis more clearly on the eschatological angle found in the passage (especially with the modifying phrase that follows–ἡ ἐλπὶς τῆς δόξης).[78] The hope of glory is the confidence of future blessing in God's presence based upon the saving work and life of Christ applied to believers. The eschatological rendering of "Christ in/within you" does not require a private, individualistic notion of spirituality, since the saving presence of Christ is shared by all in the believing community, and in this case, the community (the Colossians) is representative of the Gentiles mentioned just prior to the clause (ἐν τοῖς ἔθνεσιν).[79] This interpretation then aligns closely with Col 1:12, where the Colossian believers are recognized as part of the greater community of believers destined for inheriting eschatological blessings.

Colossians 1:27, with its association of the indwelling of Christ and expectation of future glorification, corresponds well to Rom 8:9–11, where Χριστὸς ἐν ὑμῖν (8:10) is the grounds for the assurance of resurrection.[80] The compact wording of Col 1:27 (Χριστὸς ἐν ὑμῖν, ἡ ἐλπὶς τῆς δόξης) accurately summarizes the thinking from Rom 8:9–11, which is then followed by further description of δόξα (8:17–21) and ἐλπίς (8:24–25). Though the

---

77. Moo, *Letters to the Colossians and to Philemon*, 149. Some trace of this topic is present in 1:12, 3:11, and, depending on one's understanding of the Colossian threat, 2:16–17.

78. Agreeing with this position are Lightfoot, *Epistles to the Colossians and to Philemon*, 169; O'Brien, *Colossians, Philemon*, 87; Dunn, *Epistle to the Colossians and to Philemon*, 123; Moo, *Letters to the Colossians and to Philemon*, 158–59.

79. Along these lines, see Cannon, *The Use of Traditional Materials in Colossians*, 213.

80. Arnold, *The Colossian Syncretism*, 272–73; Barclay, *"Christ in You": A Study in Paul's Theology and Ethics*, 32–38, 49.

role of the Spirit is not in view in Col 1:27 as it is in Rom 8:9–11, the omission is consonant with the single-minded focus on the supremacy of Christ in Colossians.[81]

Mystery in Colossians 1:26–27 and in the Undisputed Letters

The contours of the mystery in Col 1:26–27 are consistent with Paul's thought elsewhere. Eschatological salvation is the implicit or explicit centerpiece of the mystery in 1 Cor 2:6–10, 1 Cor 15:51, Rom 11:25, and Rom 16:25–26 as well. In particular, the eschatological orientation of the mystery emerges plainly in 1 Cor 2:6–10 (and also in 1 Cor 15:51) as it does in Col 1:27. The once hidden, now revealed paradigm parallels the presentation in Rom 16:25–26, and to a lesser degree, 1 Cor 2:6–10. The involvement in the mystery of revealer, mediators, recipients, and beneficiaries is similar in Col 1:26–27 and 1 Cor 2:6–16. The inclusion of the Gentiles in God's saving plans recalls the testimony in Rom 11:25 (and Rom 16:26). On the whole, the ideas about mystery in Col 1:26–27 match most impressively with 1 Cor 2:6–16, even though the wording is rarely the same.[82] In no case does the wording of Col 1:26–27 appear to have been copied from these passages or conflated from multiple passages.[83]

---

81. Barclay, *"Christ in You": A Study in Paul's Theology and Ethics*, 49. *Contra* Wolter, *Der Brief an die Kolosser*, 105, who detects in Col 1:27 a collective and eschatological drift away from an individual and pneumatological direction in Rom 8:9–11. In response to Wolter, the fact that the thinking in Col 1:27 and Rom 8:9–11 reflects the unique emphases of Colossians and Romans as a whole supports common authorship, especially since the perspectives are compatible, and any sign of literary dependence is absent.

82. Percy, *Die Probleme der Kolosser- und Epheserbriefe*, 82–83. Leppä, however, contends that Col 1:26–27 borrows from 1 Cor 2:7, as evidenced by duplication of key words and phrases such as μυστήριον, ἀποκρύπτω, θεός(!), δόξα, and πρὸ/ἀπὸ τῶν αἰώνων (Leppä, *The Making of Colossians*, 108). The final correlation is the most interesting, since the phrases modify different ideas in the two passages. In 1 Cor 2:7, God's blessings for believers are foreordained before the ages, whereas in Col 1:26 the blessings are hidden in ages past. Both ideas communicate the involvement of an eternal God in the plans of salvation, and along with the other terms in common exhibit a shared perspective about central Pauline themes (revelation, apostolic ministry, eschatology). Literary dependence is unlikely, since none of the expressions is that unusual, some of them (mystery, God, and glory) reflect themes in Colossians, and many of them belong together (glory and the ages, mystery and hidden, God and all of the above).

83. *Contra* E. P. Sanders, "Literary Dependence in Colossians," 39; Leppä, *The Making of Colossians*, 109–10. See n75 above.

Portrait of an Apostle

The Activities and Goal of Paul's Ministry—Colossians 1:28

The next two verses, 1:28–29, supplement the discourse from the previous verses by showing how Paul carries out his role as an intermediary agent of the mystery.[84] Chief among Paul's responsibilities is the commission to proclaim Christ. The same verb for "proclaim" (καταγγέλλω) makes an appearance in 1 Cor 2:1, which at the very least precedes the discussion of mystery in 2:6–10 and is linked directly to μυστήριον in some manuscripts of 1 Cor 2:1.[85] Additionally, placement of Christ as the object of proclamation has a precedent in Phil 1:17–18, where Paul speaks favorably of any activity that spreads the message of Christ.[86]

With the participles νουθετοῦντες ("admonishing") and διδάσκοντες ("teaching"), which are dependent upon the main verb καταγγέλλομεν, Paul further expounds on the nature of his ministry as God's spokesperson. The verb νουθετέω is seen as part of Paul's specific ministry in 1 Cor 4:14, as part of the role of ministers in general in 1 Thess 5:12, and as the responsibility of all believers in Rom 15:14 and 1 Thess 5:14 (cf. Col 3:16). Teaching (διδάσκω) surfaces as a descriptor of a general task within Paul's ministry in 1 Cor 4:17. This teaching is implemented "in all wisdom" (ἐν πάσῃ σοφίᾳ), which is a characteristic of Paul's service that is especially pronounced in 1 Corinthians 1–2, where the aim of refuting false quests for spiritual knowledge is similar to that of Colossians 1–2.

Colossians 1:28 underscores Paul's view that the benefits of the mystery of Christ apply to all people without distinction. Paul stresses this universal accessibility of the gospel through his repetition of πάντα ἄνθρωπον (three times in verse 28).[87] The scope of Paul's ministry extends to all people, whether Jew or Gentile (Col 3:11), and this limitless aim mirrors

---

84. The occurrences of "we" in these verses have the probable referent of Paul and his associates (cf. 1 Cor 2:6–10; 4:1).

85. Leppä notes the common appearance of καταγγέλλω, λόγος, σοφία, and θεός in 1 Cor 2:1 and Col 1:25–28 to conclude that literary dependence is tenable (Leppä, *The Making of Colossians*, 113–14). But the terms are far too common to bear the weight of proving dependence. More feasibly, they support a coherence of thought between the two passages, in support of a broader consistency between 1 Cor 2:1–10 and Col 1:25–28.

86. For more discussion about Paul's use of the verb καταγγέλλω, see O'Brien, *Colossians, Philemon*, 87.

87. The use of the singular form of ἄνθρωπος as the object of Paul's ministry captures the personal touch that characterizes Paul's ministry in 1 Thess 2:11–12, where similar wording is selected (O'Brien, *Colossians, Philemon*, 88; cf. Abbott, *Epistles to the Ephesians and to the Colossians*, 235).

the universal reach of the gospel (Col 1:6, 23) and the absolute sufficiency of Christ (Col 2:3; 3:11). The credible view has also been posited that the emphasis on all people is purposefully included as a contrast to the restricted availability of knowledge in the false teachers' system.[88]

Paul's obligation entails ministering effectively to people within his sphere of influence so that he may present (παρίστημι) them to God (Col 1:28).[89] The occurrence of the verb recalls Col 1:22, where Paul points to the believer's expectation of being presented (παρίστημι) as holy and blameless to God based on the reconciling work of Christ. This theme opens the door to a collection of similar passages from Paul's earlier letters. In 2 Cor 11:2 Paul states that his ultimate agenda with the Corinthian believers is to present (παρίστημι) them to Christ as exclusively devoted disciples. Paul describes this presentation using marriage imagery in 2 Cor 11:2. The language of presentation occurs within the context of Paul's profession of commitment to believers under his care in both 2 Cor 11:2 and Col 1:28. Though Paul offers believers to God in Col 1:28 rather than to Christ against a marriage backdrop, the concept is similar in the two verses. In 1 Thess 3:13 and 5:23, Paul portrays the believer's future appearance before Christ in blamelessness and holiness, in parallel with the scene from Col 1:22 (though there, the eschatological orientation is not as explicit).[90] Likewise, in 2 Cor 4:14 Paul depicts the presentation of believers to Christ when he returns. Most likely, Paul's offering of believers in Col 1:28 is to be understood eschatologically as well.[91] In short, the image of presenting believers complete before God on the last day (Col 1:28), besides having the conceptual overlap with the language of offering in Rom 15:16, as mentioned earlier, aligns well with Paul's vision elsewhere of the anticipated appearance before Christ and God of prepared and "presentable" believers.

---

88. Abbott, *Epistles to the Ephesians and to the Colossians*, 235; Lohse, *Colossians and Philemon*, 77; Ernst, *Die Briefe an die Kolosser*, 188; O'Brien, *Colossians, Philemon*, 88; Harris, *Colossians and Philemon*, 72; Sappington, *Revelation and Redemption at Colossae*, 186; Aletti, *Colossiens*, 145.

89. It is probable that God is the understood recipient of the presentation, as is the case in Rom 12:1.

90. Barth and Blanke, *Colossians*, 267, reject any eschatological sense in the use of παρίστημι in Col 1:22 and 28, but the emphasis on the eschatological hope in 1:5, 23, 27 (the latter two of which are in the immediate context of the verses in question) indicate that an eschatological viewpoint is being assumed (see also 3:4, 24).

91. See also 1 Thess 2:19–20; 1 Cor 1:8; Phil 1:10.

Portrait of an Apostle

Paul specifically wants to present his believers to God in a mature or completed spiritual condition. The word τέλειος ("mature" or "complete") calls to mind the same term in 1 Cor 2:6.[92] There is significant continuity in the two depictions of maturity. First, τέλειος is a desired state in both passages.[93] In Colossians 1 τέλειος describes the outcome of maturity Paul and his associates strive to inculcate in the people they serve.[94] In 1 Corinthians 2–3 the readers are recognized as deficient in their spiritual growth but are never excluded from the ideal of maturity. Second, both passages associate becoming τέλειος with appreciating the wisdom of God, revealed in the mystery of Christ. Third, neither maturity nor growth in the knowledge of the mystery is a given in the passages (this fact becomes more explicit in Col 2:1–3 and Col 4:12). Fourth, descriptors of Christian maturity (Col 1:28) or immaturity (1 Cor 3:1) are qualified with the phrase ἐν Χριστῷ.[95] The main differences between the use of τέλειος in the two passages are (1) in Col 1–2 Paul reveals a more positive assessment of his audience's potential for growth into maturity, whereas with the Corinthians, he has more reason to be skeptical of their maturity, and (2) maturity is seen as an end result in Colossians (in keeping with the eschatological language of presentation), as opposed to a present descriptor of character (or lack thereof) in 1 Cor. In either case, maturity and growth in the knowledge of the wisdom and mystery of Christ go hand and hand.

---

92. The appearance of τέλειοι in Phil 3:15occurs in a much different context, and the mere occurrence of the word in both Phil 3:15 and Col 1:28 does not lend support to Kiley's theory that the author of Colossians depends on Philippians as one of his two written sources (Kiley, *Colossians as Pseudepigraphy*, 89).

93. This claim must be carefully nuanced for 1 Cor 2:6. As seen in chapter 2 of the book, τέλειος is best understood as referring to all believers rather than to a select group of initiates. The designation is applied based on the reception to the preached message of Christ crucified. Those who are mature (τέλειος) respond in faith to that message. The Corinthians Christians exhibit a jarring inconsistency by valuing worldly wisdom in a way that is contradictory to their confession of faith. The rebuke of 1 Cor 3:1–4 is a challenge for them to attain to the maturity that should characterize their lives as believers. In other words, the usage of τέλειος is heavily shaped by rhetorical goals in this passage.

94. See also Col 4:12. Bruce makes the connection between the believer's perfection and the perfection of Christ, made manifest at his return, in 1 Cor 13:10–12 (Bruce, *Epistles to the Colossians, to Philemon, and to the Ephesians*, 87–88).

95. In Col 1:28 ἐν Χριστῷ, other than specifying in a compact way that those being presented to God are those who share in the life of Christ (for another example of Paul's use of this shorthand see Col 1:2), serves to highlight Christ as the only grounds for spiritual advancement, previewing the contrast between Christian enlightenment and sham alternatives in chapter 2 (see especially the use of ἐν αὐτῷ in Col 2:10–12).

Paul's Identity in Colossians

A comparison of the two passages presents no compelling evidence that a later author has misunderstood the original use of the term in 1 Cor 2–3.

Paul's Personal Investment as a Minister—Colossians 1:29

Paul's shift from plural in Col 1:28 to singular in 1:29 is probably best explained as his perception of sharing in the church's broader task in terms of proclamation but a narrower calling in terms of the unique trials and obstacles he endures as part of his ministry. This is consistent with Paul's personal focus from Col 1:24 as well.[96] Paul's depiction of determination and personal investment in his ministry strengthens the sincerity with which he addresses his readers. He is committed to laboring and sacrificing on their behalf (see also Col 2:1).

Paul's approach to ministry requires wholehearted commitment to the task. He describes his activity as laboring (κοπιάω) and struggling (ἀγνίζομαι) in the power of God.[97] Paul uses the cognate term ἀγών in the following verse (2:1) to emphasize further his efforts. Paul describes his ministry on behalf of his churches using κοπιάω in Gal 4:11; 1 Cor 4:12; 15:10; Phil 2:16 and κόπος in 1 Thess 2:9; 3:5; 2 Cor 6:5; 11:23. The latter two passages fall within the context of sufferings encountered in the course of Paul's ministry. Though the challenges of Paul's ministry are not described in detail in Col 1:29—2:1 as they are in 2 Cor 6:4–10 or 2 Cor 11:23–33, the language used in Col 1:29-2:1 might summarize the suffering and hardship Paul has endured as part of his divine calling.[98] In that case, Col 1:29—2:1 would continue the focus on suffering started in Col 1:24. Paul's incorporation of ἀγνίζομαι is observed in 1 Cor 9:25 with reference to the type of undivided athletic commitment that characterizes his

---

96. Barth and Blanke, *Colossians*, 167–68.

97. Kiley notes that for both Paul (Col 1:23—2:1) and Epaphras (Col 4:12) ministry is described using the terms διάκονος, τέλειος, and ἀγνίζομαι. He suggests that Epaphras may be the author and is using the parallel depictions to adopt the status and authority of Paul for himself (Kiley, *Colossians as Pseudepigraphy*, 96; cf. Dübbers, *Christologie und Existenz im Kolosserbrief*, 164). More likely than either of these suggestions, Paul the author portrays Epaphras in similar terms because Epaphras serves as Paul's delegate to the Colossians. Thus the ministry of Epaphras is an extension of Paul's ministry.

98. Making the connection between Col 1:29—2:1 and the so-called "catalogues of hardship" in 2 Corinthians is MacDonald, *Colossians and Ephesians*, 93–94. See also Pfitzner, *Paul and the Agon Motif*, 111. For a discussion of Paul's accounts of his hardships, see Hodgson, "Paul the Apostle and First Century Tribulation Lists," 62–67.

ministry.⁹⁹ Paul's use of ἀγών is found in 1 Thess 2:2 and Phil 1:30. In those two instances Paul likely alludes to his struggles in the face of opposition. The verb in Col 1:29 and the noun in 2:1 appear to have a more general meaning of expended effort (for a conceptual parallel, see 2 Cor 12:15), though with the transition to repelling false teaching in Col 2:4, it is possible that Paul already has struggle against opponents in mind in Col 2:1.¹⁰⁰ Also plausible is that Paul envisages his prayer for the Colossian believers as his struggle, since the same verb when applied to Epaphras (Col 4:12) describes his prayers.¹⁰¹ In short, the appearance of κοπιάω and ἀγνίζομαι as descriptors of ministry reflects Paul's custom and can thus reasonably be traced to his own way of speaking, even though the precise context assumed by Paul in Col 1:29–2:1 is not known with certainty.¹⁰²

Paul's struggle is not perceived as his own expenditure of effort for a good cause but instead as a product of God's work in him (κατὰ τὴν ἐνέργειαν αὐτοῦ τὴν ἐνεργουμένην ἐν ἐμοὶ ἐν δυνάμει). This statement reflects both wording and concepts from passages in the undisputed letters. A similar pairing of God's energy and power is found in Phil 3:21 (κατὰ τὴν ἐνέργειαν τοῦ δύνασθαι αὐτόν), where it is applied to God's eschatological provision of resurrected bodies for believers. Kiley insists that this and other examples of comparable wording in divergent contexts reveal literary dependence.¹⁰³ But the literary dependence observed in the *Epistle to the Laodiceans* and *3 Corinthians* was characterized by near reproduction that either was not appropriate to the surrounding discourse or misunderstood the original thinking of Paul. The use of the language in Col 1:29 fits naturally within the broader discourse of Col 1:23—2:5 and accurately represents Paul's mindset from other letters. In particular, Paul adopts a

---

99. Other occurrences of the verb are found in Rom 15:30 and Col 4:12.

100. Along these lines, see Pfitzner, *Paul and the Agon Motif*, 110, 128; Hay, *Colossians*, 78; Moo, *Letters to the Colossians and to Philemon*, 162.

101. Lightfoot, *Epistles to the Colossians and to Philemon*, 172; Pfitzner, *Paul and the Agon Motif*, 110-11; Harris, *Colossians and Philemon*, 79.

102. The connections between Col 1:29—2:1 and scattered verses in the undisputed Pauline letters that contain words such as κοπιάω, ἀγνίζομαι, ἐνεργέω, ἐνέργεια, πρόσωπον, and δύναμις, and the construction θέλω γὰρ (δὲ) ὑμᾶς εἰδέναι are enlisted as evidence for conflation or dependence in Leppä, *The Making of Colossians*, 114-16. But since these words and variations of the construction are found quite often, in different passages in letters from the undisputed corpus and are thus indicative of Paul's typical speech, nothing suggests the need to attribute the wording of Col 1:29—2:1 to a later author. The easier explanation is that Paul once again is speaking like Paul in this letter.

103. Kiley, *Colossians as Pseudepigraphy*, 90.

similar perspective about the source of strength in ministry in Rom 15:18, though the wording is somewhat different (οὐ γὰρ τολμήσω τι λαλεῖν ὧν οὐ κατειργάσατο Χριστὸς δι' ἐμοῦ). Furthermore, the juxtaposition of Paul's labor (κοπιάω) and God's enablement emerges side by side in 1 Cor 15:10 as well, showing that Paul was prone to moderate any attention given to his work by attributing any success to God's grace.[104] Finally, the appearance in Col 1:29 of wording that resembles Phil 3:21 does not indicate that the author misunderstood the passage from Philippians, because there is no evidence that the author was trying to replicate its viewpoint about the resurrection.[105] On the topic that is shared, crediting God with supernatural work, the positions of Col 1:29 and Phil 3:21 are in harmony. With familiar wording, Paul communicates a familiar understanding about his ministry in Col 1:29.

Paul's Hope for the Colossian Believers in Colossians—2:1–3

Colossians 2:1 begins with a standard expression of "disclosure" (Θέλω γὰρ ὑμᾶς εἰδέναι) that is employed by Paul almost identically in 1 Cor 11:3 (cf. Phil 1:12) and with a negative counterpart in 1 Thess 4:13; 1 Cor 10:1; 12:1; 2 Cor 1:8; Rom 1:13; 11:25.[106] The mixed contextual evidence from these passages demonstrates that the construction itself does not indicate the initiation of a new topic.[107] The content of Col 2:1 does, however, exhibit a slight shift in the discourse, as Paul moves from a focus on God's servants to those being served.[108] Concern for these recipients of ministry is central to Paul's ministry persona, as expressed in his reiteration of his devoted ministry (ἀγών) on behalf of believers such as the Colossians (ὑπὲρ ὑμῶν).

Speaking to an audience that he addresses as Christians (1:2), Paul now expresses his desire for their encouragement (παρακληθῶσιν) in the faith (2:1). The inclusion of this verb (παρακαλέω) may not be incidental.

---

104. See also 2 Cor 3:5, 12:9.

105. And in fact, in Col 2:12, the author reveals his Pauline understanding of the connection between God's power (ἐνέργεια) and the resurrection of Christ.

106. Mullins, "Disclosure: A Literary Form in the New Testament," 91.

107. Abbott, *Epistles to the Ephesians and to the Colossians*, 237; Barth and Blanke, *Colossians*, 270.

108. The shift is not absolute, since Paul has already included reference to the final recipients in phrases like ὑπὲρ ὑμῶν (1:24), εἰς ὑμᾶς (1:25), ἐν τοῖς ἔθνεσιν (1:27), Χριστὸς ἐν ὑμῖν (1:27), and πάντα ἄνθρωπον (1:28).

Barth and Blanke suggest that the close proximity of παρακαλέω to descriptions of Paul's suffering recalls the pairing of suffering and comfort in 2 Cor 1.[109] The use of ἵνα at the beginning of Col 2:2 supports the fact that Paul's struggle (ἀγών) is endured with his readers' strengthening (παρακαλέω) in mind. This fits within the greater picture in Colossians 1:24–2:5 of Paul seeing the Colossians' (and related believers') comfort and progress as one of the driving forces behind his sacrificial labors, as is the case also in 2 Cor 1:6; 4:7–15; 6:10. With this language Paul reinforces his care for the spiritual health of the believers.

The nature of this health is specified in what follows. The verb παρακαλέω is modified by the aorist participial clause συμβιβασθέντες ἐν ἀγάπῃ. The meaning of this clause is disputed, with options for the verb συμβιβάζω being identified as "to bring together in a unit, unite," and "to advise by giving instructions."[110] Either meaning is possible here. The stress on knowledge throughout the letter, including in the surrounding context of Col 1–2, and examples of this meaning from the LXX and NT persuades some that the meaning is "taught."[111] On the other hand, it should be noted that in the occurrence of the same word in Col 2:19, the meaning of "bonded" is unavoidable.[112] Furthermore, in Col 3:14, love is singled out as the virtue that unites believers, and so the addition of ἐν ἀγάπῃ to συμβιβάζω in Col 2:2 is telling.[113] In conclusion it is likely that the clause is envisioning the building up of the believers as a community of faith. The picture of unity that is fostered by love as a goal for Paul in his missionary labors is consonant with a number of passages from his early letters (1 Cor 1:10; Phil 1:27; 2:2; 2 Cor 13:11; Rom 15:5–6).[114] This familiar hope for growth in unity forms the first part of the description of

---

109. Barth and Blanke, *Colossians*, 275–76.

110. BDAG, "συμβιβάζω," 956–57.

111. Dibelius, *Die Briefe des Apostels Paulus II*, 77; O'Brien, *Colossians, Philemon*, 93.

112. Lightfoot, *Epistles to the Colossians and to Philemon*, 173; Lohse, *Colossians and Philemon*, 80–81; Martin, *Colossians and Philemon*, 75; Wolter, *Der Brief an die Kolosser*, 110; MacDonald, *Colossians and Ephesians*, 85; Moo, *Letters to the Colossians and to Philemon*, 166.

113. Martin, *Colossians and Philemon*, 75; Wolter, *Der Brief an die Kolosser*, 110; Barth and Blanke, *Colossians*, 278; Moo, *Letters to the Colossians and to Philemon*, 166.

114. MacDonald's contention that after his death Paul's associates are displaying a portrait of Paul as an "authoritative teacher" using the language of exhortation (παρακαλέω) and unity (συμβιβάζω) suffers from the fact that the goals expressed are consistent with Paul's goals from his earlier letters (MacDonald, *Colossians and Ephesians*, 92).

what Paul expects the readers' strengthening to look like as a result of his ministry efforts.

The second aspect of the believers' encouragement consists of insight into spiritual truth. The language of wisdom and knowing permeates Col 2:2–3 (σύνεσις, ἐπίγνωσις, σοφία, and γνῶσις).[115] This is consistent with Paul's interest in the topic of knowledge throughout Colossians, especially in contrasting true knowledge centered in Christ and false knowledge that finds its source apart from Christ.[116] Paul's characterization of spiritual growth in terms of advancement in the knowledge of Christ resembles passages such as Phil 1:9 (with the connection to love, as here); 2 Cor 4:6–7 (with the connection to treasure, as here); Rom 15:14; Phlm 6. The assertion that the emphasis on language of wisdom and knowledge places Paul in the role of a "mystagogue" who guides seekers into paths of enlightenment again is weakened by the continuity between the image of Paul here and in earlier writings.[117]

The final goal of godly wisdom that Paul has in view for the Christians addressed is expressed by the phrase εἰς ἐπίγνωσιν τοῦ μυστηρίου τοῦ θεοῦ ("unto the knowledge of the mystery of God").[118] Here, τοῦ μυστηρίου is an objective genitive (the object of the believer's knowledge), and τοῦ θεοῦ is indicating the author and revealer of the mystery. Fully comprehending the depth and significance of God's mystery is seen as the culmination of Christian growth in this passage. This mystery, while finding its context in God's eternal plans, is specifically related to Christ in the following genitive Χριστοῦ. This genitive has created problems for ancient scribes and modern scholars alike.[119] But once the reading in the NA²⁷ is adopted with

---

115. It is doubtful that anything should be made of the common occurrence of πλοῦτος, σοφία, and γνῶσις in Col 2:2–3 and Rom 11:33 (as noted by Kiley, *Colossians as Pseudepigraphy*, 94). The three appear in immediate proximity to one another in Rom 11:33, but πλοῦτος is quite far removed from σοφία and γνῶσις in Col 2:2–3. The resemblance is likely incidental.

116. On the ample use of language of knowledge and wisdom in Colossians, see Aletti, *Colossiens*, 132–33; Moo, *Letters to the Colossians and to Philemon*, 148.

117. For the description of Paul as a mystagogue, see Pokorný, *Colossians*, 107; Furnish, "On Putting Paul in His Place," 5; W. Wilson, *The Hope of Glory*, 70.

118. Harris, *Colossians and Philemon*, 81, explains that "this fourth and final aim (telic εἰς) is not introduced by καί, which suggests that Paul is here redefining his aim or stating it comprehensively."

119. Agreeing with Metzger's summary, the reading in NA27 is preferred "(a) because of strong external testimony and (b) because it alone provides an adequate explanation of the other readings as various scribal attempts to ameliorate the syntactical ambiguity" (Metzger, *A Textual Commentary on the Greek New Testament*, 622).

confidence, the grammatical awkwardness of taking Χριστοῦ in loose apposition to the entire phrase τοῦ μυστηρίου τοῦ θεοῦ can be accepted as a device to move the reader's focus back to Christ.[120] Bockmuehl is correct in rejecting the impulse to see Christ as the ontological equivalent to God's mystery in this passage, given the overwhelming epistemological focus.[121] Paul's point is not that the mystery equals Christ, but that knowledge of the mystery can be found only in Christ. A similarly strong christocentric focus for the mystery is attested indirectly in 1 Cor 1:18–2:10. There, the mystery is tied to wisdom, which is anchored in Christ (1 Cor 1:23-24, 30; 2:8). And if μυστήριον rather than μαρτύριον is the original reading of 1 Cor 2:1, then 2:1-2 communicates a more direct relationship between Christ and the mystery. Once again the concept of "mystery" in Colossians remains closely in line with the earlier testimony from 2 Cor 2:1-10.

Colossians 2:3 (ἐν ᾧ εἰσιν πάντες οἱ θησαυροὶ τῆς σοφίας καί γνώσεως ἀπόκρυφοι) confirms that Paul is not seeking to make Christ the definition of mystery but to make him the focal point for the quest for the wisdom situated in the mystery. All of verse 3 modifies "Christ," with the effect of driving home the point that no true wisdom can be accessed apart from Christ.[122] Christ is the one ἐν ᾧ εἰσιν πάντες οἱ θησαυροὶ τῆς σοφίας καί γνώσεως ἀπόκρυφοι.[123] The knowledge of the mystery that is revealed conclusively to the saints is still a process that is dependent upon pursuing Christ.[124] There is yet wisdom to be gleaned from pursuing an understanding of Christ. Paul expects the Colossian believers to persist in turning to Christ for the type of enlightenment that leads to wise and fruitful living.

Two more points of agreement between Colossians 1–2 and 1 Corinthians 1–2 emerge from this section. First, in Col 2:1-3, Paul claims that the knowledge of the mystery is available to all without distinction but is nonetheless fully grasped only as believers grow as a unit and stay

120. Dunn, *Epistle to the Colossians and to Philemon*, 131.

121. Bockmuehl, *Revelation and Mystery*, 188.

122. Along these lines, see also Brown, *The Semitic Background of the Term "Mystery" in the New Testament*, 55; Arnold, *The Colossian Syncretism*, 274; MacDonald, *Colossians and Ephesians*, 86.

123. The use of "hidden" (ἀπόκρυφος) is not implying that the knowledge of the mystery is still hidden, in contradiction to 1:26. The use of the term correlates well with the "treasure" imagery, and these two themes are occasionally found together in Jewish literature (Lightfoot, *Epistles to the Colossians and to Philemon*, 174; Dunn, *Epistle to the Colossians and to Philemon*, 131–32; Hay, *Colossians*, 79; Moo, *Letters to the Colossians and to Philemon*, 171).

124. See Brown, *The Semitic Background of the Term "Mystery" in the New Testament*, 63–64.

oriented towards Christ. An emphasis on the recipients' spiritual readiness to receive the revelation of the mystery appears in 1 Cor 2:1–16 as well.[125] Second, Paul contrasts the knowledge of the mystery of Christ with competing ideas of wisdom in Col 2:2–3 and 1 Corinthians 1–2. In both cases, God's revealed mystery, with Christ as the focus, is described as the expression of God's superior wisdom.[126] While there is minimal verbal overlap between the two passages, time after time similar topics and perspectives are expressed within comparable contexts.

Affirmation of Paul's Concern—Colossians 2:5

A final demonstration of Paul's concern for the Colossians in this section appears in Col 2:5. The conjunction (γάρ) shows that the verse follows on the heels of 2:4, where Paul has begun to warn his readers of the dangers of false teaching. In Col 2:5 Paul encourages the Colossians with the assurance that despite being removed from them geographically, he is still with them in spirit (εἰ γὰρ καὶ τῇ σαρκὶ ἄπειμι, ἀλλὰ τῷ πνεύματι σὺν ὑμῖν εἰμι).[127] The rhetorical purpose of this statement is to strengthen the bond that exist between Paul and his readers.[128] Through Epaphras, Paul can stay abreast of the Colossians' situation and can thus sincerely affirm his

---

125. See Barth and Blanke, *Colossians*, 282–83. Similar examples are found in 4 Ezra 12:36 and Mark 4:1–12 and parallels.

126. For further development of the theme of revelation in Colossians, especially as it stands in opposition to the opponents' perspective on knowledge, see Smith, *Heavenly Perspective*, 187, 191. See also Arnold, *The Colossian Syncretism*, 272–74.

127. This geographical separation is more likely than Betz's claim that Paul was separated from them as a result of his death (Betz, "Paul's 'Second Presence' in Colossians," 513–14, 517; see also Pokorný, *Colossians*, 106; Wolter, *Der Brief an die Kolosser*, 113–14; Standhartinger, "Colossians and the Pauline School," 582–83; Dübbers, *Christologie und Existenz im Kolosserbrief*, 173–74). Betz bases his claim primarily on his understanding from 1:24 that Paul is already dead and on the observation that σάρξ instead of σῶμα (1 Cor 5:3) is used (Betz, "Paul's 'Second Presence' in Colossians," 513–14, 517). But while Betz is right in asserting that σῶμα would not likely be used to represent Paul's absence after death, nothing would prevent Paul from using σάρξ to describe his bodily location, whether in terms of presence or absence, before death (see for instance Phil 1:22, 24; 2 Cor 7:5). The use of σάρξ in relation to Paul's physical presence also recalls ὅσοι οὐχ ἑόρακαν τὸ πρόσωπόν μου ἐν σαρκί in Col 2:1.

128. Dibelius notes this function for 2:5 and observes parallels between Romans (1:8–15; 15:14–29) and Colossians (1:24—2:5) regarding how Paul attempts to forge warm bonds with readers yet unknown to him (Dibelius, *Die Briefe des Apostels Paulus II*, 74). The formulaic quality of the phrase is explored by Karlsson, "Formelhaftes in Paulusbriefen?," 140–41.

ongoing involvement in their affairs.[129] In view of the phrase immediately following, which pictures Paul's active interest in the believers' progress (χαίρων καὶ βλέπων ὑμῶν τὴν τάξιν καὶ τὸ στερέωμα τῆς εἰς Χριστὸν πίστεως ὑμῶν), the idea is unlikely that the letter itself transmits the presence of Paul.[130] The bond Paul attempts to forge adds weight to his warnings (Col 2:4) and his encouragement (Col 2:5b).

Paul's turn of phrase in Col 2:5a has its closest precedent in 1 Cor 5:3 (ἐγὼ μὲν γάρ, ἀπὼν τῷ σώματι παρὼν δὲ τῷ πνεύματι), where Paul asserts his presence in spirit as part of a display of his authority over a controversy brewing in the church.[131] The pattern of thought in Col 2:5 approximates that of 1 Cor 5:3, even though the wording is not close enough to suggest literary dependence.[132] The degree of variation in terms (εἰ καί . . . ἀλλὰ instead of μέν . . . δέ, σάρξ instead of σῶμα, different ways of communicating presence), form (finite verbs rather than participles), and word order casts doubt on the theory of literary dependence. Elsewhere Paul incorporates similar expressions for his presence and absence.[133] While

---

129. See Col 1:7, where Epaphras is introduced as a faithful minister of Christ (ὑπὲρ ὑμῶν), and Masson, *L'épître de Saint Paul aux Colossiens*, 119.

130. As propagated by Nielsen, "The Status of Paul and His Letters in Colossians," 115; Meeks, "To Walk Worthily of the Lord," 44; Standhartinger, "Colossians and the Pauline School," 584, 588, 592.

131. Schweizer detects significant difference between the two passages because of his judgment that Paul is referring to the Holy Spirit in 1 Cor 5:3 (Schweizer, *Colossians*, 119–20). More likely though, both 1 Cor 5:3 and Col 2:5 reflect an extension of Paul's theology of union with Christ (O'Brien, *Colossians, Philemon*, 98). Marguerat points to Col 2:5 as an example of applying the authoritative heritage of Paul for the purposes of perpetuating orthodox teaching (Marguerat, "Paul après Paul," 322), but the presence of the parallel usage in 1 Cor 5:3 demonstrates that Paul himself spoke this way to guard the truth.

132. Dependence is considered by Leppä, *The Making of Colossians*, 121–22. Among the possibilities explored by Schweizer is that a disciple of Paul intentionally or unintentionally adapted 1 Cor 5:3 (Schweizer, "The Letter to the Colossians: Neither Pauline nor Post-Pauline?," 9). Standhartinger, "Colossians and the Pauline School," 579, doubts that Col 2:5 reflects literary dependence upon 1 Cor 5:3.

133. 2 Corinthians 10:11, 13:2, and 13:10 (cf. Phil 2:12) follow 1 Cor 5:3 in pairing ἄπειμι with πάρειμι, while Phil 1:27 and 2 Cor 10:1 are similar to Col 2:5 in that they contain only the first half of the pair, with presence expressed in other ways. For further discussion of the themes of presence and absence in these verses, see Betz, "Paul's 'Second Presence' in Colossians," 510–12. Kiley enlists the similarity between Col 2:5 and Phil 1:27 as part of his argument for the literary dependence of Colossians upon Philippians, but the existence of other close parallels from the undisputed letters reduces the likelihood that an author used Phil 1:27 in particular as a source (see Kiley, *Colossians as Pseudepigraphy*, 89).

in many of those passages there is an accompanying discussion of Paul's travel plans and intended visits, the Colossian church is representative of churches Paul has not known in person (2:1) and apparently does not expect to encounter first-hand.[134] Nonetheless, Paul still hopes to have an indirect impact upon these churches through his letters, prayers, and the ministry of his associates.

Against Dependence Restricted to Philippians and Philemon

In this extended section (Col 1:23—2:5), parallels from a number of different undisputed Pauline epistles have been identified. Kiley, on the other hand, sees dependence upon only two letters in Colossians: "Col may have known only two genuine letters of Paul's, Phil and Phlm. I will suggest that the material in Col which cannot reasonably be assigned to an extrapolation based on either of these letters might be seen as a product of the oral tradition in the Pauline churches, perhaps in a kind of deutero-Pauline school."[135] He then suggests that this limited collection of source material is typical of pseudepigraphy, drawing on the *Epistle to the Laodiceans* as an example.[136] The specific connections in Col 1:23—2:5, however, to such a variety of passages from Paul's undisputed letters appear to undermine Kiley's proposal.[137] The most likely explanation is that Paul himself is portraying his ministry with familiar terms and images in a fresh situation after a number of years had passed since his original letters were written.

---

134. Dübbers alleges that the omission of Paul's anticipation of release from imprisonment or future visits is best explained by the reality that Paul has already died (Dübbers, *Christologie und Existenz im Kolosserbrief*, 160; cf. R. Collins, *Letters That Paul Did Not Write*, 207). But more likely is the fact that the large scope of Paul's ministry and resulting requirement to prioritize his visits kept many churches off of his travel agenda. He relied instead on his trusted associates to maintain relationships with churches such as the one in Colossae. Both Standhartinger and Dübbers read the perfect form ἑόρακαν in Col 2:1 as an indication of the permanence of Paul's situation (Standhartinger, "Colossians and the Pauline School," 582; Dübbers, *Christologie und Existenz im Kolosserbrief*, 160), but a sense of finality in the perfect tense is not required by either old or new models of verbal aspect theory.

135. Kiley, *Colossians as Pseudepigraphy*, 32.

136. Ibid., 24, 27.

137. Even other skeptics of the Pauline authorship of Colossians recognize a much more diverse group of writings behind the formation of Colossians (see for instance E. P. Sanders, "Literary Dependence in Colossians," 29; Leppä, *The Making of Colossians*, 260–61).

Portrait of an Apostle

Paul the Prisoner in Colossians 4

Paul's self-depiction surfaces again in Colossians 4. The predominant feature of Paul's situation highlighted in this chapter is his imprisonment. Paul's captivity is raised in three places: 4:3-4, 4:10, and 4:18. The first passage displays Paul's missionary concern in the midst of his suffering and his awareness of his need for diligent prayer from his readers. Paul asks for prayer that God would "open up to us a door for the word" (ἀνοίξῃ ἡμῖν θύραν τοῦ λόγου).[138] Similar language occurs in 1 Cor 16:9 (θύρα γάρ μοι ἀνέῳγεν μεγάλη καὶ ἐνεργής) and 2 Cor 2:12 (θύρας μοι ἀνεῳγμένης ἐν κυρίῳ).[139] The pairing of ἀνοίγω and θύρα in all three cases expresses the same idea of new ministry opportunities. It is unclear, however, whether the wording of Col 4:3 refers to ministry possibilities sought even in the current setting of hardship, as in Phil 1:12-18, or to the hope of deliverance from hardship in order to make new ministry frontiers accessible, as in Phil 1:19, 2 Cor 1:10-11, and Rom 15:30-31.[140] Either way the wording reflects an understanding similar to that in 1 Cor 16:9 and 2 Cor 2:12 and is applied in an appropriate context in Col 4:3-4. Thus Col 4:3-4 carries the same conceptual and verbal (ἀνοίγω and θύρα) nuances about avenues for propagating the gospel as in earlier correspondence.[141]

As was the case in Col 1:26-27 and 2:2, μυστήριον is Paul's preferred term in Colossians for denoting his gospel message in 4:3. This term effectively relates the cosmic dimensions of the message, in keeping with the cosmic slant found elsewhere in the letter. Once again, the mystery is tied immediately to Christ (τὸ μυστήριον τοῦ Χριστοῦ). Just as Paul's gospel is often described as the good news of Christ elsewhere (Gal 1:7; 1 Thess 3:2; 1 Cor 9:12; Phil 1:27; 2 Cor 2:12; 9:13; Rom 15:19), so here Paul's divine message derives its significance from the identity and work of Christ in

---

138. A ἵνα clause presents the substance of the prayers sought or offered in Phil 1:9; Rom 15:30-31. The genitive τοῦ λόγου should be seen as equivalent to the gospel, which is further unpacked in terms of mystery in the second half of the verse (*contra* Barth and Blanke, *Colossians*, 453).

139. See also Acts 14:27.

140. Preferring the first option are Gnilka, *Der Kolosserbrief*, 229; Moo, *Letters to the Colossians and to Philemon*, 322. Opting for the second choice are Lohse, *Colossians and Philemon*, 165; Martin, *Colossians and Philemon*, 127; Schweizer, *Colossians*, 233; Cassidy, *Paul in Chains*, 90. Seeing aspects of both possibilities is Müller, *Anfänge der Paulusschule*, 185.

141. The incorporation of a familiar image using common wording is attested, rather than the conscious imitation of a specific passage (*contra* Leppä, *The Making of Colossians*, 194).

salvation history. While the mystery is associated with God as revealer elsewhere (1 Cor 2:7; 4:1; cf., 1 Cor 2:1), the emphasis is on the mystery's focal point in Colossians. The two perspectives are certainly conducive to Paul's overall theology on the shared work of the Father and Son in revelation and salvation.

This very mystery Paul wants to proclaim is then identified as the reason for his imprisonment (δι' ὃ καὶ δέδομαι). It has been alleged that the reference to imprisonment here serves only to add an authentic feel to the letter, by means of resorting to a commonly known detail of Paul's life.[142] But a better explanation is that when Paul reminds himself and his readers that his imprisonment has been brought about because of allegiance to his calling and to Christ, his aim is to resist the overwhelmingly shameful associations of imprisonment in the ancient world.[143] Paul is no ordinary criminal, suffering as a result of shameful behavior. Instead, his imprisonment is endured for the sake of the higher calling of proclaiming the mystery of Christ.

It is not certain how the ἵνα clause of Col 4:4 relates grammatically to 4:3.[144] First, it may continue specifying the substance of Paul's prayer request, being subordinate to προσεύχομαι ("I pray") and parallel to the ἵνα clause of 4:3.[145] Second, it may develop the idea of speaking the mystery of Christ, being dependent upon the first ἵνα clause.[146] Third, it may further elaborate on the reason that Paul is bound, explicating δι' ὃ καὶ δέδομαι.[147] The assumption of God's calling of Paul is often seen to lie behind the wording (ἵνα φανερώσω αὐτὸ ὡς δεῖ με λαλῆσαι). With this reading of Col 4:4 Paul would be recalling the divine necessity (δεῖ) of faithfully articulating only what God has ordained for him to speak.[148] This obligation to obey

---

142. Wolter, *Der Brief an die Kolosser*, 211; Moreschini and Norelli, *Early Christian Greek and Latin Literature*, 20–23; Dübbers, *Christologie und Existenz im Kolosserbrief*, 158.

143. For Paul's proclivity in his earlier letters to challenge cultural attitudes towards shame in view of Christ's calling, see Corrigan, "Paul's Shame for the Gospel," 23–27. For examples of imprisonment bringing shame from the ancient world, see *Dig.* 49.7.1; Josephus, *J.W.* 4.628; Lucian, *Toxaris* 28; Seneca, *Epistula Morales* 9.8–9.

144. See Moo, *Letters to the Colossians and to Philemon*, 324–25 for a helpful presentation of the three main options.

145. Harris, *Colossians and Philemon*, 195.

146. Lightfoot, *Epistles to the Colossians and to Philemon*, 231–32; O'Brien, *Colossians, Philemon*, 240; Moo, *Letters to the Colossians and to Philemon*, 325.

147. Barth and Blanke, *Colossians*, 454.

148. The idea of faithful execution of his commission is supported by HCSB; NET; Gnilka, *Der Kolosserbrief*, 230; Wolter, *Der Brief an die Kolosser*, 211; Dunn, *Epistle*

his calling would resemble the perspective found in 1 Cor 9:16, where Paul asserts that his ministry is more compulsory (ἀνάγκη) than voluntary, and in Rom 1:14, where Paul speaks of the obligation (ὀφειλέτης εἰμί) to carry out his ministry to all types of people. As attractive as this understanding of Col 4:4 is, it falls short because a parallel use of δεῖ appears in relation to Paul's readers in Col 4:6 (εἰδέναι πῶς δεῖ ὑμᾶς ἑνὶ ἑκάστῳ ἀποκρίνεσθαι). This use of δεῖ in Col 4:4 and 4:6 approximates Paul's manner of speech in Rom 8:26 (τὸ γὰρ τί προσευξώμεθα καθὸ δεῖ οὐκ οἴδαμεν) in the sense of "something that should happen because of being fitting."[149]

In Col 1:23, Paul subsumed his own ministry under the broader expanse of the gospel itself. Likewise, in Col 4:4 Paul's calling finds meaning only in its association with the worth of the mystery (αὐτό) he has been commissioned to reveal. The message gives value to the mission. As is the case in other passages (1 Cor 2:10; Rom 15:25–26; Col 1:26–27) employing the term μυστήριον, Paul uses revelatory language (φανερόω) to designate the unveiling of the divine message.[150] Though with the use of φανερόω in Col 4:4 God is not portrayed as the ultimate source behind the manifestation, as is the case in Paul's undisputed letters,[151] no incompatibility with Paul's thought is present in light of the emphasis in the broader context on God opening the door for the message (4:3) and giving Paul the energy for service (Col 1:29).

Looking at Col 4:3–4 as a whole, Paul's association with imprisonment, persistent ministry, and the divine calling to proclaim the mystery of Christ is familiar from the undisputed letters. His request for prayer and the recognition of his accountability to God also corresponds to the earlier picture and has the effect of presenting Paul in a humble, human light. Charges that Paul is presented as "the evangelist *par excellence*" who makes "bold proclamations" are unwarranted if such claims are meant to cast doubt on the authenticity of the portrayal.[152]

---

to the Colossians and to Philemon, 264; Garland, *Colossians and Philemon*, 273; Hay, *Colossians*, 152; MacDonald, *Colossians and Ephesians*, 172; Moo, *Letters to the Colossians and to Philemon*, 326. The thought that Paul simply wants to make the message intelligible in whatever setting he finds himself has advocates in NIV; NRSV; NASB; ESV; NLT; Dibelius, *Die Briefe des Apostels Paulus II*, 92.

149. BDAG, "δεῖ," 214. See also 1 Thess 4:1, 1 Cor 8:2.

150. The revelatory sense of the verb is preferred because of similar uses in Col 1:26 and 3:4 (Dunn, *Epistle to the Colossians and to Philemon*, 264; MacDonald, *Colossians and Ephesians*, 172).

151. Müller, *Anfänge der Paulusschule*, 185.

152. MacDonald, *Colossians and Ephesians*, 176–77.

Paul's Identity in Colossians

There is a passing reference to Aristarchus, Paul's συναιχμάλωτος ("fellow prisoner") in Col 4:10, which finds a parallel in Rom 16:7, with the appellation of Andronicus and Junia, and in Phlm 23, where the label is applied to Epaphras. As mentioned briefly in chapter 2 of this book, the term can be understood either literally or metaphorically.[153] The possibility that Paul's co-workers shared the burden of accompanying him in prison allows for a literal meaning in at least some of these instances.[154]

In Col 4:18, Paul includes in his closing remarks the request for "remembrance" of his imprisonment (μνημονεύετέ μου τῶν δεσμῶν). There is no precedent for this specific turn of phrase, though the ideas of "remembering" in relation to prayer (1 Thess 1:2–3; Rom 1:9; cf., Phlm 4) and "chains" in relation to imprisonment (Phil 1:7, 13, 14, 17; Phlm 10, 13) are attested in Paul's earlier letters.[155] In addition, in 1 Thess 5:25 and Rom 15:30–31 Paul beseeches his readers for prayer as part of his concluding thoughts.[156] The prayer request in Col 4:18 may reflect the physical and emotional hardships of prison life, or it could reiterate the prayer sought in Col 4:3–4. At first glance Gal 6:17, which also occurs at the end of a letter and accentuates Paul's suffering, is tempting as a parallel, but the tone in Gal 6:17 is combative, which is not the case in Col 4:18.[157] Still, the exhortation to remember Paul's chains in Col 4:18 could, at least in part, function to enhance the effectiveness of the rhetoric of the letter, as

---

153. In favor of the metaphorical interpretation in Col 4:10 are Moule, *Epistles to the Colossians and to Philemon*, 136; Ladd, "Paul's Friends in Colossians 4:7–16," 508–9; Houlden, *Paul's Letters from Prison*, 220; Harris, *Colossians and Philemon*, 206.

154. For an example of someone accepting imprisonment for the sake of a friend, see also Lucian, *Toxaris* 31 (Harmon, LCL).

155. Kiley (*Colossians as Pseudepigraphy*, 89) detects direct dependence upon Philippians and Philemon in Col 4:18: "[T]he several references to Paul's chains, δεσμοί, ([Phil] 1.7, 13f., 17) as well as those in Phlm 10, 13 are epitomized in Col 4.18." Kiley appeals to this as an example of the "tiny details which give verisimilitude to a pseudepigrapher's work," and suggests that in the same way "the Laodicean pseudepigrapher borrows from Phil in order to portray the Apostle in chains (v.6) and to greet the saints (v.18)." Kiley draws a false parallel between *Ep. Lao.*, which borrows from Philippians almost word for word, and Colossians, which connects with Philippians ("epitomizes") at most on a conceptual level.

156. Interpreting this clause as a call to prayer are O'Brien, *Colossians, Philemon*, 260; Moo, *Letters to the Colossians and to Philemon*, 353.

157. Lightfoot (*Epistles to the Colossians and to Philemon*, 245) sees Gal 6:17 as "somewhat similar" to Col 4:18. The terse wording in both cases may reflect Paul's unedited style, since these sections were inscribed in Paul's own hand, as is noted in Gal 6:11 and Col 4:18 (Richards, *Paul and First-Century Letter Writing*, 175).

a reference to Paul's sincerity as attested by his chains.[158] In view of these legitimate options for interpretation, one need not resort to the solution that the entreaty was appended simply as a final attempt to pass off the letter as Pauline through the use of a predominant image associated with Paul's memory.[159] It continues the theme of imprisonment found in Col 4:3-4, and 4:10.

What Is Missing in Colossians

The perspective in this chapter so far has been to examine the discourse of Colossians and explain it with reference to material in Paul's earlier letters. In the process, a number of points of connection, some direct and some more subtle, have been detected. But it is also helpful to proceed in the opposite direction: to examine the portrait of Paul in the early letters and observe what significant areas have not been reflected in Colossians. Revisiting the ground explored in chapter 2 of this book, one finds that the most striking omissions in Colossians are (1) the purposeful rooting of Paul's calling and God's ministry plans to the Gentiles in the soil of OT expectation, (2) description of God's dramatic grace and revelation in calling Paul to ministry, and (3) Paul's definition of his ministry with reference to other apostles. For a short letter such as Colossians, omissions of some sort are to be expected, and earlier letters likewise do not treat every aspect of Paul's calling and ministry.[160] But each instance of missing emphasis in

---

158. Those interpreting the appeal primarily in this way or as a show of authority include Lightfoot, *Epistles to the Colossians and to Philemon*, 245; Moule, *Epistles to the Colossians and to Philemon*, 139; Lohse, *Colossians and Philemon*, 177; Gnilka, *Der Kolosserbrief*, 247; Martin, *Colossians and Philemon*, 141; Pokorný, *Colossians*, 196. Upon observing the clause's insertion at the end of the letter and immediately after the personally written greeting, Cassidy remarks on the "startling" nature of the appeal, an appeal designed to capture the readers' attention and create motivation for similar expressions of devotion (Cassidy, *Paul in Chains*, 93).

159. Kiley, *Colossians as Pseudepigraphy*, 89; Wolter, *Der Brief an die Kolosser*, 222; Leppä, *The Making of Colossians*, 208. As Cassidy points out, it is far from established that emphasizing imprisonment would have helped the letter gain a hearing during the era in which a pseudepigraphal letter would have been penned (Cassidy, *Paul in Chains*, 87). Even less likely is the theory that the recollection of Paul's chains is a subtle acknowledgment by the pseudonymous author that Paul is no longer alive (R. Collins, *Letters That Paul Did Not Write*, 207).

160. For instance, 1 Corinthians does not present any OT foundation for Paul's calling or discussion of his focus on Gentiles in his ministry. Romans contains no account of Paul's encounter with Christ on the road to Damascus, no treatment of Paul's standing in relation to other apostles, and no reflection on the sufferings he endured

Colossians needs to be examined in order to offer plausible explanations for why the material is lacking, to ensure that oversights do not reflect the work of an imitator who has overlooked something essential.

For the first point, the exclusion of an OT backdrop to Paul's ministry calling to the Gentiles in Colossians matches with the relative scarcity of OT references, allusions, and echoes in the letter as a whole. This neither supports nor weakens the view that Paul instead of a later imitator wrote the letter, but it does show that the portrayal of Paul's calling is not deficient when considered within the surrounding discourse. More telling are the reasons for which Paul emphasized the OT foundation of his ministry to the Gentiles in the undisputed letters (especially in Gal 1:15–16, 2 Cor 5:18—6:10, and Rom 15:21). In letters such as Galatians and Romans, one of Paul's main goals was to establish the full rights of Gentiles to receive the saving benefits of Christ's sacrifice. Part of his argument required showing the OT precedent for God sending his servants to reach the Gentiles with this message. Such a message and the legitimacy of its messengers are assumed in Colossians, where Paul is addressing a Gentile audience made up of people who had already welcomed the blessings of salvation (1:5–6; 2:6). A second consideration is that Paul's gospel ministry was having difficulty gaining acknowledgment as being on par with that of other preachers in Galatians and 2 Corinthians. In Gal 1:15–16, the connection to the call of Jeremiah and/or the Isaianic servant helped highlight the divine origins of Paul's ministry and message. In 2 Cor 6:2, Paul's association with the servant of Isaiah lent support to his overall depiction of power through weakness (seen most immediately in the verses that followed, 2 Cor 6:3–10). In contrast, Paul is able to comfortably align himself with the orthodox, catholic gospel in Colossians (1:23), without needing to defend his validity as a minister (see further discussion on Paul's relationship to other apostles below). While Paul still perceives his calling as divine and involving both suffering and proclamation in Colossians, he only describes this calling instead of defending it. As a result, he does not need to employ OT patterns in the ways demonstrated in Galatians and 2 Corinthians.

The second noticeable strand of material missing from Paul's portrait in Colossians is his position as a privileged and undeserving recipient of divine revelation and a divine calling to ministry. In other words, Paul does not recall his past as a persecutor or marvel at the grace of God in revealing divine plans to him in spite of it. In response, the theme of grace

---

as a byproduct of his ministry. Philippians devotes no attention to the mystery, OT connections, other apostles, or Paul's responsibility to reach the Gentiles.

is not under investigation elsewhere in Colossians, so it is not surprising that it does not surface in connection with Paul's calling. Second, Paul underscores his unworthiness as a servant of God in other places (Gal 1:13–16; 1 Cor 15:9–10) in order to attribute his dramatic enlistment into ministry even more to God, in defense of his full standing as an apostle and minister of the gospel. As already mentioned, Paul does not need to contend for a hearing in Colossians. For a third possibility, Aletti proposes that Paul does not emphasize his special reception of revelation because his opponents were abusing the idea of divine knowledge privy to only a select group.[161] A focus on Paul's extraordinary access to divine revelation through a special calling would run the risk of interfering with Paul's goal of pointing people to wisdom found in Christ and the revealed gospel preached openly to everyone.[162]

The third problem needing resolution is the charge that the writer of Colossians has accorded Paul an exclusive apostolic prestige that does not surface in the "authentic" letters, as suspected from the observation that no other apostles are mentioned in the letter.[163] Apart from being an argument from silence, the theory does not rule out other possible reasons for the omission of the other apostles.

A look at Paul's undisputed letters demonstrates that first, Paul mentions well-known apostles in cases such as Gal 1:19, 1 Cor 9:5, and 1 Cor 15:5–11, when he intends to establish the validity of his apostleship. This concern is not part of Paul's agenda in Colossians.[164] Second, Paul applies the label ἀπόστολος to lesser-known co-workers in places such as Phil 2:25 and 2 Cor 8:23. Though others are not called apostles in Colossians, a similar result is attained when Paul ascribes the title διάκονος to both himself and his co-workers (Col 1:7, 23, 25; 4:7).[165] Third, Paul acknowledges the presence of other apostles, without naming specific apostles, by speak-

---

161. Aletti, *Colossiens*, 141.

162. See also Smith, *Heavenly Perspective*, 187, 191; Arnold, *The Colossian Syncretism*, 272–74.

163. Lohse, *Colossians and Philemon*, 6, 72; De Boer, "Images of Paul in the Post-Apostolic Period," 364; Penny, "The Pseudo-Pauline Letters of the First Two Centuries," 346; Nielsen, "The Status of Paul and His Letters in Colossians," 107–9; Kiley, *Colossians as Pseudepigraphy*, 60–61; R. Collins, *Letters That Paul Did Not Write*, 203; Beker, *Heirs of Paul*, 68. Also, tentatively, R. Wilson, *Colossians and Philemon*, 67.

164. *Contra* Nielsen, "The Status of Paul and His Letters in Colossians," 109, who says, "To omit the notion of the Twelve from a discussion of authority could surely be seen as an attack upon and rejection of their apostolic status."

165. See also σύνδουλος in Col 4:7.

ing of himself as one of the apostles in instances including 1 Thess 2:6 and 1 Cor 4:9. In those cases the characteristics or experiences of an apostle are pertinent to specific arguments Paul is making. In Colossians, after the reference to Paul's apostolic calling in Col 1:1, the designation ἀπόστολος is not applied to Paul in Colossians.[166] Instead, as was seen in the analysis of Col 1:23, he is described as a minister (διάκονος), who shares a small part of a larger ministry. The specific issue of apostleship does not appear to concern Paul in this letter, so he has no reason to mention the other apostles. As demonstrated from this brief analysis of the three categories of references to the apostles in the undisputed letters, there exists no compelling reason for Paul to mention other apostles in Colossians.

Upon examination of the nature of the three categories of omissions regarding Paul's ministry in Colossians, a common thread is that the portrait of Paul as it stands aligns well with the occasion and audience of the letter. In Colossians Paul shows little interest in grounding his identity and calling with reference to Jewish texts and Jewish apostles and in response to Jewish opponents.[167] Paul is addressing Gentile believers who were brought to faith under the oversight of Paul, through Epaphras, without any evident contact with other well known apostles. As a result, issues relating to the OT basis for his apostleship, Paul's history as a Jewish persecutor transformed and appointed to service through God's grace,

166. Hobson attempts to make διάκονος and ἀπόστολος virtual synonyms, but his reasoning is unconvincing (Hobson, "The Authorship of Colossians," 145). Ernst rightly rejects this hypothesis, noting that the title "apostle" would more effectively convey the rhetorical effect a pseudonymous author would hope to achieve (Ernst, *Die Briefe an die Kolosser*, 182).

167. This explanation aligns with the position that the opponents in Colossians were not predominantly Judaizers. Opinions vary over the precise origins and affiliation of the so-called "Colossian heresy." Some scholars gravitate towards the view that Paul's opponents were Jews (Wright, *Colossians*, 24–30, and Dunn, *Epistle to the Colossians and to Philemon*, 25–34; Smith, *Heavenly Perspective*, 38). A group resembling the Judaizers faced in Paul's earlier ministry is unlikely in any case, since references to the distinguishing characteristics of Judaism, so clear in Paul's other letters, are at best veiled in Colossians (there is no reference to the Law, the mention of Sabbaths (2:16) is ambiguous, and the theme of circumcision (2:11–13) is left rather undeveloped (Moo, *Letters to the Colossians and to Philemon*, 56–7). Other scholars rightly minimize the Jewish elements of the false teaching and believe that a syncretistic belief system is presupposed by the contents of the letter (see especially Arnold, *The Colossian Syncretism*, 3, 243). It is also possible that a well-organized "heresy" group did not exist but that Paul was simply providing pre-emptive teaching to help ground the Colossian believers in Christ. Paul's main concern is to promote a view of wisdom that is founded on Christ rather than on philosophy, human tradition, and the principles of the world (Col 2:8).

and his validity in the eyes of the other apostles do not demand attention in the letter. The omissions reflect topics that do not fit the occasion.

Conclusion

At the beginning of this chapter three questions were identified as central for the task of weighing the relative merits of Pauline authorship and pseudonymous authorship of Colossians. The first question consisted of looking at how the concepts of Paul's calling and ministry reflected in Colossians contributed to a coherent overall discourse in Colossians. There is consistency in the way Paul is portrayed throughout Colossians: he is characterized by a divine calling to serve, suffer for, instruct, and build up churches under his supervision, focusing on Christ as the source of meaning and growth. These features are shared as part of the natural discourse of the letter: in the introduction, in a section functioning as an apostolic apology, and in prayer requests and personal comments at the end of the letter. These discrete sections in turn have natural points of connection with other parts of the letter, with themes such as wisdom, hope, glory, and the universal and cosmic relevance of the gospel uniting the sections focused on Paul with the sections relaying his teaching for his readers.

For the second avenue of research, correspondence in words and thought between Colossians and earlier Pauline letters is best explained by the hypothesis that Paul echoed and adapted portions of his previous teachings for specific churches with specific problems, but churches with which Paul had no prior relationship. Similar vocabulary, especially when the terms identified surface in more than one of Paul's undisputed letters, which is the case for the majority of examples cited, is insufficient for establishing literary dependence.[168] The pattern of affinity between Colossians and the undisputed letters varies drastically from the effects seen in *Epistle to the Laodiceans*, where very little variance from Paul's letters was witnessed, and *3 Corinthians*, where wording was followed quite closely and only in areas that needed to support the letter's claim to authorship rather than in sections advancing fresh teaching. Conceptually, Colossians faithfully reproduces the theological viewpoints from Paul's earlier letters, even though there are still surprising arrangements of words and ideas, such as in Col 1:24, that demonstrate the freedom of Paul to be Paul. In

---

168. The tendency to be too quick to identify dependence or conflation based on scattered common wording is particularly characteristic of Leppä, *The Making of Colossians*.

short, the portrayal of Paul's ministry and persona in Colossians has too little verbal overlap and too much conceptual overlap with earlier letters to betray any obvious attempt of a later admirer to mimic Paul's speech and authority.

Finally, snapshots of Paul from earlier letters not observed in Colossians are of such nature that Paul had no compelling reason to include them. There is no indication from elsewhere in the letter that the Colossian believers had been influenced by other specific apostles or that they were dubious of Paul's legitimacy as a minister. The apostolic apology of Col 1:23—2:5 provides a brief overview of Paul's calling and ministry with the specific intent of establishing his rationale for addressing them as one who had not founded their church. And even in that section the focus is more on the content and character of Paul's teaching rather than on his personal history, since the teaching about divine wisdom in Christ was what they needed as a corrective to the urge to find wisdom elsewhere.

In summary, Colossians stands apart from the documents analyzed in chapter 2. Paul's authoritative and familiar yet fresh voice is transmitted consistently throughout the letter.

5

Paul's Identity in Ephesians

Guiding Questions for the Analysis of the Letter

IN THIS CHAPTER PAUL's projected persona in Ephesians will be examined in detail. The procedure will resemble the approach taken with Colossians, but with a substantial new consideration. The portrayal of Paul will be analyzed in comparison to Paul's image both in the undisputed letters and in Colossians, since Colossians was most likely written before Ephesians. Once a brief overview of research on the relationship between Colossians and Ephesians has been set forth, material in Eph 1:1; 3:1–13; 4:1; and 6:19–20 will be investigated more closely.

Criteria for detecting authenticity will follow those put forward in chapter 4 with respect to Colossians. First, attention will be paid to whether the author has offered a plausible portrayal of Paul that is consistent with both material from earlier letters and the discourse elsewhere in Ephesians. If both of these standards have been met simultaneously, then the probability is that Paul himself is responsible. Second, the nature of verbal parallels will be examined to see whether literary dependence or additional articulation of familiar themes by the same author is the more likely scenario. Finally, rationale for the absence of any typical feature of Paul's self-description will be supplied, and comparison to the omissions in Colossians will be explored. It will be shown that though many scholars contend that the presentation of Paul in Ephesians reflects the perspective of an imitator, on a consistent basis the different features of Paul's image in Ephesians are best explained by recourse to the assumption that Paul himself wrote the letter.

The Relationship between Colossians and Ephesians

The first section of this chapter will engage the important and complex issue of the relationship between Ephesians and Colossians. The letters have a remarkable degree of similarity in the areas of vocabulary, style, structure, and content, but actual reproduction of long strings of words in the book is quite uncommon, and the similar or identical words are often incorporated into contexts that vary somewhat.[1] Scholars skeptical of the Pauline authorship of Ephesians often explain these insights by alleging that the author of Ephesians borrows from Colossians, though disagreement persists over whether Colossians was in the author's possession at the time of writing or whether the dependence was based on memory and great familiarity with the letter.[2] But this view has been contested. Occasionally someone will support the opposite conclusion that Colossians relies upon Ephesians.[3] Both of these views suffer from the fact that in specific passages dependence can be argued in either direction.[4] At times scholars have contended for a multiple-stage process involving successive alterations of existing documents.[5] The overall coherence, however, of both Colossians and Ephesians in their present forms supports their integrity. Another position holds that two authors, neither of whom were Paul but were from the same close circle, wrote independently of one another.[6]

---

1. See Mitton, *Ephesians: Its Authorship, Origin, and Purpose*, 57–58; Polhill, "The Relationship between Ephesians and Colossians," 439–40; Lincoln, *Ephesians*, xlviii–lv.

2. Preferring at least some degree of direct literary dependence are Benoit, "Rapports littéraires entre les épîtres aux Colossiens et aux Éphésiens," 20; Lindemann, *Der Epheserbrief*, 11; Müller, *Anfänge der Paulusschule*, 301. In favor of indirect influence based on memory are Mitton, *Ephesians: Its Authorship, Origin, and Purpose*, 58, 63; Schnackenburg, *Ephesians*, 32. Remaining open to either alternative or some combination are Merklein, *Das kirchliche Amt nach dem Epheserbrief*, 39; Lincoln, *Ephesians*, lv.

3. This view can be traced back to Mayerhoff, *Der Brief an die Colosser: mit vornehmlicher Berücksichtigung der drei Pastoralbriefe*, 105–6. See also Coutts, "The Relationship of Ephesians and Colossians," 201–7.

4. Polhill, "The Relationship between Ephesians and Colossians," 444; Barth and Blanke, *Colossians*, 72–85; Best, "Who Used Whom?," 77–93.

5. Holtzmann, *Kritik der Epheser- und Kolosserbriefe*, 35–193. See also Muddiman, *Ephesians*, 20–21.

6. Best, "The Relationship of Ephesians and Colossians," 93–96.

Portrait of an Apostle

Various other views have been proposed as well.[7] The view accepted in the early church and for centuries thereafter is that Paul wrote both letters.[8]

Connected with the problem of authorship and the relationship between Ephesians and Colossians is the puzzle of audience and destination. Many scholars have pointed to evidence that the letter to the Ephesians does not appear to have been written to the church in that specific city.[9] In some early manuscripts (P[46], the originals of ℵ and B, and in 6 and 1739) Eph 1:1 lacks a named addressee (ἐν Ἐφέσῳ is missing). One solution is that the reference to Ephesus had once been included but was omitted for some reason.[10] Or perhaps some other destination city (or more than one) had appeared in the original letter.[11] A further complicat-

---

7. Van Roon believes that an original Pauline letter was expanded upon to create both Colossians and Ephesians (van Roon, *The Authenticity of Ephesians*, 429–32). Boismard suspects that an original letter, attributable to Paul or his writing assistant, was supplemented with additions from Colossians by someone else after Paul's lifetime (Boismard, *L'Énigme de la letter aux Éphésians*, 11). Benoit detects in Ephesians the "voice" of Paul but the "hand" of a disciple who exercised extensive freedom in transmitting Paul message on Paul's behalf, using Colossians as a guide (Benoit, "Rapports littéraires entre les épîtres aux Colossiens et aux Éphésiens," 21–22).

8. This conclusion, preceded by an extensive analysis of the evidence and various positions, is supported by Barth and Blanke, *Colossians*, 72–126. See also a list of writers supporting Paul's authorship of Ephesians in particular in Hoehner, *Ephesians*, 9–18. For recent defenses of the Pauline authorship of Ephesians, see O'Brien, *Ephesians*, 4–47; Hoehner, *Ephesians*, 30–38; Carson and Moo, *An Introduction to the New Testament*, 480–86.

9. A few scholars (Black, "The Peculiarities of Ephesians and the Ephesian Address," 59–73; Arnold, "Ephesians," 244–45; Hoehner, *Ephesians*, 78–79, 144–48; Heil, *Empowerment to Walk in Love for the Unity of All in Christ*, 6–8) identify the Ephesians as the exclusive or primary recipients of a genuine letter written by Paul. Boismard believes that a shorter, original version of the letter was written to the Ephesians specifically, but that a later editor excised the reference to the Ephesians in order to adapt the expanded letter for a wider audience (Boismard, *L'Énigme de la letter aux Éphésians*, 80).

10. Black points to the possible parallels of references to Rome being removed from several manuscripts (most notably G) in Rom 1:7 and 1:15 (Black, "Ephesians and the Ephesian Address," 67–68; cf. Arnold, "Ephesians," 244). Best, though, protests that the reading τοῖς ἁγίοις τοῖς οὖσιν ἐν Ἐφέσῳ καὶ πιστοῖς, with the place name dividing the two substantive titles, is awkward enough to cast doubt on its originality (Best, "Ephesians 1.1 Again," 275; Best, *Ephesians*, 98).

11. Tertullian (*Marc.* 5.11.12; 5.17.1) contends that Marcion (wrongly) recognized a letter to the Laodiceans in place of the one to the Ephesians. Goulder opts for an original destination to the Laodicean church, with copies later circulating elsewhere (Goulder, "The Visionaries of Laodicea," 16). Whether or not one accepts such a specific destination for the letter, Goulder's proposed reconstruction of the errant views

ing factor, however, is that the letter's contents (especially Eph 1:15, 3:2 and the lack of personal greetings and recollection of past encounters) indicate the author's assumption that many people reading the letter were not well acquainted with Paul, which would not match the history of Paul's relationship with the Ephesians. On the other hand, without a specific addressee the resulting wording is stilted and unlikely to have been intended as the final reading in the original.[12] In response, some have proposed that a gap existed from the beginning to allow a number of locations to be inserted.[13] A more complex theory supposing a number of textual changes from an initial generic address (τοῖς ἁγίοις καὶ πιστοῖς) to the wording that eventually won the day respects the general character of the letter while avoiding the weaknesses of the gap hypothesis, though it too has its own drawbacks.[14]

Beyond textual issues, Col 4:16 provides evidence that Paul was already beginning to conceive of a wider circulation for his letters when he wrote Colossians. The widening scope of Paul's ministry at the time the letters would have been written would have necessitated a more wide-ranging scope for Paul's writing ministry. The most probable reconstruction of events is that Paul wrote Colossians to assist Epaphras in his oversight of the church. Paul then planned to write a letter to neighboring Laodicea, with the aim of encouraging and instructing them as well (Col 4:16; cf. Col 2:1). Either after writing the letter to the Laodiceans, or as a substitute for a letter specifically to that church, Paul wrote a general letter that would serve the needs of any number of churches, particularly those

---

on spiritual elitism countered by Paul is attractive in its explanatory power. It is possible that Paul was aware of this propensity to esteem supernatural phenomena in the broader region of Asia Minor when he penned his circular letter. This would explain the emphasis on the heavenly realms, Christ's supremacy over the whole universe, and resistance to satanic forces in the letter. See further Goulder, "The Visionaries of Laodicea," 24-25, 27-29, 37.

12. This is all the more true if, with P46, the article is lacking before οὖσιν in τοῖς ἁγίοις οὖσιν καὶ πιστοῖς. See BDF §413.3; Best, "Ephesians 1.1 Again," 275; Lincoln, *Ephesians*, 2. Others, to the contrary, see as the least problematic the hypothesis that the text never contained nor was meant to contain a place name (Kümmel, *Introduction to the New Testament*, 355; Schnackenburg, *Ephesians*, 40–41).

13. See J. Robinson, *Ephesians*, 11, 141; Wikenhauser and Schmid, *Einleitung in das Neue Testament*, 485–86; Witherington III, *The Letters to Philemon, the Colossians, and the Ephesians*, 218–19. Discussing the strengths and weaknesses of this view are Guthrie, *New Testament Introduction*, 530–31; Carson and Moo, *Introduction to the New Testament*, 488–89.

14. Supporting this theory while acknowledging its defects is Best, "Ephesians 1.1 Again," 276–78; Best, *Ephesians*, 99–101.

in Asia Minor.[15] If, according to this theory, Colossians and Ephesians shared similar recipients and were crafted within a short period of one another, then the overlap between the two letters in terms of content and language would not be unexpected.

In view of the lack of consensus about the exact relationship between Colossians and Ephesians, in the rest of this chapter the specific passages related to Paul's identity will be inspected on a case by case basis. Sensitivity will be shown to commonalities with material in Colossians, but correspondence to other material in the undisputed letters will be observed as well. Special attention will be given to the *nature* of the correlations between Ephesians and Paul's earlier letters, including Colossians. It will be demonstrated that Ephesians exhibits strong conceptual relationships to a number of Paul's letters without the trademark verbal or syntactical rigidity that pseudepigraphal works tend to reflect in their relationship to their source material.[16] Alternate explanations, other than the hypothesis that a pseudonymous author of Ephesians borrowed language and concepts from Colossians and earlier Pauline letters, will be explored in support of the view that the portrait of Paul reflects Paul's own presentation.

---

15. Mitton objects to the circular hypothesis on the grounds that Paul had written a number of churches in his letter to the Galatians without needing to create a generic letter for those churches (Mitton, *Ephesians: Its Authorship, Origin, and Purpose*, 224–25). In response, the occasion for the letter was quite different (Paul was much more personally involved in the discord with the Galatians and the threats were more urgent), the specific churches being addressed in Galatia may have been more identifiable and fewer in number, and the scope and organization of Paul's ministry had changed since he wrote Galatians (he now had oversight of many more churches and through the mediation of a greater number of co-workers).

16. Mitton attempts to pair Ephesians with the *Epistle to the Laodiceans* with regard to how they incorporate Paul's earlier letters (not even including the use of Colossians by the author of Ephesians), according to two tests he devised to expose the work of a pseudepigrapher (Mitton, *Ephesians: Its Authorship, Origin, and Purpose*, 111–13, 116–17, 134–36). The flaw in his method is that he has constructed his tests based on intuition rather than upon observed characteristics in what is known to be pseudepigraphal literature. When letters such as the *Epistle to the Laodiceans* and *3 Corinthians* are examined, it is found that they betray close verbal and syntactical correspondence to specific passages from the Pauline corpus while occasionally faltering on conceptual fidelity. It will be shown in this chapter that Ephesians faithfully echoes the concepts of Paul's earlier letters while straying from the script in its sentence formation and choice of vocabulary (with the exception of Colossians, which will receive special treatment in this chapter and was not considered in the section in which Mitton applied his tests). In other words, the use of the undisputed letters of Paul by the author of Ephesians in no way resembles the work of the pseudonymous author of the *Epistle to the Laodiceans*.

Paul's Identity in Ephesians

PAUL'S GREETING – EPHESIANS 1:1

The opening salutation that includes Paul's self-description (Eph 1:1) follows the same wording as that in Col 1:1 (Παῦλος ἀπόστολος Χριστοῦ Ἰησοῦ διὰ θελήματος θεοῦ). These both mirror 2 Cor 1:1 and approximate 1 Cor 1:1. The literary dependence of Eph 1:1 upon Col 1:1 (and/or 2 Cor 1:1 or 1 Cor 1:1) is not the obvious conclusion, since in 2 Cor 1:1 (and Col 1:1) Paul has already shown the propensity to conform to an existing pattern in his self-identification at the beginning of a letter. As was the case with Colossians, this general identification conforms well to the broad tenor of a letter penned to a relatively unfamiliar audience. The additional reasoning in favor of the authenticity of Col 1:1 (as listed in chapter 4 of this book) also applies to Eph 1:1.

Notably, Paul stands alone as the stated sender in Ephesians, in contrast to Colossians and 1 and 2 Corinthians. Some scholars detect this narrowed focus on Paul as a sign of a later author's attempts to elevate Paul and his authority.[17] But the appearance of Paul alone accords better with the theory that Ephesians was intended to be as general as possible for use in multiple churches, many of which had no prior relationship with Paul and his associates.[18]

AN INTRODUCTION TO PAUL'S MINISTRY – EPHESIANS 3:1–13

Ephesians 3:1–13 delivers an extended discussion of Paul's ministry. There are significant similarities to what is noted in Col 1:23–29. In fact, two of the closest verbal parallels in the letters (Eph 3:2 with Col 1:25 and Eph 3:9 with Col 1:26) are found in these sections.[19] The bulk of the overlap occurs between Col 1:23–29 and Eph 3:2–7, but the verses do not follow the same exact order.[20] A careful examination of the parallel material sug-

---

17. Ernst, *Die Briefe an die Epheser*, 260, 263; Houlden, *Paul's Letters from Prison*, 253; Penny, "The Pseudo-Pauline Letters of the First Two Centuries," 243, 264; Schnackenburg, *Ephesians*, 42; Furnish, "Ephesians" 2:540; MacDonald, *Colossians and Ephesians*, 194, 272; Sterling, "From Apostle to the Gentiles to Apostle of the Church," 77-78.

18. As noted by van Roon, Romans, a letter directed to believers largely unknown to Paul, is addressed from Paul alone as well (van Roon, *The Authenticity of Ephesians*, 85).

19. Mitton, *Ephesians: Its Authorship, Origin, and Purpose*, 58.

20. For presentation of the parallel material in two columns for the two passages, see Merklein, *Das kirchliche Amt nach dem Epheserbrief*, 159-60; Lincoln, *Ephesians*, 169; Aletti, *Saint Paul Épître aux Éphésiens*, 171.

gests that no certain conclusion can be drawn about whether one section is dependent upon the other.[21]

Both sections may be described as an "apostolic apology," which is also observed in some of Paul's undisputed epistles (Gal 1:10–2:21; 1 Thess 2:1–12; Phil 1:12–26; 2 Cor 1:12–17).[22] The section is not an artificial presentation designed to allow a later author to speak with the idealized authority of Paul.[23] Instead, it is Paul's own depiction of his relationship to the grand vision of the outworking of God's plans to bring all things under Christ's authority and to deliver salvation to the new humanity of redeemed Jews and Gentiles.

Paul's Summary of His Imprisonment and Its Purpose— Ephesians 3:1

Paul begins the next section with an anaphoric construction (Τούτου χάριν) that is picked up again in Eph 3:14 as a prelude to a prayer for the readers.[24] Though τούτου χάριν is unusual for Paul (χάριν is used on its own in Gal 3:19, and the word or phrase surfaces again only in the disputed Paulines) the virtual synonyms διό (2:11; 3:13; 4:8, 25; 5:14) and διὰ τοῦτο (1:15; 5:17; 6:13; cf. 5:6), which are more typical in Paul's undisputed letters, appear elsewhere in Ephesians. The construction τούτου χάριν looks back to the grand vision of Jews and Gentiles together being reconciled to God and built up as God's holy temple (2:11–22). Paul's prayer is offered so that his readers' experience in Christ will be consonant with this great

---

21. See the compact summary of the salient points of such an analysis in Best, *Ephesians*, 310–11. Best's conclusion that two separate authors both influenced by Paul's writings are responsible for the passages does not follow though (ibid., 311). It is unlikely that two separate authors would arrive at such similar material with similar wording based solely upon a shared theological heritage or apprenticeship. More plausible is that Paul himself penned the two sections within a short period of time.

22. Boers, "The Form Critical Study of Paul's Letters," 153; Penny, "The Pseudo-Pauline Letters of the First Two Centuries," 244.

23. W. Knox, *St. Paul and the Church of the Gentiles*, 185, 189; Penny, "The Pseudo-Pauline Letters of the First Two Centuries," 231; MacDonald, *The Pauline Churches*, 125; Schnackenburg, *Ephesians*, 130, 132; Lincoln, *Ephesians*, xiii; Furnish, "Ephesians," 2:540; Beker, *Heirs of Paul*, 72; Dunn, "Pauline Legacy and School," 890.

24. Seeing τούτου χάριν in Eph 3:14 as resumptive of the same phrase in 3:1 are Abbott, *Epistles to the Ephesians and to the Colossians*, 77; Caragounis, *The Ephesian Mysterion*, 55; Schnackenburg, *Ephesians*, 128; Lincoln, *Ephesians*, 167. Fay disagrees with the resumptive theory, contending that τούτου χάριν in 3:14 builds upon 3:1–13 (Fay, "Paul the Empowered Prisoner," 190–92).

vision. Before proceeding with the prayer, Paul introduces himself with his apostolic apology. The wording ἐγὼ Παῦλος is reminiscent of the transition to Paul's self-presentation found in Col 1:23. Once again, this Pauline expression (Gal 5:2, 1 Thess 2:18, 2 Cor 10:1, and Phlm 19) might serve to delineate the transition to a distinct topic or place emphasis on Paul as the subject of focus.

Paul's name is further modified by the appositional phrase ὁ δέσμιος τοῦ Χριστοῦ. In contrast to what was seen in Colossians, Paul's imprisonment is stated overtly fairly early in the letter. The term δέσμιος has reference to Paul elsewhere in Phlm 1 and 9, where it is similarly specified that Paul is δέσμιος Χριστοῦ Ἰησοῦ.[25] In those instances the article precedes neither the head noun nor the genitive modifier, as is the case in Eph 3:1. According to Apollonius' Canon and Corollary, it is expected that both nouns would either possess the article or lack the article, and that anarthrous genitive nouns in the construction tend to carry the same semantic force.[26] These observations suggest that there is not necessarily any semantic difference between δέσμιος Χριστοῦ Ἰησοῦ and ὁ δέσμιος τοῦ Χριστοῦ In any case, it is unlikely that the author of Eph 3:1 wished to confer a venerated status upon Paul in a way that was foreign to Phlm 1 and 9.[27] If any rhetorical force is intended, it is more probable that the article sets Paul apart from the prisoners around him or highlights the irony of his situation.[28]

A literal imprisonment in Eph 3:1 should be understood in the light of Eph 6:20, where Paul's imprisonment is not qualified by any association with Christ, as is the case here. The clarification that Paul's imprisonment is τοῦ Χριστοῦ demonstrates the way in which Paul interprets his imprisonment. He does not suffer randomly or according to the whims of human rulers but according to his calling to serve Christ. As seen in the analysis

---

25. Though Eph 3:1 mirrors Phlm 1 quite closely (see Mitton, *Ephesians: Its Authorship, Origin, and Purpose*, 132), titles such as ἀπόστολος (1 Cor 1:1; 2 Cor 1:1; Col 1:1), δοῦλος (Gal 1:10; Phil 1:1; Rom 1:1), and δέσμιος (Phlm 1, 9) surface often enough to be an expected part of Paul's speech.

26. See Wallace, *Greek Grammar beyond the Basics*, 239–40; 250–51.

27. As advanced by Gnilka, *Der Epheserbrief*, 162 (who claims the statement alludes to Paul's martyrdom); R. Collins, *Letters That Paul Did Not Write*, 167; Furnish, "Ephesians," 2:540; Kitchen, *Ephesians*, 30–31; Dunn, "Pauline Legacy and School," 890; MacDonald, *Colossians and Ephesians*, 260. Though not a supporter of Paul's authorship of Ephesians, Best does not believe that the presence of the article indicates a status of "prisoner *par excellence*" (Best, *Ephesians*, 295).

28. Cassidy, *Paul in Chains*, 96; cf. Heil, *Empowerment to Walk in Love for the Unity of All in Christ*, 134.

Portrait of an Apostle

of his earlier letters (chapter 2 of the book), Paul's suffering is typically understood in terms of his intimate affiliation with Christ (Gal 6:17; 1 Cor 4:10; Phil 1:13; 3:10; 2 Cor 1:5; 4:11; Phlm 1, 9).

Just as was the case in the undisputed letters, the value of the people Paul serves contributes additional meaning to Paul's hardships. In Eph 3:1 Paul's imprisonment is further understood in relation to the benefit imparted to Gentile believers (ὑπὲρ ὑμῶν τῶν ἐθνῶν). A similar perspective is repeatedly emphasized in Colossians (1:24a,b, 25; 2:1), without the explicit reference to the believers' Gentile background. In keeping with the overt interest in the unification of Jews and Gentiles under Christ, Paul makes his advocacy for Gentile believers more clear in Eph 3:1. Paul's assurance that personal hardship is withstood for the benefit of other believers is witnessed in Phil 1:25; 2 Cor 1:6; 4:15; 12:15. A specifically Gentile-directed ministry emerges clearly in Gal 1:16; 2:7–9; Rom 1:5, 13; 11:13; 15:15–21.[29] These verses place no limits on the scope of Paul's ministry to the Gentiles, and Paul's sense of obligation to minister to all Gentiles is attested in the aforementioned Romans passages in particular. Thus Paul's introduction in Eph 3:1 is in comfortable agreement with his depiction in the earlier letters.

Paul's Ministry and Knowledge of God's Mystery—Ephesians 3:2

In the course of describing his current situation and ongoing calling Paul makes a detour in 3:2, a detour that is not concluded until the end of 3:13.[30] The combination εἴ γε, which is seldom present in the undisputed letters (Gal 3:4; 2 Cor 5:3, in some manuscripts; Rom 5:6, in codex B; cf. Col 1:23; Eph 4:21) appears abruptly and changes the direction of the discourse.[31] As a protasis (εἰ) without an explicit apodosis, the apodosis must be inferred.[32] In this case, Paul may be indicating that he is assuming the readers' acceptance of his identity as stated in Eph 3:1. With εἴ γε ἠκούσατε then, Paul signals a willingness to revisit the cause of his imprisonment and the

---

29. See the extensive discussion of this theme in chapter 2 of this book.

30. It is not in any way an incidental detour though, since the themes of this section support many of the main themes of the letter as a whole. See Fay, "Paul the Empowered Prisoner," 679–83.

31. For the use of γε following εἰ, see Denniston, *The Greek Particles*, 126, 142, 146; Thrall, *Greek Particles in the New Testament*, 86–92; BDAG, "γέ," 190.

32. For the idea of εἴ γε specifying an unstated assumption, see Lincoln, *Ephesians*, 173; O'Brien, *Ephesians*, 226; Gombis, "Ephesians 3:2–13," 316.

justification for his overtures towards the Gentile churches for an audience that was potentially only vaguely acquainted with these points.[33] Unlike the situation in Col 1:23—2:5, where Paul's apostolic apology is delivered to readers who already have a relationship with Paul through Epaphras, in Eph 3:2 Paul allows for a wider audience that includes people who have no such bond with the apostle.[34]

Paul uses ἀκούω followed by the accusative in Eph 1:15; 3:2; 4:21 in the context of second-hand rather than first-hand familiarity with someone.[35] In Gal 1:13 Paul enlists ἀκούσατε as a way of acknowledging his readers' general familiarity with the story of his calling before spelling it out in detail. Likewise, in Eph 3:2, Paul raises the possibility that some of his readers have already heard about his divine appointment to ministry.

The substance of what Paul speculates that they have heard is recounted in 3:2–13. Paul begins by referring to τὴν οἰκονομίαν τῆς χάριτος τοῦ θεοῦ τῆς δοθείσης μοι εἰς ὑμᾶς. This is similar to what was said in Col 1:25 (τὴν οἰκονομίαν τοῦ θεοῦ τὴν δοθεῖσάν μοι εἰς ὑμᾶς) but in Eph 3:2 grace is included in the formulation. Moreover, in Eph 3:2 τῆς δοθείσης μοι modifies χάρις rather than οἰκονομία. This suggests that Paul associates grace with being designated by God for special service. As seen from chapter 2 of this book, Paul is fond of depicting the grace of his ministry in a similar fashion (Gal 2:9; 1 Cor 3:10; Rom 12:3; 15:15).[36] But as compared

---

33. For a similar conclusion from a rhetorical perspective, see Jeal, *Integrating Theology and Ethics in Ephesians*, 166; Witherington III, *Letters to Philemon, the Colossians, and the Ephesians*, 264. Van Roon notes a similarly cautious approach in Paul's letter to the Romans and suggests that the two letters are both intentional in establishing Paul's authority to address an audience relatively unacquainted with him upon the foundation of God's gracious appointment of Paul to reach the Gentiles (van Roon, *The Authenticity of Ephesians*, 87). Colossians differs somewhat from Romans and Ephesians in that Paul's associates had been more intimately involved in the founding of the church in that city, and so Paul's self presentation does not stand out in such a pronounced way in Colossians (ibid.).

34. Thus the statement is not "quite unnecessary and rather strange" (Lincoln, *Ephesians*, 173; see also Mitton, *Epistle to the Ephesians: Its Authorship, Origin, and Purpose*, 14).

35. See Barth, *Ephesians*, 10.

36. The implications of the earlier Pauline conception of gracious ministry to the meaning of Eph 3:2 will be explored in a later paragraph in this section. Mitton provides an example of his overall thesis from the correlation in wording between Gal 2:9 and Eph 3:1–2 (Mitton, *Ephesians: Its Authorship, Origin, and Purpose*, 131–32). The argument is not strong though, since other passages from the undisputed Pauline letters reflect similar constructions, and the additional feature in common (εἰς followed by a specification of Paul's ministry audience) exhibits some conceptual

to Col 1:25, this yields a slightly different overall accent to the wording of Eph 3:2 and prompts further investigation about the meaning of οἰκονομία and the nature of the genitive relationship between οἰκονομία and χάρις.

The term οἰκονομία is found two other times in Ephesians, both times in association with μυστήριον (Eph 1:9–10; 3:9; cf. 1 Cor 4:1; Col 1:25–26), as is the case with the occurrence in Eph 3:2 (see 3:3). The possibility of different but overlapping nuances for these uses of οἰκονομία in Ephesians has been noted by a number of scholars.[37] God's broader oversight and implementation of his eternal plans is more clearly in view in Eph 1:9–10 and 3:9. Ephesians 3:2, on the other hand, occurs in a context in which Paul is the subject of focus. Thus the image of οἰκονομία in Eph 3:2 is likely extended to include Paul's reception of the responsibility to serve as God's agent in carrying out his plans.[38] The term retains the active force observed in 1:9–10 and 3:9 but is accompanied by Paul as the primary subject. As such, the resulting application of οἰκονομία in relationship to God and Paul approximates that which is found in Col 1:25.[39]

As already mentioned in chapter 4 of this book, stewardship and grace are ideas that belong together, since Paul regularly relates both ideas to his ministry.[40] The genitive chain (τὴν οἰκονομίαν τῆς χάριτος τοῦ θεοῦ) found in Eph 3:2 makes this connection more explicit. Percy supposes that τῆς χάριτος has the force of an adjective, making Paul's stewardship one that is characterized by grace.[41] Also credible is the view that τῆς χάριτος

---

correspondence but little similarity in placement (εἰς occurs immediately after the shared formula in Eph 3:2 but 19 words after in Gal 2:9!) or wording (εἰς ὑμᾶς versus εἰς τὰ ἔθνη) between the two passages.

37. Tooley, "Stewards of God," 81; Reumann, "Οἰκονομία," 164–65; Merklein, *Das kirchliche Amt nach dem Epheserbrief*, 173–74; Lincoln, *Ephesians*, 174; O'Brien, *Ephesians*, 227–28. Muddiman drives a wedge between the varying uses in Ephesians and doubts that they can be attributed to a single author (Muddiman, *Ephesians*, 150, 159).

38. See Percy, *Die Probleme der Kolosser- und Epheserbriefe*, 343; Barth, *Ephesians*, 328–29; Kim, *The Origin of Paul's Gospel*, 22; Hübner, *An die Epheser*, 186; O'Brien, *Ephesians*, 227–28. In contrast, detecting an exclusive reference to God's work is Mitton, *Ephesians: Its Authorship, Origin, and Purpose*, 93–94; Kümmel, *Introduction to the New Testament*, 360; Best, *Ephesians*, 298–99.

39. Reumann, "Οἰκονομία," 164–65; *contra* Mitton, *Ephesians: Its Authorship, Origin, and Purpose*, 93; J. T. Sanders, "Hymnic Elements in Ephesians 1–3," 230–32; Kümmel, *Introduction to the New Testament*, 360; Gnilka, *Der Epheserbrief*, 12, 163. See also chapter 4 of this book for how the term functions in Col 1:25.

40. For grace and ministry, see Gal 1:15; 2:9; 1 Cor 3:10; 15:10; Phil 1:7; Rom 1:5; 12:3; 15:15–16. Stewardship and ministry are associated together in 1 Cor 4:1–2; 9:17.

41. Percy, *Die Probleme der Kolosser- und Epheserbriefe*, 343–44.

operates either as an objective or epexegetical genitive, so that the grace of God is a shorthand descriptor for the ministry over which Paul is expected to exercise responsibility.[42] The precise force of the genitive is difficult to pin down in this instance, and all options present complementary ideas that tie grace to stewardship. Paul proceeds to unfold further the specific components of this ministry of grace in the verses that follow.

The close association of grace and ministry in the undisputed letters was discussed extensively in chapter 2 of this book (see Gal 1:15; 2:9; 1 Cor 3:10; 15:9–10; Phil 1:7; Rom 1:5; 12:3; 15:15–16). Paul's emphasis on grace was seen to further several goals: (1) to recall his conversion from hostility towards God's plans in Christ to cooperation with God's mission, (2) to establish the divine source of Paul's authority in ministry, (3) to indicate that God is the one who enables a fruitful outcome in Paul's efforts, (4) to highlight the privilege of participating in groundbreaking outreach to the Gentiles, (5) to insinuate that with such a gracious calling comes the urgency to carry out the ministry wholeheartedly. Taking into account the other references to grace in Eph 3:7, 8 and the overall direction of Eph 3:1–13, any of the above purposes might be in effect with Paul's mention of grace in the context of Eph 3:2. Most likely though, following on the heels of the accent on the Gentiles in verse 1, in connection with οἰκονομία, and as part of the introduction to Paul's ministry in the passage, the mention of grace in Eph 3:2 accords most closely with some combination of the second, fourth, and fifth options above.

In Eph 3:3 the theme of a revealed mystery resurfaces, after having first been advanced in Eph 1:9. In both settings μυστήριον and γνωρίζω appear in tandem to denote God's action in disclosing his eternal plans, but unlike in Eph 1:9, where Paul and his readers are together identified as recipients of God's mystery, Paul alone is pictured as receiving knowledge of the mystery in Eph 3:3. This difference can be explained by recourse to two observations. First, Paul's specific role as a mediator of divine truth is under investigation in Eph 3:1–13. Second, Gentile inclusion in the blessings of salvation, a cause with which Paul is particularly yoked (Eph 3:1), is the particular facet of the mystery that is drawn out the verses that follow. Nonetheless, even given the emphasis on Paul's involvement in God's work, in Eph 3:5 Paul proceeds to recognize the fact that other gifted ministers have also received the revelation of God's savings plans for the world.

---

42. Schlier, *Der Brief an die Epheser*, 148; Kim, *The Origins of Paul's Gospel*, 22; Jeal, *Integrating Theology and Ethics in Ephesians*, 166–67.

Paul is made privy to this specific aspect of God's plans κατὰ ἀποκάλυψιν, in which κατά probably indicates God's manner or mode of making known the mystery to Paul and has the rhetorical effect of recalling the authoritative source of Paul's understanding of the mystery.[43] The term ἀποκάλυψις also depicts the unveiling of the mystery in Rom 16:25 (κατὰ ἀποκάλυψιν μυστηρίου), where a corresponding interest in the mystery's application to the Gentiles (Rom 16:26) is evident (cf. Rom 11:25).

Paul's transformative Damascus road experience is most likely being recalled in Eph 3:3. This prompts exploration of another passage employing the term ἀποκάλυψις. As is the case in Eph 3:3, ἀποκάλυψις in Gal 1:12 is found within the broader context of Paul's justification for his Gentile-focused ministry and directs attention to the supernatural means by which the gospel was revealed to Paul. The same purpose is attested in Eph 3:3, though the divine source of revelation is not insisted upon to the same extent as in the polemical environment of Galatians 1. Nor is the memory of Paul's Damascus road event recalled as vividly in Ephesians 3 as it was in Galatians 1. The order of events (Paul's encounter with God and his exposure to the apostles) is a central part of the argument in Galatians 1 whereas it is not in Ephesians 3, so this may explain the difference. In any event, the similarities between the two passages are more significant and demonstrate a shared understanding of ἀποκάλυψις in relation to Paul's ministry.

The revealed mystery of Eph 3:3 is given by revelation to Paul in particular (ἐγνωρίσθη μοι). The point of this emphasis is not to deny the existence of other appointed mediators of the mystery, as Eph 3:5 makes clear, but to indicate that Paul's role as an emissary is the topic at hand.[44] Likewise, Rom 16:25 equates the mystery with τὸ εὐαγγέλιόν μου without requiring the restriction of the responsibility of preaching to Paul alone,

---

43. For a helpful discussion of the tension between the typical meaning of κατά and its use in this context, see Merklein, *Das kirchliche Amt nach dem Epheserbrief*, 197–98. Merklein eventually settles on a modal understanding of κατά in this passage. Also agreeing with a modal use of κατά are Schlier, *Der Brief an die Epheser*, 148; Caragounis, *The Ephesian Mysterion*, 99; Best, "Revelation to Evangelize the Gentiles," 24; Hoehner, *Ephesians*, 426; contra BDAG, "κατά," 512, where Eph 3:3 is mentioned under a category in which "*in accordance with* and *because of* are merged"; cf. O'Brien, *Ephesians*, 229.

44. The broader aim for Paul to introduce himself and his ministry to his readers accounts for the sustained focus on Paul throughout the passage (*contra* de Boer, "Images of Paul in the Post-Apostolic Period," 364–65; Penny, "The Pseudo-Pauline Letters of the First Two Centuries," 242; Brown, *The Churches the Apostles Left Behind*, 48; R. Collins, *Letters That Paul Did Not Write*, 168; Furnish, "Ephesians," 2:540).

and Gal 1:6–2:10 insists upon the validity of Paul's unique calling without downplaying the priority of the other apostles (Gal 1:17) or the authenticity of their ministry (Gal 2:7–8).[45]

The curious clause καθὼς προέγραψα ἐν ὀλίγῳ implies that what Paul is reporting about his reception of God's mystery is in line with what he has already told them. The verb προγράφω can refer either to what was written earlier in the same letter or to material in a different letter.[46] Goodspeed, adopting the second position, believes that the wording presupposes a later era, in which at least some of Paul's letters exist in a collection.[47] More likely, the aorist προέγραψα denotes prior content in the same letter.[48] Ephesians 1:9 (γνωρίσας ἡμῖν τὸ μυστήριον τοῦ θελήματος) is probably the intended reference, since γνωρίζω and μυστήριον are common pairings in both 1:9 and 3:3.[49] Even though Eph 1:9 lacks any treatment of Paul's role of proclaiming the mystery, it is not unknown for Paul to assume but not comment upon the role of intermediaries in the dissemination of the contents of the mystery (1 Cor 2:7–10; cf. Rom 16:25–26; Col 1:26–27). Some commentators have sought an additional connection to Eph 2:11–22, but καθώς relates more naturally to the verbal idea of making known the mystery (as in Eph 1:9) rather than to the substance of the mystery itself (as with Eph 2:11–22).[50] In addition Eph 1:10, which follows soon after the affirmation of divine revelation in 1:9, already provides a crisp summary statement of the mystery, so further recourse to Eph 2:11–22 is unnecessary.[51] The qualifying prepositional phrase in Eph 3:3 (ἐν ὀλίγῳ) suggests a

---

45. For more extended discussion on these passages, see chapter 2 of the book. It should be noted that just as in Eph 3, in Gal 1–2 Paul's overlapping roles as recipient and disseminator of the gospel message stand side by side (*contra* Marguerat, "Paul après Paul," 328, who finds significance in what he discerns to be a newly emerging emphasis on Paul's proclamation activity in Eph 3 and Col 1, as compared to earlier letters).

46. See BDAG, "προγράφω," 867.

47. Goodspeed, *The Meaning of Ephesians*, 40–43; cf. Mitton, *Ephesians: Its Authorship, Origin, and Purpose*, 234–36; Kitchen, *Ephesians*, 31.

48. See Paul's use of the aorist of γράφω to indicate that which is inscribed already in the same letter in Rom 15:15; Phlm 21. Of note also is the combination δι' ὀλίγων ἔγραψα in 1 Pet 5:12.

49. Barth, *Ephesians*, 329; Barth and Blanke, *Colossians*, 84; Hübner, *An die Epheser*, 186.

50. A relative pronoun would connect προέγραψα ἐν ὀλίγῳ to the content of the mystery more transparently than καθώς would.

51. As noted by Lincoln, Eph 1:21–23 (not to mention Eph 3:9–10) attests to the author's vision of uniting both church and universe under Christ's authority,

brevity that is more compatible with the momentary focus on the revealed mystery in Eph 1:9–10 than with the extended discourse on its contents in Eph 2:11–22 or the sum of Paul's teaching on the subject in earlier letters. In short, the clause καθὼς προέγραψα ἐν ὀλίγῳ reminds the readers of the divine basis for everything Paul is teaching in the letter.

Introduction to the Mystery and the Mystery's Substance— Ephesians 3:3–6

The relative clause beginning with πρὸς ὅ connects grammatically either to 3:3a (κατὰ ἀποκάλυψιν ἐγνωρίσθη μοι τὸ μυστήριον) or to Eph 3:3b (καθὼς προέγραψα ἐν ὀλίγῳ).[52] The difference is not significant, because the revelation of the mystery and Paul's reference to that event are overlapping ideas. The preposition πρός followed by a substantive in the accusative case may contain a sense of either "movement" or "orientation."[53] The latter option is probably in force here, with the specific meaning of "with regard to"[54] or "with reference to."[55] The resulting function of πρὸς ὅ would be to direct the readers' focus back to the divinely revealed mystery they have already encountered in the letter in order to make an additional comment about it.[56]

The appearance immediately following of the verb-infinitive construction δύνασθε . . . νοῆσαι is read as a statement of fact ("you are able to understand"), in accordance with the indicative mood form of the head verb. It suggests that the readers' grasp of Paul's insight into the mystery is made possible by the revelation Paul has received and recorded.

Reading (ἀναγινώσκοντες) is the means by which the specific readers of Ephesians are able to understand the truth Paul has grasped. No object

---

demonstrating that the ecclesiological mystery of Eph 3:1–7 is closely related to the cosmic one of Eph 1:9–10 (Lincoln, *Ephesians*, 181, 188). This supports the hypothesis that Paul is alluding to Eph 1:9–10 in Eph 3:3b.

52. The former option construes καθὼς προέγραψα ἐν ὀλίγῳ as a parenthetical aside.

53. BDAG, "πρός," 874–75.

54. Ibid., 875 (option β).

55. BDF §239.6.

56. For this use of πρός, see Hoehner, *Ephesians*, 434. It is probably reading too much into the preposition to infer a sense of conformity to standard (for this translation, see BDAG, "πρός," 875 [option δ]; Lincoln, *Ephesians*, 175–76; O'Brien, *Ephesians*, 229). In possible parallel passages (Gal 2:14; 2 Cor 5:10; Luke 12:47) πρός can be explained more simply, without requiring such a specific meaning.

for the participle is specified, but the letter as a whole is probably what is in mind at this point. The believers' access to divinely revealed truth comes by way of Paul's letter to them. The inclusion of ἀναγινώσκοντες is also a reminder of the fact that Paul is ministering to his readers indirectly, by means of a letter, rather than directly through his actual presence among them.[57]

By reading Paul's letter, the readers are able to gain an understanding of Paul's insight into the mystery of Christ (νοῆσαι τὴν σύνεσίν μου ἐν τῷ μυστηρίῳ τοῦ Χριστοῦ). It is not startling to see Paul's insight isolated, because it is his letter that the recipients are reading, and he wants them to understand what he is saying.[58] Moreover, Paul has already attributed his insight into the mystery to the grace and revelation granted him (Eph 3:2–3), and he will later highlight God's grace again (Eph 3:7, 8), so reference to Paul's revelatory insight does not amount to a vain boast.[59]

Paul is making one of two points with the components examined in Eph 3:4 so far. First, he might be encouraging his readers to recognize the *fact* that he has unusual insight into God's plan, as a result of God's revelation to him.[60] This places the accent on Paul as an approved messenger. Second, Paul might be inviting his readers to understand the *content* of his insight into the revealed mystery.[61] This shifts the focus to the readers' growth in comprehension.[62] The two options are of course related,[63] even though they fulfill slightly different purposes in the discourse. With the first option, Paul would be highlighting that what he has written is the fruit of his revelatory experience and its aftermath, confirming the claim that he is a minister to the Gentiles according to divine decree. This conforms well

---

57. See Barth, *Ephesians*, 362; Heil, *Empowerment to Walk in Love for the Unity of All in Christ*, 9, 137. Discussion of Paul's presence and absence in Col 2:5 further supports this line of thinking.

58. Paul is quite direct about his insight into a divinely revealed mystery in 1 Cor 15:51 as well (ἰδοὺ μυστήριον ὑμῖν λέγω).

59. See also Percy, *Die Probleme der Kolosser- und Epheserbriefe*, 350 (and note the possible parallel to 2 Cor 11:6); Best, *Ephesians*, 303–4; Hoehner, *Ephesians*, 436.

60. See Barth, *Ephesians*, 330–31; Gombis, "Ephesians 3:2–13," 318–19. The CEV and NCV translations adopt this meaning as well.

61. See BDAG, "σύνεσις," 970; Best, *Ephesians*, 303–4; O' Brien, *Ephesians*, 229–30; Hoehner, *Ephesians*, 436; Heil, *Empowerment to Walk in Love for the Unity of All in Christ*, 137.

62. Paul has already expressed this sentiment in the prayer for his readers in 1:17–18 (see O'Brien, *Ephesians*, 229).

63. The readers' ability to benefit from Paul's insight depends upon the legitimacy of his apostleship.

to the ground covered in preceding verses. In the second case, Paul would be emphasizing his calling as one of God's intermediaries, with the role of helping his readers share in the knowledge of God's plans. Paul would be illuminating the two-stage process of revelation (from God to Paul and from Paul to his audience) that was only implied in Eph 1:9-10. Though God has made known his mystery to all believers, the means by which this becomes a reality is through the preaching of a message that was initially revealed to specially appointed heralds such as Paul (as further developed in 3:5).[64] The verses would explain the way in which Paul's ministry is ὑπὲρ ὑμῶν τῶν ἐθνῶν (Eph 3:1) and εἰς ὑμᾶς (Eph 3:2).

Either of the above explanations reflects a coherent line of thinking and thus helps repel the charge that the author is being redundant or including the statements merely to inflate the value of his own teaching throughout the letter.[65] Instead, Paul is relaying significant information about the legitimacy of his apostleship or about how access to divine revelation is ultimately enjoyed by all in the church.

The mystery of Christ reflects the same centrality of Christ in the mystery that is witnessed in Col 4:3 (cf. Col 1:27; 2:2). The forthcoming emphasis on the equal standing of Jews and Gentiles before God as the essence of the mystery is based on the presupposition that Christ's person and work makes that shared position possible. This interaction of Christological and ecclesiological themes preserves the balance seen between vertical and horizontal reconciliation in Eph 2:11-22. Charges that the referents of μυστήριον in Colossians and Ephesians are different enough to call common authorship into question artificially divides concepts such as Christology, soteriology, and ecclesiology.[66]

---

64. The claim that Paul is displayed in Eph 3:4 as a "mystagogue" who initiates others into privileged access to truth (Fischer, *Tendenz und Absicht des Epheserbriefes*, 99; Penny, "The Pseudo-Pauline Letters of the First Two Centuries," 264; Meade, *Pseudonymity and Canon*, 148; Furnish, "Ephesians," 2:540; Beker, *Heirs of Paul*, 71) overstates the point and fails to deal adequately with the existence of the other gifted recipients of revelation (apostles and prophets) mentioned in Eph 3:5.

65. As espoused by Merklein, *Das kirchliche Amt nach dem Epheserbrief*, 217-18; Lincoln, *Ephesians*, 176-77.

66. Using the different shading of mystery in the two letters as fodder in the argument against common authorship of the letters are Ochel, "Die Annahme einer Bearbeitung des Kolosser-Briefes im Epheser-Brief," 3; Mitton, *Epistle to the Ephesians: Its Authorship, Origin, and Purpose*, 89-90; Kümmel, *Introduction to the New Testament*, 359-60; Gnilka, *Der Epheserbrief*, 12; Houlden, *Paul's Letters from Prison*, 298; Beker, *Heirs of Paul*, 69-70; Sterling, "From Apostle to the Gentiles to Apostle of the Church," 88. Conceding the point that there are differences that may reflect an author

The mystery is further defined according to the contours of the so-called "revelation pattern" (ὃ ἑτέραις γενεαῖς οὐκ ἐγνωρίσθη τοῖς υἱοῖς τῶν ἀνθρώπων ὡς νῦν ἀπεκαλύφθη) observed in the early church.[67] This first part of the description conforms closely on a conceptual level to the representation of the mystery in Col 1:26. The wording in Eph 3:5, however, varies considerably from that of Col 1:26, both in terms of vocabulary and sentence construction. Of particular note is the incorporation of the phrase "the sons of men" (οἱ υἱοὶ τῶν ἀνθρώπων), which adds a note of universality to the prior hiddenness of God's mystery and highlights the church's great privilege of having access to that revelation now through the preaching of chosen ministers. This sweeping horizon also accords well with the cosmic scope that surfaces later in the section (Eph 3:10). The concealment of God's mystery does not eliminate the OT foundations of the gospel message but does accentuate the novel aspect of full incorporation of the Gentiles into the blessings of salvation (as will be seen in Eph 3:6).

A more significant difference in thought surfaces as the pattern continues. In Eph 3:5, the mystery is now revealed τοῖς ἁγίοις ἀποστόλοις αὐτοῦ καὶ προφήταις, whereas the groundbreaking revelation is given τοῖς ἁγίοις αὐτοῦ in Col 1:26.[68] Departing from the usage of Col 1:26, in Eph 3:5 Paul uses ἁγίοις not as a noun but as an adjective, modifying ἀποστόλοις and perhaps προφήταις as well.[69] The resulting sense is that a more restricted

for Ephesians other than Paul but reluctant to allow too much weight to this argument are Merklein, *Das kirchliche Amt nach dem Epheserbrief*, 31–32; Best, *Ephesians*, 302. Refuting this argument by highlighting the compatibility of Christology and ecclesiology are Percy, *Die Probleme der Kolosser- und Epheserbriefe*, 380–81; Brown, *The Semitic Background of the Term "Mystery" in the New Testament*, 58; Kim, *The Origin of Paul's Gospel*, 22–24; Bockmuehl, *Revelation and Mystery in Ancient Judaism and Pauline Christianity*, 202; O'Brien, *Ephesians*, 237; Hoehner, *Ephesians*, 436–37.

67. The pattern can be understood as relatively fixed (Dahl, "Form-Critical Observations on Early Christian Preaching," 32) or more fluid (Bockmuehl, *Revelation and Mystery*, 208–10).

68. The prophets mentioned are probably Christian-era prophets, based on the interpretation of the similar pairings of apostles and prophets (always in that order) in Eph 2:20 and 4:11 and on the fact that the mystery is recounted in 3:5 as having been revealed only now as opposed to during past generations.

69. Most likely, προφήταις has been appended to the end of τοῖς ἁγίοις ἀποστόλοις αὐτοῦ as an afterthought (though certainly not an insignificant one). The additional pieces modifying ἀποστόλοις should thus be understood to apply to προφήταις as well. The fact that one article governs both ἀποστόλοις and προφήταις is a grammatical point in favor of this view, since this feature associates the two groups closely together (see discussion of the use of the article in constructions such as these in Wallace, *Greek Grammar beyond the Basics*, 278–90; see also Eph 2:20; 3:12, 18; 4:11).

group has been identified as recipient of the revelation of the mystery. This deviation in Eph 3:5 from Col 1:26 is not contradictory though, since in Col 1:26, the interest is in the readers (and other believers) as the ultimate recipients of the truth of the mystery, and so the intervening service of Paul and others is circumvented.[70] This treatment is appropriate to the context, since the readers' growth in maturity and comprehension of the mystery of Christ is a distinct objective being pursued in Col 1:23–2:5. The apostolic apology of Eph 3:1–13 retains more of a singular focus on Paul's role in the fulfillment of God's plans, and so as part of this spotlight on Paul as a chosen instrument, other agents, rather than final beneficiaries, are mentioned.[71] Furthermore, as was noted in chapter 4 of this book, Colossians as a whole reveals little interest in how Paul's ministry and role in salvation history fares in comparison to that of the other apostles. On the other hand, in Ephesians Paul's place in the broader landscape of the early church is hinted at in several other places (Eph 2:20; 3:8). And Eph 3:5 follows naturally on the heels of Eph 2:20 by identifying apostles and prophets as having a foundational role in the growth and teaching of the church.[72] In short, the reference to apostles and prophets is both suit-

---

70. The same could be said for Rom 16:25–26, which, as noted by Merklein, also envisions an unlimited audience for revelation, in contrast to Eph 3:5 (Merklein, *Das kirchliche Amt nach dem Epheserbrief*, 167). Since Rom 16:25–26 is a brief statement of Paul's gospel and its effects on people rather than an analysis of his ministry calling, it is not surprising that the role of a smaller intermediary group is not investigated there either.

71. The inclusion of the apostles and prophets only after Paul's own ministry has been introduced does not reflect the theological agenda of promoting Paul's ministry above all others (see Sterling, "From Apostle to the Gentiles to Apostle of the Church," 88; cf. Houlden, *Paul's Letters from Prison*, 253; Schnackenburg, *Ephesians*, 131) but rather serves the discourse purpose of locating Paul's call in the broader story of God's plan to disseminate the revealed message through various gifted ministers in the church. Paul surfaces at the beginning of the section (and before the apostles and prophets in general) because he is the letter writer and it is his apostolic apology being unfolded.

72. A similar perspective on the apostles is witnessed in 1 Cor 15:1–11. The presentation of Christ as the unrivaled foundation of the church in 1 Cor 3:11 is respected in the clarification that Jesus Christ is the cornerstone of the foundation in Eph 2:20 (see Clark, "Apostleship," 64; Hoehner, *Ephesians*, 403–4; Beisser, "Wann und von wem könnte der Epheserbrief verfasst worden sein?" 157–58). The addition of prophets to the circle of select recipients of revelation has been seen as a possible mark of pseudonymity (Sandnes, *Paul—One of the Prophets?*, 237–38), or explained away as a misreading of a phrase that designates a single group of "apostle-prophets" (Grudem, *The Gift of Prophecy in the New Testament and Today*, 45–62). But Paul's inclusion of a distinct class of prophets (some of whom were probably counted among

able to the overall discourse of Ephesians and coherent within the overall framework of Paul's thought in earlier letters.

The earlier undisputed letters of Paul also view Paul's ministry as part of a larger advance of the gospel, with the contributions of other apostles duly noted.[73] For instance, in Gal 2:7-9 the shared task of ministry is shouldered by both Paul and the other apostles. Though different arenas of ministry are specified, a common gospel is affirmed (2:7). The same perspective emerges from 1 Cor 9:1-6 and 15:3-11, where Paul aligns himself with the other apostles and insists that they are all proclaiming the same good news (see 15:11).

The supposed adulatory tone of ἅγιος as an adjective has also been seen as problematic for the insistence on Pauline authorship.[74] In the uncontested Pauline corpus, ἅγιος modifies an array of nouns, including a kiss (1 Thess 5:26; 1 Cor 16:20; 2 Cor 13:12; Rom 16:16), the temple consisting of believers (1 Cor 3:17; cf. Eph 2:21), children of a believer (1 Cor 7:14), the OT Scriptures (Rom 1:2), and God's law (Rom 7:12). The connotations of the word need not exceed "consecrated to the service of God,"[75] which corresponds well to the role being depicted for ministers here.[76] In addition, as a substantive ("saints"), ἅγιος is a typical appellation given to Christians (1 Thess 3:13; 1 Cor 1:2; 6:1; Phil 1:1; 2 Cor 1:1; Rom 1:7; 8:27; Phlm 5; etc.), and no sharp wedge should be driven between the noun and adjective.

---

his co-workers) can be explained simply as the acknowledgment of their central role in the church's early growth, as noted in Acts 11:27-28; 13:1-3; 15:32; 21:10-11; 1 Cor 12:28; Rev 18:20 (see also Aletti, *Éphésiens*, 161-62). Moreover, Barth argues that it would be more likely for a later author to highlight apostles alone rather than both apostles and prophets (Barth, *Ephesians*, 316-17).

73. Thus the alignment with established apostolic authority should not be viewed as an innovation betraying the hand of a later author (as contended by MacDonald, *Colossians and Ephesians*, 269).

74. Mitton, *Ephesians: Its Authorship, Origin, and Purpose*, 19; Kümmel, *Introduction to the New Testament*, 360; Gnilka, *Der Epheserbrief*, 167; Penny, "The Pseudo-Pauline Letters of the First Two Centuries," 264; Schnackenburg, *Ephesians*, 133; Lincoln, *Ephesians*, 179; Furnish, "Ephesians," 2:540; Muddiman, *Ephesians*, 29, 154.

75. BDAG, "ἅγιος,"10; cf. Schlier, *Der Brief an die Epheser*, 150; Barth, *Ephesians*, 335; Houlden, *Paul's Letters from Prison*, 299; Hoehner, *Ephesians*, 443.

76. Van Roon sees a correlation to the idea of being called (κλητός) and set apart (ἀφορίζω) in Gal 1:15 (van Roon, *The Authenticity of Ephesians*, 389-90; cf. Merklein, *Das kirchliche Amt nach dem Epheserbrief*, 190-91). Snodgrass notes a similar parallel to Rom 1:5, where Paul is set apart (ἀφορίζω) for God's service (Snodgrass, *Ephesians*, 26-27).

Portrait of an Apostle

The final prepositional phrase of 3:5 (ἐν πνεύματι) modifies ἀπεκαλύφθη and specifies the means by which God has disclosed the mystery of Christ. The inclusion of the Spirit's contribution to the revelation process continues an emphasis on the Spirit in the rest of the letter (1:13–14; 2:18; 4:4; 4:30; 5:18; 6:17; cf. 1:17). Even more significantly, the prominence of the Spirit's role in unveiling the mystery recalls the detailed exposition in 1 Cor 2:7–16, which is punctuated with an attribution of the mystery's reception to the Spirit's work (ἡμῖν δὲ ἀπεκάλυψεν ὁ θεὸς διὰ τοῦ πνεύματος).[77] The shared wording and thought in the two passages (Eph 3 and 1 Cor 2) further points to the seemingly effortless blending in Ephesians 3 of Col 1:24–29 with material from the undisputed letters.[78] This results in an always coherent, often familiar, but freshly worded portrayal of Paul that, as has been demonstrated from an investigation of later pseudepigraphal works, is extremely difficult to counterfeit.

The actual content of the mystery is unfolded in 3:6. The Gentiles (τὰ ἔθνη) are revealed to be included in the blessings of God's people in Christ Jesus (συγκληρονόμα καὶ σύσσωμα καὶ συμμέτοχα τῆς ἐπαγγελίας ἐν Χριστῷ Ἰησοῦ). Immediately evident here is a return to the συν- prefixed terms that were interspersed throughout Eph 2:19–22 (and in Eph 2:5–6). The prefix is perfectly fitted to communicate Paul's idea of Gentiles completely sharing in the blessings bestowed on the Jews through the Messiah.[79] This is the aspect of the mystery that so captivates Paul at this juncture. He has not discarded a christocentric mystery to make this ecclesiological point, since the mystery is still the mystery of Christ (Eph

---

77. See also Bockmuehl, *Revelation and Mystery*, 201. Though in 1 Cor 2 the recipients of the Spirit-inspired revelation are not confined to apostles and prophets (as noted by Merklein, *Das kirchliche Amt nach dem Epheserbrief*, 168), Paul does insist on a special preaching role for apostles later in the letter (1 Cor 15:6–11), and so the difference should not be pressed to the point that Ephesians is seen as injecting a novel concept out of the blue.

78. As was the case with Col 1:26, 1 Cor 2:10 is not concerned with the intermediate step of how chosen agents first encountered the revelation of the mystery, but that intermediate step is still assumed, without being highlighted (as in Eph 3:5).

79. The interest in the Gentiles' invitation to enjoy the blessings promised to the Jews is not incompatible with the authentic Paul's alleged primary emphasis on "the freedom of Gentiles *from* Judaism" (Meade, *Pseudonymity and Canon*, 151, emphasis his; cf. Fischer, *Tendenz und Absicht des Epheserbriefes*, 99–100), since the earlier letters of Paul (for instance, in Rom 11:17–24) also reveal a recognition of the unification of Jewish and Gentile Christians (Carson and Moo, *Introduction to the New Testament*, 483), and the accent in the earlier letters was upon removing barriers that prevented Gentiles from enjoying the same promised benefits that are invoked in Eph 3:6.

3:4). But here Paul begins to contemplate the reverberating effects of the mystery to all people and in the whole universe (see 3:10).[80]

The term συκληρονόμα, besides supplementing an already strong emphasis on κληρονομία in Ephesians (1:14, 18; 5:5), reflects the rich heritage of the inheritance theme in earlier letters. A similar truth is stated in Col 1:12 (with the cognate term κλῆρος), without an overt distinction between Jews and Gentiles, in keeping with the characteristics of that letter. Other inheritance imagery of note surfaces in Gal 3:18; 3:29–4:7; 4:28–30; Rom 4:13–14; 8:17.[81] In Gal 3:18; 4:28–30; and Rom 4:13 in particular, inheritance is linked with God's promise (ἐπαγγελία), as is true in Eph 3:6.[82] The inheritance awaiting believers is identified as the kingdom of God in several passages (Gal 5:21; 1 Cor 6:9; 15:50; Eph 5:5), and that is probably the implied context of the inheritance in Eph 3:6 as well (cf. Eph 5:5).[83] The thought of being co-heirs (συγκληρονόμος) with the Jews in Christ (Eph 3:6) builds upon the notion of being co-heirs with Christ (Rom 8:17) and reflects the novel ecclesiological contribution of Ephesians (and presupposes the careful balance between vertical and horizontal reconciliation seen throughout the letter, especially Eph 2:14–18).

Neither σύσσωμος nor συμμέτοχος surface outside of Ephesians (see 5:7) in the Pauline corpus, but Paul was inclined to employ συν- prefixed terms with a similar force elsewhere (see for instance Gal 2:19; 1 Cor 1:20; 12:26; Phil 2:2; 3:10, 17; Rom 6:4–8; 8:17, 29; 15:30), and the cognates σῶμα

---

80. This also picks up the theme that was announced in Eph 1:10 (Gnilka, *Der Epheserbrief*, 168).

81. Mitton includes the mention of συγκληρονόμα in Eph 3:6 as part of a list of passages in Ephesians that share terms in common with Rom 8:9–39 (Mitton, *Ephesians: Its Authorship, Origin, and Purpose*, 122–23). In response to Mitton, the similarities in wording are not at all striking given the coverage of common themes and the large amount of material from which the connections are drawn. In other words, recognizing that Ephesians covers theological perspectives that resemble those from Rom 8 (which certainly does not weaken the claim that Paul wrote Ephesians), it is difficult to see how the inexact and scattered verbal connections can bear any additional weight in either establishing or undermining common authorship.

82. Of course, the tie between the two is not direct in Eph 3:6, since ἐπαγγελία modifies only συμμέτοχα grammatically (Reynier, *Évangile et Mystère*, 106; Best, *Ephesians*, 311). But there is an indirect association by sense in the passage between inheritance and promise. The resemblance between Eph 3:6 and Gal 3:20 (see Mitton, *Ephesians: Its Authorship, Origin, and Purpose*, 132) is unremarkable for the question of literary dependence, especially given the proximity of ideas of inheritance and promise in other passages.

83. The concept of kingdom functions as shorthand for the culmination of the OT promises to Israel.

Portrait of an Apostle

(denoting a group of people) and μετέχω/μετοχή (for participation) were common enough in Paul's letters. And in Ephesians σῶμα is a frequent image for the corporate community of faith (Eph 1:23; 2:16; 4:4,12, 16; 5:23, 30). Thus the reality of entering into an intimate bond with believers from divergent backgrounds reinforces this important theme (see also Gal 3:28; Col 3:11). The meaning of συμμέτοχα τῆς ἐπαγγελίας depends upon the identity of the promise. That the promises to Abraham are in view in Eph 3:6 according to the pattern from those passages is supported by the prior mention of promise in Eph 2:12, where Paul associates the promise with the covenants and with citizenship in Israel.[84] Other than supplementing the idea of Gentiles being co-heirs with the Jews, the promise may also allude to the Spirit as the promised ἀρραβών of believers' inheritance (see Eph 1:13–14; 2:18).[85] Accordingly, the Spirit is understood as the new covenant guarantee of eschatological blessings that were promised in the OT.[86] This would mirror the joining of OT promises, inheritance, Jews and Gentiles being united as one, and the Spirit in Gal 3:13–29 (see especially 3:14, 18, 28–29).[87] In short, σύσσωμος and συμμέτοχος make strong additions to συγκληρονόμος in Eph 3:6, since they draw together the old covenant and new covenant blessings experienced by Jews and Gentiles through being united with Christ as one body.

The reminder that Christ Jesus is the one in whom the promises of God are fulfilled (ἐν Χριστῷ Ἰησοῦ) is consistent with the emphasis in the rest of the letter, especially in the first three chapters. The phrase depicts Christ as the arena in which divine blessing is experienced, through believers' union with Christ. Of course, the theme of partaking in the blessings of God in Christ is prominent in Paul's other letters as well.[88]

Similarly prevalent as a theme in Paul's writings is the affirmation that spiritual blessings are proclaimed through the gospel (διὰ τοῦ εὐαγγελίου).[89] Paul's gospel is probably understood as a revealed mystery

---

84. See Grindheim, "What the OT Prophets Did Not Know," 532.

85. Schlier, *Der Brief an die Epheser*, 151; Barth, *Ephesians*, 337–38; O'Brien, *Ephesians*, 235–36. See also the combination of μέτοχος and Holy Spirit in Heb 6:4.

86. This fulfills the OT expectation that the Spirit would be poured out in a more universal way as part of the arrival of the new covenant (Ezek 11:17–20; 36:24–28; 39:25–29; Joel 2:28–32; cf. Jer 31:31–34).

87. See Hoehner, *Ephesians*, 447.

88. See for instance Gal 2:4; 3:14, 28; 1 Cor 1:4, 30; 15:22; Phil 3:9; Rom 6:11, 23; 8:32, 39. It should be noted that "in Christ" was a flexible metaphor for Paul and thus did not always have the exact same force in each instance (Seifrid, "In Christ," 433–36).

89. The gospel and mystery are bound together in Rom 16:25–26 as well.

in the sense that the full extent of the new reality experienced by Jewish and Gentile believers in Christ was never comprehensively and definitively delineated in any one passage in the OT, even though the pieces of the puzzle may have been there all along, waiting to be assembled in Christ.[90] One of these pieces was that God's reign, salvation, and peace would be announced to those waiting for his deliverance, according to Isa 52:7, where the proclamation is twice described with the verb εὐαγγελίζω in the LXX. Paul alludes to this verse later in Ephesians (6:15; cf. Rom 10:15) in relation to the gospel, so an OT backdrop should be assumed for the reference to gospel in Eph 3:6 as well. This is further supported by the aforementioned language of inheritance and promise that is applied to those who are united with Christ. Just as is the case in the undisputed letters with respect to OT and NT revelation, discontinuity is tempered with continuity, in recognition that God is sovereign over one coherent story throughout time.

Paul Called into the Service of the Gospel–Ephesians 3:7

Mirroring the structure of Col 1:23, the mention of the gospel prompts Paul to define himself in a relationship of accountability to it (οὗ ἐγενήθην διάκονος).[91] Unlike in Col 1:23, Paul does not employ ἐγὼ Παῦλος as part of the formula, since Col 1:23 begins the section while Eph 3:7 does not (see the use of ἐγὼ Παῦλος in Eph 3:1).[92] Also, Eph 3:7 contains the passive form of γίνομαι in contrast to the active (deponent) form of Col 1:23, perhaps to frame Paul even further as the passive recipient of God's calling. The two passages betray a parallel thought-pattern but with difference in wording and with the presence or absence of material determined by the context.

---

90. See O'Brien, *Ephesians*, 232; Grindheim, "What the OT Prophets Did Not Know," 547, for additional discussion on the unexpected features of Christ's work reflected in the use of the term μυστήριον.

91. The precedent of the gospel governing Paul's ministry from the undisputed letters was explored in chapter 4 of this book. Also noted in that chapter, διάκονος denotes one who in his or her activities represents the interests of someone or something else. See BDAG, "διάκονος," 230; cf. J. Collins, "The Mediatorial Aspect of Paul's Role as *Diakonos*," 42–43.

92. The subordination of Paul's ministry to the gospel does, however, signal a slight movement towards Paul's personal experience in receiving and carrying out his ministry (Eph 3:8–9).

Portrait of an Apostle

Paul's ministry was received from God's gracious hand (κατὰ τὴν δωρεὰν τῆς χάριτος τοῦ θεοῦ τῆς δοθείσης μοι), which continues to highlight the divine origin of Paul's calling and perhaps foreshadows the idea that Paul is unworthy of this blessed commission. As was the case with the identical wording in Eph 3:2 (τῆς χάριτος τοῦ θεοῦ τῆς δοθείσης μοι), an earlier pattern of Paul's is reflected (Gal 2:9; 1 Cor 3:10; Rom 12:3; 15:15).[93] The association of gift and grace, besides being intuitive based on the overlapping meaning, is attested in 2 Cor 9:14–15 and Rom 5:15 (cf. Rom 3:24). In conjunction with the foregrounding of grace in Eph 3:2 and 3:8, Paul broadcasts the importance of grace for his vocation just as he already has for the Christian life in general (Eph 2:1–10).

A second phrase beginning with κατά (κατὰ τὴν ἐνέργειαν τῆς δυνάμεως αὐτοῦ) follows immediately after the first one. But the second κατά phrase probably modifies the first, as a description of how God's gracious ministry was given to Paul, rather than building upon ἐγενήθην διάκονος. The linking of ἐνέργεια and δύναμις in Eph 3:7 is congruent to that in Col 1:29 (κατὰ τὴν ἐνέργειαν αὐτοῦ τὴν ἐνεργουμένην ἐν ἐμοὶ ἐν δυνάμει), though the idea is stated more crisply in Eph 3:7. Both passages reflect Paul's habit, as seen in 1 Cor 15:10; 2 Cor 3:5; 12:9; Rom 15:18, of attributing his ministry's validity or progress to God's intervention. The verb ἐνεργέω, along with its participle form ὁ ἐνεργήσας, fulfills a similar function in Gal 2:8, where God's active involvement is seen as the reason (γάρ) for both Peter's and Paul's ongoing claim to be engaged in ministry (Gal 2:7). The emphasis on the activation of God's power (combination of ἐνεργέω and δύναμις) also links Eph 3:7 thematically with other sections of the same letter (Eph 1:19–20; 3:20).[94] With the reference to God's active involvement in Paul's calling, there may be an allusion to Paul's Damascus road encounter, especially in view of the content that follows.

Paul Proclaims a Cosmic-Scaled Mystery—Ephesians 3:8–11

The coupling of God's power and Paul's role as recipient rather than initiator in his ministry installation has been building in momentum in the passage, and that dynamic should probably be viewed as the key to

---

93. Mitton (*Ephesians: Its Authorship, Origin, and Purpose*, 123–24) tentatively draws attention to the connection to Rom 12:3 in particular, in conjunction with two other verbal similarities between the Rom 11:32—12:5 and Eph 3:7–10 (one of which, σοφία τοῦ θεοῦ, is an inexact match of an already unspectacular pairing of words!).

94. See Gombis, "Ephesians 3:2–13," 317.

unlocking the significance of Eph 3:8. In other words, the author is not injecting an artificial note of humility at this point but rather is continuing an emphasis already initiated in the preceding verses.[95] Paul proclaims that he is unworthy to have been entrusted such a lofty ministry: Ἐμοὶ τῷ ἐλαχιστοτέρῳ πάντων ἁγίων ἐδόθη ἡ χάρις αὕτη. The sentiment echoes 1 Cor 15:9 (Ἐγὼ γάρ εἰμι ὁ ἐλάχιστος τῶν ἀποστόλων)[96] and resembles the later adaptations of the expression in the *Letters of Ignatius* (*Eph.* 21:2; *Trall* 13:1; *Rom* 9:2; *Smyrn.* 11:1). Ephesians 3:8 betrays a similar context to that of 1 Cor 15:9, since in both cases, a discussion of God's grace as related to Paul's ministry stands in the background (see 1 Cor 15:10).[97] In contrast, no such emphasis supplements the discussions in the *Letters of Ignatius*.[98] Already implied in Eph 3:2-7 is Paul's unworthiness to be engaged in God's service, since this is necessarily the reverse side of God's grace (see Eph 2:8-9). This acknowledgment of unworthiness is the explicit accompaniment to Paul's humble self-assessment in 1 Cor 15:9 (οὐκ εἰμὶ ἱκανὸς καλεῖσθαι ἀπόστολος). There, the reason given for Paul's

95. With Abbott, *Epistles to the Ephesians and to the Colossians*, 85; Percy, *Die Probleme der Kolosser- und Epheserbriefe*, 412. Mitton believes that the author's attribution of humility to Paul in Eph 3:8 is awkward and unprovoked (Mitton, *Ephesians: Its Authorship, Origin, and Purpose*, 136, 152). But this disregards the development of the theme of grace throughout Ephesians. Paul applies that concept to his own ministry in this context. Others suspecting the author of conveying false humility or fostering an exaggerated characterization of Paul's own self-assessment are Kümmel, *Introduction to the New Testament*, 361; Gnilka, *Der Epheserbrief*, 170; Fischer, *Tendenz und Absicht des Epheserbriefes*, 96; Schnackenburg, *Ephesians*, 136; Lincoln, *Ephesians*, 183; Furnish, "Ephesians," 2:540. Allowing for a spotlight on both grace and humility is Jeal, *Integrating Theology and Ethics in Ephesians*, 170.

96. The comparative of the superlative form (ἐλαχιστότερος), as opposed to ἐλάχιστος, is used for rhetorical flourish in Eph 3:8, heightening the sense of wonder that Paul was entrusted with such a ministry (see BDF §60.2; 61.2; Barth, *Ephesians*, 339-40; Wallace, *Greek Grammar beyond the Basics*, 302; O'Brien, *Ephesians*, 240; Aletti, *Éphésiens*, 185).

97. See also 1 Tim 1:15. Mitton includes the parallel between Eph 3:8 and 1 Cor 15:9 in his long list of parallels and finds it "remarkable" that two other parallels from Ephesians are found in 1 Cor 15:24-28, so close to 1 Cor 15:9-10 (Mitton, *Ephesians: Its Authorship, Origin, and Purpose*, 128-29). The strong conceptual affinity between Eph 3:8 and 1 Cor 15:9-10 is supported by little overlap of vocabulary and syntax. As seen from the examples of the *Epistle to the Laodiceans* and *3 Corinthians*, pseudepigraphers tend to betray themselves through mimicking the wording and sentence structure of their source material.

98. MacDonald makes too much of the parallel between Eph 3:8 and the similar statements by Ignatius (MacDonald, *Colossians and Ephesians*, 270-71). The pronouncements by Ignatius arise from a backdrop that is considerably different from that of 1 Cor 15:11, which is not the case with Eph 3:8.

Portrait of an Apostle

unworthiness is his history of persecuting the church (διότι ἐδίωξα τὴν ἐκκλησίαν τοῦ θεοῦ). That reason is likely the unstated assumption of Eph 3:8 as well, though it is not included this time.[99]

A second difference is that in Eph 3:8 Paul is no longer found wanting in comparison to the apostles alone but in comparison to all the saints. This expanded object of comparison is not surprising. Paul's relationship to the other apostles is not a primary issue in Eph 3:1–13, and his ministry is not even described using the term "apostle." Indeed it would have been more unusual for Paul to have suddenly brought in the topic of apostleship at this point in the discourse. Paul's definition of himself in relation to all the saints, on the other hand, reinforces the unity and equal standing among believers that Paul has been promoting throughout the letter.

Paul finally proceeds to define fully and directly the grace (= ministry) given to him in an extended statement that runs from Eph 3:8b to 3:12. First, he highlights the Gentiles as beneficiaries of the unfathomable riches of Christ. Paul's primary task is thus identified as preaching the gospel to the Gentiles. This same activity was seen at the forefront of Paul's ministry according to earlier letters (Gal 1:16; 2:7–9; Rom 15:15–21; cf. Gal 2:2). The wording is most similar to Gal 1:16 (ἵνα εὐαγγελίζωμαι αὐτὸν ἐν τοῖς ἔθνεσιν), with the repetition of one of Paul's central tasks (preaching the good news) and his audience (the Gentiles) expressed in a different overall construction.[100] The gospel is portrayed as "the unsearchable riches of Christ" (τὸ ἀνεξιχνίαστον πλοῦτος τοῦ Χριστοῦ), which accords with the idea of finding manifold blessings through salvation in Christ (cf. Eph 1:3–14, 18–19; 2:4–7, 19). In Rom 11:33 as part of a doxology, Paul extols

---

99. Supporting this view are Abbott, *Epistles to the Ephesians and to the Colossians*, 86; Barth, *Ephesians*, 340; Kim, *The Origin of Paul's Gospel*, 24; Reynier, *Évangile et Mystère*, 93; Best, *Ephesians*, 317; O'Brien, *Ephesians*, 240; Muddiman, *Ephesians*, 157. For opposing views, Penny believes that a reminiscence of Paul's past would detract from his position as a preeminent figure in the church (Penny, "The Pseudo-Pauline Letters of the First Two Centuries," 263, 265–66), and Lindemann speculates that the author passed over what was the troubling image of Paul as persecutor (Lindemann, *Der Epheserbrief*, 60).

100. Mitton notes further that both passages combine grace with this calling to preach to the Gentiles (Mitton, *Ephesians: Its Authorship, Origin, and Purpose*, 131; cf. Gnilka, *Der Epheserbrief*, 170; Leppä, *The Making of Colossians*, 38–39). Beyond this conceptual similarity though, the forms of χάρις and the immediate contexts in which it appears is quite dissimilar. Moreover, labeling Eph 3:8 as the product of the conflation of 1 Cor 15:9–10 and Gal 1:15–16 rests on too slim of a connection, the single word χάρις (Mitton, *Ephesians: Its Authorship, Origin, and Purpose*, 152–53; Leppä, *The Making of Colossians*, 39).

the unsearchable (ἀνεξοχνίαστος) judgments of God.[101] One purpose of describing the blessings of salvation using this elevated term in Eph 3:8 is to foreshadow the attainment of the lofty spiritual comprehension envisioned in the prayer of Eph 3:14-21 (especially verses 18-19). Describing the benefits of salvation as the riches (πλοῦτος) of Christ creates a compact pairing of riches and Christ that is unique to the NT, but similar groupings are observed in Phil 4:19 (κατὰ τὸ πλοῦτος αὐτοῦ ἐν δόξῃ ἐν Χριστῷ Ἰησοῦ) and Col 1:27; 2:2 (where riches are part of the adornment of the Christ-centered mystery). In addition, as is the case in Eph 3:8 Paul targets the Gentiles as beneficiaries of God's riches in Rom 9:23-24; 10:12; 11:12.

A second feature of Paul's ministry consists of illuminating God's implementation of his eternal plans. The inclusive indirect object (πάντας) stands in contrast to the restricted reference to the Gentiles in the verse before. This move to universal proclamation of God's wisdom becomes more prominent in Eph 3:10.[102] The preferred verb for Paul's activity here is φωτίζω, which occurs only once in the undisputed letters, and in reference to God's activity rather than Paul's (1 Cor 4:5; cf. Eph 1:18). But the association of light (φωτισμός) with the gospel Paul proclaims in 2 Cor 4:4 demonstrates that the adoption of φωτίζω in Eph 3:9 is not strained.[103] Moreover, there is a possible correlation to the light imagery (εἰς φῶς ἐθνῶν) that occurs in the servant passages of Isa 42:6 and 49:6, which are both passages that are associated with Paul's ministry elsewhere in the NT.[104]

101. Mitton adds the appearance of ἀνεξοχνίαστος in both Rom 11:33 and Eph 3:8 to the roster of affinities between portions of Ephesians and Rom 11:32–12:5 (Mitton, *Ephesians: Its Authorship, Origin, and Purpose*, 123–34). As is the case with other purported instances of influence from Romans upon the pseudonymous author of Ephesians, the parallels are unremarkable in their verbal and syntactical correspondence, given the large amount of material brought into the comparison. It should also be noted that ἀνεξοχνίαστος surfaces in similar contexts in Job 5:9; 9:10; 34:24 (LXX).

102. The shift to a more universal scope does not betray the hand of a redactor (as alleged by Muddiman, *Ephesians*, 158–62), but reflects the consistent and seamless interest throughout the letter. Paul envisions Jews and Gentiles, and indeed everything in the whole created order, being brought together as one as part of God's cosmic plans (see Eph 1:9–10, 22–23; 2:15–16; 4:4–6).

103. A similar fluidity in referents (God and Paul) in revelatory contexts also occurs with terms such as γνωρίζω (Rom 9:22; Rom 16:26; Col 1:27; Eph 6:19) and φανερόω (Rom 1:19; 3:21; 16:26; 2 Cor 2:14; Col 1:26; 4:4).

104. Acts 26:18 draws upon Isa 42:7 in describing Paul's commission, and the connections between Isa 49:1–8 and Gal 1:15–16 and 2 Cor 6:2 are developed in chapter 2 of this book. Linking Eph 3:8–9 to Isa 49:6 is Stettler, "An Interpretation of Colossians 1:24 in the Framework of Paul's Mission Theology," 192. For the proposal that the whole passage Eph 3:1–13 bears a resemblance to the servant passages of Isaiah, see Reynier, *Évangile et Mystère*, 102–3.

Portrait of an Apostle

The evidence suggests that the use of φωτίζω to describe Paul's preaching ministry has a claim to Paul's own expression of this perspective.

The familiar terms οἰκονομία and μυστήριον emerge once again in conjunction with one another, and at first glance the return to the topics seems superfluous, in view of what was already said in Eph 3:2-6. But Paul approaches the themes from a different direction this time. It is God and his purposes that are divulged. God's present execution of his plans (ἡ οἰκονομία τοῦ μυστηρίου) is set in contrast to his past decision to conceal his intentions (τοῦ ἀποκεκρυμμένου ἀπὸ τῶν αἰώνων). These final four words are identical to what is found in Col 1:26, and in both cases, the mystery is what is being modified. Nonetheless, literary dependence upon Col 1:26 is not a foregone conclusion here.[105] A similar grouping of terms is first witnessed in 1 Cor 2:7, and the association of eternity past and God's concealed plans is fairly intuitive. The wording from Col 1:26 repeated in Eph 3:8 may exhibit the development of a stock phrase in Paul's habit of speech.

The designs for the world were hidden "in God." which makes explicit Paul's vantage point in the verse by suggesting the divine origin of the mystery and its revelation according to divine decree alone.[106] The additional depiction of God as creator brings together creation and revelation and roots them both in God's sovereign decrees. It may also reinforce the connection between salvation and God's creative power as seen in Eph 2:10 and 2:15.[107]

The ἵνα clause of Eph 3:10 is subordinate to ἀποκεκρυμμένου, expressing the purpose or result for the past concealment of God's mystery. The logical connection made by ἵνα highlights the temporal reasons for the hiddenness. Paul asserts that the mystery was kept secret until the arrival of the church on the scene. The idea of the church's actual existence as a new entity established in Christ (see also Eph 2:14–16), rather than its missionary endeavors, is understood to be the primary means of displaying the wisdom of God.

The recipients of this disclosure are unique as compared to other mystery passages in Paul, but the interest in the heavenly places simply continues a theme that is being pursued throughout Ephesians (Eph 1:3, 20; 2:6; 6:12). The rulers (ἀρχή) and authorities (ἐξουσία) surface in a

---

105. Contra Boismard, *L'Énigme de la letter aux Éphésians*, 107.

106. This is different from seeing Christ as the one in whom divine wisdom is hidden (ἀπόκρυφος) in the present age (Col 2:3).

107. Heil, *Empowerment to Walk in Love for the Unity of All in Christ*, 143–44.

cosmic context in 1 Cor 15:24 (both) and Rom 8:38 (the former), (cf. Eph 1:21; 6:12; Col 1:16; 2:10, 15), reflecting Paul's belief in the relevance of the unseen world. That the wisdom of God is on display is consonant with not only Col 2:2–3 but also 1 Cor 2:7 (cf. 1:30), since in both places wisdom is associated with mystery.[108] The term πολυποίκιλος is a *hapax legomena* in the NT but an embellishment of ποικίλος, which is common enough in the NT but unattested in the undisputed Pauline letters. The prefixed word is well suited to the overall doxological tone of Ephesians. The overall picture of ἡ πολυποίκιλος σοφία τοῦ θεοῦ highlights the wonderful complexity of God's plans, followed by the culmination of all of those plans in Christ (Eph 3:11).

This striking picture of God making his divine wisdom manifest on a cosmic scope through his church adds an innovative touch to Paul's treatment of the significance of Christ's saving work in his people, though the advance is more akin to shining additional light onto an already expansive vision than to redirecting it toward a different trajectory. Paul's conception of salvation's effects is never constrained purely to the level of the individual, though it certainly includes this. The people of God are being constructed into a holy temple (1 Cor 3:10–17) and formed into a body (1 Cor 12:12–14; Rom 12:4–5; cf. Gal 3:26–28). Paul even perceives creation-wide repercussions to Christ's work (Rom 8:19–21). This vision is further unfolded in Colossians and Ephesians (Col 1:18; 3:10–11; Eph 1:9–10; 2:15–22) and supplements the emphasis on Christ's victory over all powers (Col 1:16; 2:10, 15; Eph 1:20–21; cf. 1 Cor 15:24–28). And just as in 1 Cor 4:9 Paul imagines an angelic audience for his own ministry labors, in Eph 3:10 he spotlights the heavenly witness to the church's glory.[109]

Ephesians 3:11 injects two additional summative perspectives about God's overarching enactment of salvation history. First, his revelatory display through the church was implemented according to his eternal plans (κατὰ πρόθεσιν τῶν αἰώνων), which revisits ideas from Eph 1:3–14.[110] This

108. On the connection between mystery and wisdom, especially in Daniel 2, see Caragounis, *The Ephesian Mysterion*, 124–25; Aletti, *Éphésiens*, 184.

109. Similarly noting the relevance of 1 Cor 4:9 to this passage are Percy, *Die Probleme der Kolosser- und Epheserbriefe*, 254; Arnold, *Ephesians: Power and Magic*, 63. Bruce, *Ephesians*, 65, also posits a connection to the fleeting reference to angels in 1 Cor 11:10.

110. See also ἣν προέθετο ἐν αὐτῷ in Eph 1:9 and κατὰ πρόθεσιν in Eph 1:11. In Eph 1:4 the time frame of God's formulation of his plans is stated as being πρὸ καταβολῆς κόσμου. For a discussion of possible parallels between Eph 1:1–14 and 3:1–13, some of which are more likely than others, see Karakolis, "A Mystery Hidden to be Revealed?," 89–104.

prepositional phrase is another indicator of the temporal interests in Eph 3:1-13. It also resembles the wording in Rom 8:28 (τοῖς κατὰ πρόθεσιν κλητοῖς οὖσιν) and Rom 9:11 (ἵνα ἡ κατ' ἐκλογὴν πρόθεσις τοῦ θεοῦ μένῃ). Paul's use of πρόθεσις in all instances helps show Paul's insistence on God's sovereign determination and oversight of events that are unfolding. Additionally, the association between mystery and God's eternal purposes is familiar from Rom 16:26, where the mystery is made known in the present era κατ' ἐπιταγὴν τοῦ αἰωνίου θεοῦ.

The second qualifier of the substance of the mystery is that all saving plans were determined with Christ as the central feature of the plans' fulfillment (ἣν ἐποίησεν ἐν τῷ Χριστῷ Ἰησοῦ τῷ κυρίῳ ἡμῶν). The language forges a link to the perspective of Eph 1:3-14, where the believers' blessings in Christ are shown to be foreordained according to God's perfect grace and pleasure. Ephesians 3:11 is also a significant verse since, in conjunction with 3:4, it places the ecclesiological/missiological arches of the mystery upon christological pillars. The resulting structure stands in comfortable harmony with both that of Colossians 1-2 and those of the undisputed letters.

The Implications of the Mystery for Believers–Ephesians 3:12

In Eph 3:12 Paul continues to travel down a long and winding path in his discourse about his ministry. His reiteration of the centrality of Christ (ἣν ἐποίησεν ἐν τῷ Χριστῷ Ἰησοῦ τῷ κυρίῳ ἡμῶν) likely prompts a return to a theme initiated in Eph 2:18, where Christ was seen as the means of access (προσαγωγή) to God in the Spirit for both Jews and Gentiles. Such a turn would also confirm Paul's inclination throughout the letter to recount the blessings all believers share in Christ. In contrast to the prior resolution of God's plans in Christ (Eph 3:11), Eph 3:12 puts forward the present implications (ἔχομεν) for believers being in Christ.

Several observations support the fact that ἐν ᾧ ἔχομεν τὴν παρρησίαν καὶ προσαγωγὴν ἐν πεποιθήσει διὰ τῆς πίστεως αὐτοῦ refers to relational privileges granted to all believers rather than to a ministry openness experienced by Paul and his associates. First, the first person plural form ἔχομεν in Eph 3:12 probably denotes both Paul and his readers, since Paul is building upon the reference of Jesus Christ *our* Lord in 3:11, where the plural (ἡμῶν) is understood more readily as encompassing both Paul and his readers.[111] Second, being in Christ is more typically seen as the

---

111. See for instance Best, *Ephesians*, 329. This reference to Paul and his readers

grounds for which believers can find assurance or hope in the Lord, both in Ephesians (1:3–8; 2:6–7, 13) and in Paul's earlier letters.[112] Third, the single article preceding the two nouns παρρησία and προσαγωγή expresses the conceptual affinity between the two words, so that the ambiguity about the sense of παρρησία is resolved by the greater certainty about the meaning of προσαγωγή. Finally, elsewhere in Ephesians the faith mentioned in διὰ τῆς πίστεως αὐτοῦ is connected to a saving relationship rather than to a ministry perspective (Eph 1:15; 2:8; 3:17).[113] It will be shown that the individual components in the verse align reasonably with this interpretation as well.

The term παρρησία appears occasionally in Paul's undisputed letters, usually in the context of the bold way Paul engages in ministry towards people (Phil 1:20; 2 Cor 3:12; 7:4; Phlm 8; cf. 1 Thess 2:2), and this is the setting in which the word (and a cognate) is used twice in Eph 6:19–20. Usage outside the undisputed Paulines shows that the word can be used relationally towards God (see especially Heb 4:16; 10:19; 1 John 2:28).[114] The reference is somewhat uncertain here, but the immediate context, as well as the pairing with προσαγωγή, suggests that Paul is describing boldness towards God as a relational privilege given to all believers.

Though παρρησία surfaces with a ministry application in Eph 6:19–20, the parallel idea of access (προσαγωγή) carries a relational sense in an even nearer context (Eph 2:18), and as has already been observed, Eph 3:1–13 develops several other themes from Eph 2:14–22. Though God is not mentioned as the goal of the access in Eph 3:12, the precedent from Eph 2:18 suggests that God is the one to whom believers enjoy access through Christ.[115] This resultant meaning closely resembles Rom 5:2, where believers are also said to have access to God's grace through Christ and by means of faith.[116] These observations tip the scales towards a rela-

---

recalls the shared blessings recited in Eph 1:3–10; 2:10, 14. The distinction between Paul and his readers elsewhere does not eliminate the presence of inclusive first person plural references interspersed throughout.

112. See BDAG, "ἐν," 328 (under heading 4), where examples such as Gal 5:10; Phil 1:14; Phlm 8 are given.

113. The debated subject of the faith in 3:12 will be explored in a subsequent paragraph.

114. For a thorough treatment of the term see Unnik, "The Christian's Freedom of Speech in the New Testament," 273–89; Marrow, "Parrhèsia in the New Testament," 431–46.

115. With NIV, TNIV, NRSV, NET, NLT.

116. Some early manuscripts (B, D, 0220) do lack the reference to faith in Rom 5:2,

tional rather than ministry application for both παρρησία and προσαγωγή, given the assumed connection between the terms reflected in the shared article governing them.[117]

The prepositional modifier ἐν πεποιθήσει further characterizes the believers' access to God. A ministry context is also sometimes present for πεποίθησις (2 Cor 8:22; 10:2; cf. Gal 5:10; Phil 1:14; 2 Cor 3:4; Phlm 21), but two passages that tie confidence to a believer's standing before God are found in Phil 3:3-4, where confidence in the viability of self-empowered living is set in contrast to trust in Christ, and in 2 Cor 10:7, where confidence in belonging to Christ is the issue.

The final addendum to the clause is the qualifier διὰ τῆς πίστεως αὐτοῦ, which recalls the ambiguous genitive pairings of faith and Christ scattered throughout the undisputed epistles (Gal 2:16, 20; 3:22; Phil 3:9; Rom 3:22, 26)[118] and further inculcates the importance of faith (1:15; 2:8; 3:17) and believing (1:13, 19) in Ephesians. The presence of the article before πίστις has been seen tentatively to support a subjective genitive reading of the verse,[119] but the typical pattern is to include an article when the noun is followed by a possessive personal pronoun.[120] Quite probably αὐτοῦ is an objective genitive denoting that it is through the believers' trust in Christ that unhindered intimacy with God is possible.[121]

---

so the parallel may not encompass that similarity (see Metzger, *Textual Commentary on the Greek New Testament*, 452–53). Mitton concludes that the author of Ephesians was "deeply impressed" with Rom 5:1–2 and thus incorporated it both in Eph 3:11–12 and 2:17–18 (Mitton, *Ephesians: Its Authorship, Origin, and Purpose*, 122, 136). Though Mitton contends that an imitator, not Paul himself, would more likely replicate wording from "passages of outstanding significance" (ibid., 112) such as Rom 5:1–2, since access to God through Christ by faith arguably expresses the heart of Paul's gospel, it should not be considered unusual that Paul himself would return to that combination of ideas in several places. When he does so in Eph 2 and 3, apart from inclusion of the essential components of the composite image, the wording and syntactical structure varies significantly from the original model in Rom 5:1–2.

117. See Wallace, *Greek Grammar beyond the Basics*, 286.

118. For a snapshot of the debate over the subjective and objective readings of this pairing, see Hays, "ΠΙΣΤΙΣ and Pauline Christology: What Is at Stake?" 35–60, and Dunn, "Once More, ΠΙΣΤΙΣ ΧΡΙΣΤΟΥ," 61–81.

119. Foster, "The First Contribution to the πίστις Χριστοῦ Debate," 94. Dunn affirms the pattern but calls Eph 3:12 an exception (Dunn, "Once More, ΠΙΣΤΙΣ ΧΡΙΣΤΟΥ," 65).

120. BDF §284.1; Wallace, *Greek Grammar beyond the Basics*, 239.

121. With Caragounis, *The Ephesian Mysterion*, 111; Lincoln, *Ephesians*, 190; Jeal, *Integrating Theology and Ethics in Ephesians*, 173; Heil, *Empowerment to Walk in Love for the Unity of All in Christ*, 145; contra NET; Barth, *Ephesians*, 347; Snodgrass,

Making Sense of Paul's Suffering–Ephesians 3:13

Paul's apostolic apology concludes in 3:13, where Paul encourages the readers to not be disheartened on account of his sufferings. This is what Paul sees as a logical exhortation (denoted by διό in this context) based on what he has shared in Eph 3:2–12. His divine calling to share in a glorious ministry that results in incomparable blessing for Gentiles such as his readers is the reason that he is suffering in prison. Paul does not suffer shamefully but as a participant in a privileged ministry.[122]

Paul introduces a rhetorical request with αἰτοῦμαι. The term ἐγκακέω may have connotations of fear in some contexts, but the more probable nuance is one of discouragement.[123] Paul is comforting his readers with the assurance that his suffering is not in vain. Paul employs the word as part of an exhortation to his readers in Gal 6:9 as well and, as a close parallel to Eph 3:13, in relation to the enduring spiritual value of his ministry in 2 Cor 4:1 (ἔχοντες τὴν διακονίαν ταύτην καθὼς ἠλεήθημεν, οὐκ ἐγκακοῦμεν; cf. 4:16). In Eph 3:13 the basis for the readers' encouragement is likewise Paul's fruitful ministry in accordance with God's eternal plans.

The term θλῖψις is used to describe Paul's hardships, just as in other contexts (1 Thess 3:3–7; Phil 1:17; 2 Cor 1:4–8; 4:17; 6:4; 7:4).[124] These afflictions are tied specifically to Paul's imprisonment, since it was the identification of Paul as the prisoner of Christ for the sake of the Gentiles (Eph 3:1) that prompted Paul's digression in Eph 3:2–12 (see also Phil 1:17 for this same connection). The afflictions are likely understood to encompass both the physical stress and emotional duress of imprisonment (see Phil 1:17).

Paul's afflictions are described in two ways. First, they are endured for the sake of his readers (ὑπὲρ ὑμῶν). This is a reiteration of the point already made in Eph 3:1 (ὑπὲρ ὑμῶν τῶν ἐθνῶν), except that in Eph 3:13 the readers are addressed personally, as representatives of Gentile believers

---

Ephesians, 164–65; Wallace, *Greek Grammar beyond the Basics*, 114–16; O'Brien, *Ephesians*, 249; Gombis, "Ephesians 3:2–13," 322; Foster, "The First Contribution to the πίστις Χριστοῦ Debate," 84–95.

122. There is no need to assume that Paul's martyrdom is being reinterpreted here (*contra* Fischer, *Tendenz und Absicht des Epheserbriefes*, 104, 108; Ernst, *Die Briefe an die Epheser*, 334–35; Lincoln, *Ephesians*, 191). Suffering as a prisoner was considered shameful enough at that time (see discussion and references in chapter 2 during the discussion of Phlm 8–9).

123. BDAG, "ἐγκακέω," 272.

124. This is in contrast to Col 1:24, where θλῖψις has reference to Christ's sufferings (see Reynier, *Évangile et Mystère*, 101).

under the auspices of Paul's ministry. Second and more explicitly, Paul's afflictions result in glory for his readers (ἥτις ἐστιν δόξα ὑμῶν). Ephesians 3:1 begins with a pronouncement of Paul's imprisonment on their behalf. Paul then shows why his imprisonment was necessary: it was a byproduct of his calling to reach the Gentiles. Finally, in Eph 3:13, Paul concludes with the insistence that his afflictions yield a spiritual benefit to his readers. The same dynamic of Paul suffering for the good of those under his care appears in 2 Cor 1:6; 4:12, 15; 6:10; 12:15; Col 1:24.[125]

Though an indefinite force is not required, it may be that the indefinite relative pronoun ἥτις is included "to emphasize a characteristic quality, by which a preceding statement is to be confirmed."[126] The function of the clause would then be to provide more clarification about the way in which Paul's afflictions are endured for his readers (ὑπὲρ ὑμῶν). They are embraced for the readers' glory (δόξα ὑμῶν) in that they are offered in the service of a ministry that makes God's glorious blessings a reality for the Gentiles (as described throughout the letter and specifically in Eph 3:2–12). This use of the word δόξα places the accent on the eschatological connotations of the believers' blessings. Glory in this context envisions partaking in the divine blessedness of God (Eph 1:12, 14, 17; 3:16, 21), perhaps understood according to the distinct eschatological perspective in the letter that believers begin to participate in these eternal benefits in the present, in Christ.[127]

Ephesians 3:1–13 and Similar Passages

Several passages from Paul's earlier letters (other than Colossians) exhibit significant parallels to central themes in Eph 3:1–13. First, the section corresponds to the description of Paul's calling in Gal 1:15 and to the Damascus road revelation.[128] Second, the treatment of revelation and

---

125. The underlying contribution of the servant's calling in Isa 40–66 to Paul's self perception is a possibility in all of these passages.

126. Option listed in section 2 of BDAG, "ὅστις," 729–30; cf. Gnilka, *Der Epheserbrief*, 180.

127. Thus the tendency towards realized eschatology in Ephesians is not to the exclusion of final eschatology but indeed builds upon the presupposition of a final eschatology as part of its formulation (see for instance Eph 1:14). See also Lincoln, *Ephesians*, xc.

128. Merklein, *Das kirchliche Amt nach dem Epheserbrief*, 196–99, 204–8; Kim, *The Origin of Paul's Gospel*, 20–25; Schnackenburg, *Ephesians*, 131; Hübner, *An die Epheser*, 185–86.

mystery aligns with the expression of the same themes in 1 Cor 2:6–10 and Rom 16:25–26. Finally, the juxtaposition of proclamation (Eph 3:8–9) and suffering (3:1, 13) in ministry reflects Paul's self-understanding in 2 Cor 5–6.[129]

Thus, Eph 3:1–13 shares particular affinity with Galatians 1, 1 Cor 2:6–10, 2 Cor 5:18—6:10, and Rom 16:25–26, in addition to Col 1:24–29. The striking, though not exclusive, resemblance to Col 1:24–29 can best be explained by the theory that Paul wrote Ephesians shortly after he finished Colossians, so that his thoughts and language from that letter were still resonating clearly in his mind. But the existence of likely correspondences to other passages shows that influence was not limited to his most recent letter, but that a lifetime of articulation of his theology was exerting a pull on the way Paul expressed himself in Eph 3:1–13.

The fact that so much of Eph 3:1–13, a section devoted to presenting Paul and his ministry to the readers, further develops themes found elsewhere in the letter (especially in 3:6, 10, and 12, but also in many minor ways throughout) is no small feat. In *3 Corinthians*, for instance, the author must establish a credible claim to Paul's authorship of the letter by incorporating material that rings true of Paul. But the unique features of those excerpts do not fit naturally into the rest of the document.[130] That is because it is very difficult in a discrete discourse unit to interweave echoes of Paul and themes from the actual author's own agenda in a convincing manner. But according to proponents of the Exalted Apostle Theory, the author has done this very thing in Eph 3:1–13.[131] Much more probable is the judgment that the section exhibits the unscripted freedom of Paul to describe his ministry in terms that also advance his overall purposes in the letter. The identification of Paul as a prisoner of Christ on behalf of the

---

129. The surrounding context also exhibits an order that parallels 2 Cor 5–6, with themes of new creation and reconciliation (Eph 2:11–22) preceding an exposition on Paul's ministry (3:1–13). See Beale, "The Old Testament Background of Reconciliation in 2 Corinthians 5–7," 578–81.

130. In a related difference, the resemblances to earlier Pauline material found in Eph 3:1–13 is proportionate to affinities between the earlier letters and material in sections of Ephesians that are not related to Paul's image and ministry calling. In contrast, *3 Corinthians* adheres closely to the recognized "script" of Paul's self-presentation but then exhibits fewer connections to Pauline material in other parts of the letter.

131. See for instance Penny, "The Pseudo-Pauline Letters of the First Two Centuries," 231; MacDonald, *The Pauline Churches*, 125; Schnackenburg, *Ephesians*, 36, 132; Lincoln, *Ephesians*, xiii; Furnish, "Ephesians," 2:540; Beker, *Heirs of Paul*, 72; Dunn, "Pauline Legacy and School," 890.

Portrait of an Apostle

Gentiles in 3:1–13 is more likely the result of theological reflection than of artificial posturing for the sake of elevating Paul.

Paul's Imprisonment in Ephesians 4:1

Not too long after Paul's apostolic apology in Eph 3:1–13, Paul again designates himself as "the prisoner in the Lord" (ὁ δέσμιος ἐν κυρίῳ) in Eph 4:1.[132] The image of Paul as a prisoner resurfaces, not as a pseudepigraphal device, but again as part of Paul's perception of his ministry.[133] As with the title ἀπόστολος (Eph 1:1), ὁ δέσμιος is mentioned in passing and not as part of an intentional or elaborate attempt to place Paul on a pedestal. There is also little basis for the claim that the passage betrays simple imitation of earlier Pauline material.[134]

There are several possibilities for why Paul underscores the reality of his imprisonment in this context. First, it has been posited that the image of Paul as a prisoner is meant to bolster the force of the instructions of chapters 4–6 by granting Paul the moral high ground.[135] In Gal 6:17, where Paul calls attention to the marks of Jesus (τὰ στίγματα τοῦ Ἰησοῦ) he bears, a similar dynamic might be in operation, though Paul wields his authority more bluntly in that polemic environment.[136] In the opposite

---

132. The preposition ἐν in ἐν κυρίῳ designates "intimate association with" (BDAG, "ἐν," 328; heading 4), and thus serves to remind readers of the distinguishing characteristic of Paul's imprisonment. This also brings to mind the prominence of the theme of being united with Christ in Ephesians and in a number of Paul's other letters (Hoehner, *Ephesians*, 504). The whole phrase ἐν κυρίῳ, taking the similar expression from 3:1 as a cue, is better understood to qualify ὁ δέσμιος (Schnackenburg, *Ephesians*, 162; Aletti, *Éphésiens*, 207; Hoehner, *Ephesians*, 503) than to modify παρακαλῶ ὑμᾶς, (Muddiman, *Ephesians*, 178). The reason that an article does not govern ἐν κυρίῳ is probably because of the predicate force of δέσμιος in this context (BDF §272).

133. *Contra* Lincoln, *Ephesians*, 234.

134. The use of παρακαλῶ οὖν ὑμᾶς to introduce hortatory material in both Rom 12:1 and Eph 4:1 should not be viewed as evidence for literary dependence, even if there are a few other loose verbal connections to Rom 11:32—12:5 in Ephesians (contra Mitton, *Ephesians: Its Authorship, Origin, and Purpose*, 152; Penny, "The Pseudo-Pauline Letters of the First Two Centuries," 245; Lincoln, *Ephesians*, lvii). The same wording preceding an exhortation appears in 1 Cor 4:16 as well, and similar patterns surface quite regularly in Paul's undisputed letters.

135. Barth, *Ephesians*, 426, 453; Lincoln, *Ephesians*, 234; Reid, "Prison, Prisoner," 754; O'Brien, *Ephesians*, 274; Cassidy, *Paul in Chains*, 98; Karakolis, "A Mystery Hidden to be Revealed?," 67–68, 104–5; Byrskog, "Ephesians 4:1–16—Paraenesis and Identity Formation," 118.

136. See discussion of Gal 6:17 in chapter 2 of the book. Also relevant are Ignatius'

direction, it may be that Paul's imprisonment removes the luxury of being able to issue commands, and so he relies on a sincere appeal from a position of weakness, which is a dynamic similar to what is found in Phlm 8–9.[137] The proximity of this verse to Eph 3:13, where Paul feels that it is necessary to counter the readers' tendency to discouragement over Paul's confinement, offers additional support for this option. Another possibility is that the portrayal reinforces the exhortations that follow by presenting Paul as a model of living according to one's calling, since that is the theme stressed in Paul's introduction to the exhortatory material that follows (Παρακαλῶ οὖν ὑμᾶς . . . ἀξίως περιπατῆσαι τῆς κλήσεως ἧς ἐκλήθετε).[138] Finally, since some connection to the prior material is assumed with the use of οὖν and the reappearance of the prisoner title,[139] it is also reasonable that Paul's imprisonment is recalled in relation to his obligation to serve his Gentile readers (Eph 3:1). This sense of responsibility towards his readers was demonstrated in prayer (Eph 3:14–21) and is now expressed through delivering persuasive teaching (Eph 4–6).[140]

Prayer for Paul's Ministry — Ephesians 6:19–20

The final relevant passage for this study emerges in Eph 6:19–20, where Paul requests prayer for his proclamation ministry in the midst of confinement. After calling for prayers for all situations in Eph 6:18, Paul turns the request towards his own needs (καὶ ὑπὲρ ἐμοῦ).[141] The content of the

---

appeals to his chains as the basis of his exhortation or the proof of his sincerity (*Trall.* 12:2; cf. *Trall.* 10:1; *Phild.* 7:2; *Smyrn.* 4:2). Ignatius' relationship to his readers parallels Paul's in Eph 4:1, but his use of captivity to bolster his platform for influence is less nuanced than what is found in Eph 4:1. Ignatius takes the honor of suffering as a given in his cultural setting, whereas such a perspective is less than certain in Eph 4:1 (see Paul's conscious redefinition of suffering in Eph 3:13).

137. Aletti, *Éphésiens*, 207. For a brief discussion of this facet of Phlm 8–9, see chapter 2.

138. Muddiman, *Ephesians*, 179.

139. The relationship to antecedent material designated by οὖν is probably quite loose but present nonetheless (see BDF §451.1; Gnilka, *Der Epheserbrief*, 196; Best, *Ephesians*, 359).

140. Paul's transition to exhortation (παρακαλέω) stemming from his self-understanding as a minister parallels a move made in 2 Cor 6:1–10 (Συνεργοῦντες δὲ καὶ παρακλοῦμεν). In both cases, Paul feels responsible to motivate the readers to action based on a keen awareness of his calling.

141. By seeking prayer from his readers, he is inviting them to participate in his ministry (Barth, *Ephesians*, 808). Similar requests are seen in Phil 1:19; 2 Cor 1:10–11; Rom 15:30–31 (Gnilka, *Der Epheserbrief*, 317).

prayer sought begins with a request for enablement to proclaim the mystery of the gospel with boldness. The entreaty follows that of Col 4:3 except for at three points of note.[142] First, in Eph 6:19 the metaphor of the open door is bypassed for a more straightforward image of God opening Paul's mouth and giving him the right words.[143] This wording sidesteps the ambiguity (seen in Col 4:3) about whether Paul desires release from prison or rather opportunities for witness in the midst of imprisonment. Whatever the situation (an open door one way or the other is presupposed), Paul simply wants to be ready to communicate faithfully and skillfully. Second, Paul speaks of delivering the message with boldness and openness in Eph 6:19, choosing a word already enlisted in Eph 3:12 and familiar in ministry contexts from his earlier letters (Phil 1:20; 2 Cor 3:12; 7:4; Phlm 8). Third, the mystery is tied to the gospel rather than to Christ, which continues the missiological focus of Ephesians, as compared to the Christological bent of Colossians. The strong resemblance between the prayers in Col 4:3-4 and Eph 6:19-20 reflects the shared setting of imprisonment, the short time interval between the writing of the two letters, and the similar recipients of the letter. The alterations are consistent with the unique contributions of the letter and with Paul's perspective elsewhere.[144]

The mystery of the gospel (τὸ μυστήριον τοῦ εὐαγγέλιον) in 6:19 is modified by ὑπὲρ οὗ πρεσβεύω ἐν ἁλύσει ("on behalf of which I am an ambassador in chains") in 6:20.[145] Paul opts for ἅλυσις here instead of the synonym δεσμός (Phil 1:7, 13, 14, 17; Phlm 10, 13; Col 4:18; cf. Eph 3:1; 4:1) to describe his imprisonment. It is doubtful that this variation represents

---

142. For a side by side comparison of the two passages, see Bockmuehl, *Revelation and Mystery*, 205; Hoehner, *Ephesians*, 860. See also Smillie, "Ephesians 6:19-20: A Mystery for the Sake of Which the Apostle Is an Ambassador in Chains," 210-11. Barth and Blanke rightly caution against automatically insisting on the dependence of Eph 6:19-20 on Col 4:3-4, since material in the broader passage of Col 4:2-6 surfaces seamlessly in two other places (Eph 4:29 and 5:15-16) as well (Barth and Blanke, *Colossians*, 79-80).

143. For a similar expression, see 1 Cor 12:8. The wording also reflects a common metaphor from the LXX (Schlier, *Der Brief an die Epheser*, 302-3; Gnilka, *Der Epheserbrief*, 317).

144. Thus the entirety of Eph 6:19-20 need not be explained as the conflation of Col 4:3-4 with 2 Cor 5:20 and 1 Thess 2:2 (Mitton, *Ephesians: Its Authorship, Origin, and Purpose*, 144).

145. The tenuous correlation between Eph 6:20 and Phlm 13 (Mitton, *Ephesians: Its Authorship, Origin, and Purpose*, 133) offers no help towards identifying the work of an imitator.

anything of significance.¹⁴⁶ The pairing of ambassador and imprisonment is more intriguing, with "ambassador" recalling 2 Cor 5:20, where it is used in depiction of Paul's ministry of reconciliation. This exposes one more possible point of connection between Paul's portrayal in Ephesians and in 2 Cor 5–6.¹⁴⁷ It also underscores Paul's awareness of his ministry obligation in a setting even as extreme as imprisonment.¹⁴⁸

As was the pattern in Col 4:3–4, Paul returns to a call for prayer after mentioning his imprisonment (ἵνα ἐν αὐτῷ παρρησιάσωμαι ὡς δεῖ με λαλῆσαι). The ἵνα clause is parallel with the one in 6:19. If ἐν αὐτῷ stands as the original reading, then the prepositional phrase ties Paul's boldness to the mystery of the gospel.¹⁴⁹ Paul longs to speak boldly (παρρησιάζομαι) even while enduring difficult circumstances.¹⁵⁰ His acknowledgment that he must speak this way (ὡς δεῖ με λαλῆσαι) most likely does not recall his divine commissioning as much as it reflects his desire to be able to communicate according to the need of the hour.¹⁵¹ Besides mirroring the exact wording of Col 4:4, ὡς δεῖ με λαλῆσαι in this context exhibits a use of δεῖ that resembles instances in 1 Thess 4:1, 1 Cor 8:2, and Rom 8:26, with the gloss of "should" conveying the straightforward meaning of the term in each case.

---

146. The two terms are used interchangeably in Luke 8:29 (and in Luke-Acts as a whole), and in 2 Timothy (1:16 and 2:9).

147. It is difficult to accept that a pseudonymous author would borrow a form of πρεσβεύω from 2 Cor 5:20 just because the word was "memorable" (Mitton, *Ephesians: Its Authorship, Origin, and Purpose*, 144; cf. 137). More likely, Paul himself enlisted the terms in both places because they represented his perception of his own ministry and reflected his insistence to both honor God and expend himself for those to whom he ministered.

148. For a discussion of the background connotations to the ambassador metaphor and its sharp contrast with the status of a prisoner, see Cassidy, *Paul in Chains*, 99–103.

149. See discussion of the phrase and the preposition ἐν in Hoehner, *Ephesians*, 865. See also Bruce, *Ephesians*, 134; Barth, *Ephesians*, 783.

150. The bold speech requested in Eph 6:20 echoes the boldness Paul displayed in the midst of a hostile environment when he preached to the Thessalonians (ἐπαρρησιασάμεθα . . . λαλῆσαι πρὸς ὑμᾶς τὸ εὐαγγέλιον—1 Thess 2:2). The mention of παρρησία in Acts 28:20 is also instructive (Bruce, *Ephesians*, 134).

151. See also Smillie, "Ephesians 6:19–20," 215; *contra* Bouttier, *Éphésiens*, 269; Best, *Ephesians*, 609–10; O'Brien, *Ephesians*, 489. This should be taken at face value rather than interpreted as a call for others after the time of Paul to propagate the message of the mystery in accordance with the apostolic norm (Merklein, "Paulinische Theologie in der Rezeption des Kolosse- und Epheserbriefes," 35–36).

Some scholars see Eph 6:19–20 as part of the pseudepigrapher's portrayal of Paul as a "typological" prisoner, raised as a model to emulate.[152] More likely, Paul desires prayer on behalf of his prison ministry and wants to pass on concrete information about his circumstances (see also the reference to τὰ κατ' ἐμε and τὰ περὶ ἡμῶν immediately following in Eph 6:21–22).[153] Suffering, proclamation, and calling are intertwined in Paul's perception of his situation.

What Is Present and Missing in Ephesians

Ephesians, even more than Colossians, deals with a number of central features of Paul's persona as it is attested in the earlier letters of Paul. A ministry calling, founded in divine grace and carried out alongside other gifted ministers, to proclaim God's revealed mystery to the Gentiles and to suffer for the sake of that ministry and audience is common to both Ephesians and the undisputed letters. Only two themes are left relatively undeveloped. The direct recollection of Paul's transformation on the way to Damascus and the OT roots of Paul's self-perspective are not featured with any sustained focus, but they still linger behind the scenes and leave faint traces of themselves in the letter. First, while it is true that the deeply personal aspect of Paul's conversion and call to ministry is not recounted in Ephesians as it is in Galatians 1–2,[154] a concentration on the ministry implications of Paul's call conforms more readily to the occasion and purpose for the letter. Paul is addressing those who for the most part have not had direct personal interaction with him in the past. It is his status as a minister on his readers' behalf that concerns Paul, and so he highlights the features of his divine calling that reinforce the legitimate basis of his outreach to them. Still though, in Eph 3:3 and 3:7–8, there is a strong chance that Paul is communicating against the backdrop of the story of how God delivered him from his history of persecuting the church by dramatically revealing his Son to him on the road to Damascus.

Second, as was the case with Colossians, OT passages are not cited or obviously alluded to in order to define Paul's ministry. They are not

---

152. Wild, "The Warrior and the Prisoner," 288. See also R. Collins, *Letters That Paul Did Not Write*, 167; Schnackenburg, *Ephesians*, 135; Lincoln, *Ephesians*, 455, 458.

153. These in turn recall Col 4:7 (τὰ κατ' ἐμέ), Phil 1:12 (τὰ κατ' ἐμέ), and Phil 1:27 (τὰ περὶ ὑμῶν). See Fee, *Paul's Letter to the Philippians*, 110.

154. As noted by Sterling, "From Apostle to the Gentiles to Apostle of the Church," 88.

anticipated, however, in the occasion assumed for Paul's address to his readers in Ephesians. There is little evidence that the readers need to be convinced from the OT that Paul's ministry is valid. In spite of this state of affairs, there are several possible echoes of OT passages (Isa 42:6; 49:6; 52:7) that have associations with Paul's ministry in his earlier letters. Conceptually, the pairing of Paul's roles of pronouncing divine truth and enduring suffering in Ephesians reflects the dual focus of the servant throughout Isa 40–66. In addition, the OT covenant promises as a whole are understood as a significant component of the divine mystery revealed to Paul (3:6; cf. 2:12).

Themes such as grace and the Holy Spirit that surface in Paul's portrayal in Ephesians but were absent in his portrait in Colossians, or topics such as Paul's ministry to the Gentiles that are developed more extensively, lend support to Pauline authorship of Ephesians in two ways. First they are themes that characterize the entire letter of Ephesians but not Colossians, so they fit more naturally in the self presentation of Paul in Ephesians. Second, these are themes that are dispersed throughout the undisputed letters as well, so their presence in Ephesians strengthens the affinities between the letter and prior correspondence.

Conclusion

As has been recognized for centuries, Ephesians is a complex literary work that interacts with themes from Colossians and the undisputed letters of Paul. The relationship of Ephesians to Colossians consists of more than meets the eye. It has been shown throughout these passages that the author of Ephesians has followed much of the language of Colossians but has not misconstrued the theology found in parallel passages. The similar words employed (whether οἰκονομία or μυστήριον or αἰών or ἅγιος) and themes treated (whether Paul's calling, his suffering for his churches, or the implications of Christ's work for salvation and mission) serve the dual function of echoing Paul's perspective from Colossians and advancing the coherent discourse in Ephesians. The resultant presentation of Paul appears all the more authentic when other passages from earlier letters are observed to be embedded so comfortably in the discourse. Finally, the topics that surface in relation to Paul's calling and ministry, along with the topics that do not emerge, can be explained more satisfactorily according to Paul's aims in writing to his readers rather than to theories that propose the initiative and studied imitation of a later admirer.

6

A Better Way

Like any other letter from antiquity, Colossians and Ephesians are understood most successfully against the backdrop of the occasion that gave rise to the letters. Edgar Goodspeed says it well: "It is the glory of historical interpretation that when once the situation that called forth a document is determined, the document at once becomes luminous with meaning. The penalty of it is, that if that situation is not soundly determined, the document remains lost in obscurity. It does not yield its meaning."[1] The proponents of the Exalted Apostle Theory claim to present a reconstruction of events behind the production of Colossians and Ephesians that yields a superior meaning for how Paul is portrayed in the letters. The goal of this book has been to show that the judgment that Paul wrote the letters has greater explanatory power for the meaning of material in the letters related to Paul's persona. This applies to both the verbal and conceptual features of these sections.

As was demonstrated in chapter 1, the Exalted Apostle Theory has left its mark on recent studies of Colossians and Ephesians. A number of scholars even take the theory for granted as a starting point for their own work. Though a few reservations with the theory have surfaced from time to time, these have not stemmed the tide of confidence that someone other than Paul was responsible for the image of Paul seen in Colossians and Ephesians. Purported differences between the presentation of Paul in the undisputed letters and in Colossians and Ephesians continue to be drawn upon as confirmation of the Exalted Apostle Theory.

---

1. Goodspeed, *The Meaning of Ephesians*, 14. Though Goodspeed reached different conclusions than the ones in this book, his point still captures the common quest of identifying the plausible historical occasion behind the Pauline letters and the letters' arguments in response.

A Better Way

The persistent trend of skepticism about the Pauline authorship of the presentation of Paul's ministry in Colossians and Ephesians has created the need for the thorough and detailed response attempted in this book. The first step consisted of a careful study of the primary components of Paul's self-understanding in the undisputed letters. Chapter 2 surveyed central topics such as Paul's transformative calling, his reliance upon the OT patterns of prophet and especially servant to explain his ministry, his recognition of God's grace in appointing him to ministry, his perception of how his work fit within the context of the greater advance of the apostolic gospel, his vision of the revealed mystery that constituted the heart of his proclaimed message, the importance of the Gentiles as beneficiaries of the mystery and objects of Paul's mission, and the requirement that he suffer as a corollary to his preaching mandate. On the one hand the presence of consistency and coherence regarding these themes was attested in the various passages. On the other hand, variability owing to the divergent occasions and purposes for the discourse was observed for topics such as mystery, suffering, and the divine basis of shared apostolic truth.

The aim of chapter 3 was to provide two examples of how authors after Paul's time consciously imitated his style and theology in their depiction of calling, suffering, and ministry. In the *Epistle to the Laodiceans* and *3 Corinthians*, authors consciously adopted Paul's self-perspective in order to submit their own work under the name of Paul. These pseudonymous authors were seen to have reproduced much of the wording from Paul's earlier letters while transmitting a more simplistic form of Paul's theology, with little evidence of fresh or thought-provoking material. In both cases the portrait of Paul does not fit the literary context or supposed historical context of the letters and at times reflects a misunderstanding of the borrowed material. The portrait of Paul is not successfully integrated within the content of the rest of the letter in both cases as well. Neither of the works preserve credible Pauline viewpoints but unwillingly give voice to perspectives from the second century or later. This is especially pronounced with the topics of apostolic tradition and adulation of suffering.

In chapter 4, relevant passages from Colossians were evaluated according to verbal similarity and theological fidelity to undisputed letters, and according to contribution to the discourse of the letter. In contrast to the two pseudepigraphal letters in chapter 3, Colossians reflects relative freedom of expression, even though terms that are employed are often familiar from earlier letters. Likewise, theological presentation of Paul's calling and ministry is observed to be compatible with positions advanced in the undisputed letters, once an allowance is made for the distinct historical setting of Colossians. Moreover, wording and thinking from Colossians resembles what is found in a number of different passages rather than being limited to a few special excerpts sufficient for a pseudepigrapher's template. The passages outlining Paul's ministry support themes advanced elsewhere in the letter and are seen to contribute to Paul's rhetorical purpose, which was not the case for the *Epistle to the Laodiceans* and *3 Corinthians*. Though Colossians does not develop every theme about Paul's ministry found in Paul's earlier letters, what it does feature accords with both the established picture of Paul and Colossians as a whole, and what it bypasses is not essential for the progression of the discourse.

Ephesians likewise incorporates material related to Paul's ministry in an authentic way. The discourse closely resembles the picture from Colossians but without evidence of rigid verbal imitation by a later writer. The unique shadings of Paul's persona in Ephesians often tie into emphases elsewhere in the letter and reflect themes found in Paul's earlier correspondence with other churches. The complex interplay of ideas from Colossians, the undisputed letters, and other sections from Ephesians points to Paul as the author, since such a result would be extremely difficult to achieve by a pseudonymous writer. The material presenting Paul as prisoner, recipient of divine revelation, and minister to the Gentiles serves specific purposes within Ephesians. Paul's imprisonment emerges as a plausible circumstance behind the letter, as supported by Paul's determination to uphold the ministry benefits of his confinement, in opposition to predominant cultural appraisals of shame regarding imprisonment. Paul's insistence on having received a divine revelation initiated by God's grace functions to showcase the divine origins of his grand vision of the eternal and far-reaching plans God implemented in Christ. As part of his introduction to readers he did not know personally, Paul provides the rationale and background for his outreach to Gentile believers. These snapshots, besides serving their intended purpose in the letter, stand comfortably alongside Paul's self-descriptions in his earlier letters.

Exegetical and theological insights may be gleaned from various parts of this book, but some brief concluding reflections are offered here. The inclination to resort too quickly to the Exalted Apostle Theory risks short-circuiting the exegetical process. The temptation is to adjust the perceived background of the letter to fit a preferred interpretation. This approach has the drawback of settling prematurely on an interpretation that may be unduly influenced by the interpreter's bias. This procedure represents a failure in exegetical imagination, substituted with an overly active historical imagination. An arguably superior strategy is to begin by exploring multiple possible meanings for the discourse in the pursuit of a coherent interpretation that fits the background presented by the letter itself. If such an interpretation is found, which I believe has been the case for each passage examined in Colossians and Ephesians, then adjustments to the background become unnecessary. Of course, interpretations and proposed backgrounds shape one another, and neither side should be seen as immovable. In the cases of the *Epistle to the Laodiceans* and *3 Corinthians*, the discourse resists satisfactory explanation when viewed as a product of Paul's own mind, and so the backgrounds are adjusted accordingly. But Colossians and Ephesians have been shown to be quite different from the non-canonical letters. The assumption of Pauline authorship for Colossians and Ephesians generated meanings that were consistently superior to the often superficial ones proposed by proponents of the Exalted Apostle Theory.

There are also theological implications to be observed from the results of this book. Confirming the Pauline origins of the material portraying Paul in Colossians and Ephesians allows the letters to be admitted into evidence for constructing Paul's theology. The letters are routinely excluded when Paul's theology is discussed. If Colossians and Ephesians indeed originate with Paul, then this omission would introduce the possibility of distortion in how Paul's theology is assessed.[2] The potential theological contributions of recognizing Paul's authorship of Colossians and Ephesians extend beyond the passages dealing with Paul's perception of his ministry, but such investigation is beyond the scope of this book. Brief comment will be made instead on theological issues related to the commission and message entrusted to Paul.

The summaries of Paul's perception of his ministry in Col 1:24—2:3 and Eph 3:1–13 are significant in their length and in their function as broad summaries of his calling, ministry, and suffering. These sections consist less of defensive responses or preemptive strikes against opponents and thus are arguably more balanced formulations of Paul's identity. These passages, supplemented by the shorter excerpts about Paul's ministry in the letters, reveal that Paul is called to proclaim the gospel and suffer for it, based on a profound awareness of his Christ-shaped calling. His confidence in ministry is strengthened by his memory of God's unprovoked

---

2. See also Snodgrass, *Ephesians*, 30.

intervention in his life, while any sense of self-adulation is tempered by the same recollection. Paul's particular responsibility lies with Gentile believers both known and unknown to him. Colossians and Ephesians reveal especially how Paul expresses this devotion to relative strangers. These components of Paul's identity are present in the undisputed letters as well, but data from Colossians and Ephesians contribute to a fuller and at times (see Col 1:24) more provocative picture of Paul's ministry and attests to the stability and enduring quality of his self-understanding.

Paul's comprehension of God's overarching agenda for the world emerges more fully in Colossians and especially Ephesians. Paul unveils the cosmic dimensions of Christ's superiority and salvation in ways only hinted at in the earlier letters. This expansive vision of the divinely revealed mystery is consistent with the focused mystery of Christ's crucifixion, resurrection, and return, along with the implications of these events, as seen in the earlier letters. But the testimony of Colossians and Ephesians helps unfold the full riches of the mystery and Paul's participation in its advance.

It is hoped that at minimum the Exalted Apostle Theory will not continue to be assumed as the default position in studies in Paul's letters, theology, and legacy. The goal of this book has been to cast doubt on the viability of this paradigm and to offer alternate and ultimately more effective explanations for the ways that Paul expresses his understanding of his calling. It is concluded that the creative and unstudied voice of Paul reveals itself as powerfully and purposefully in Colossians and Ephesians as it does in Paul's earlier letters and that the resulting testimony from all of the letters provides a rich picture of the blessed apostle and his ministry.

Bibliography

Abbott, T. K. *A Critical and Exegetical Commentary on the Epistles to the Ephesians and to the Colossians*. International Critical Commentary. Edinburgh: T. & T. Clark, 1897.
Ahren, Barnabas Mary. "The Fellowship of His Sufferings (Phil 3,10): A Study of St. Paul's Doctrine on Christian Suffering." *Catholic Biblical Quarterly* 22 (1960) 1–32.
Aletti, Jean-Noël. *Saint Paul, Épître aux Colossiens*. Études Bibliques. Paris: Gabalda, 1993.
———. *Saint Paul Épître aux Éphésiens*. Études Bibliques. Paris: Gabalda, 2001.
The Ante-Nicene Fathers: The Writings of the Fathers Down to A.D. 325. Edited by Alexander Roberts and James Donaldson. 10 vols. 1885–1887. Reprint, Peabody, MA: Hendrickson, 1994.
Arnold, Clinton E. *The Colossian Syncretism: The Interface between Christianity and Folk Belief at Colossae*. Grand Rapids: Baker, 1996.
———. "Ephesians, Letter to the." In *Dictionary of Paul and His Letters*, edited by Gerald F. Hawthrone and Ralph P. Martin, 238–49. Downers Grove, IL: InterVarsity, 1993.
———. *Ephesians*. Zondervan Exegetical Commentary of the New Testament. Grand Rapids: Zondervan, 2010.
Baltzer, Klaus. *Deutero-Isaiah: A Commentary on Isaiah 40–55*. Hermeneia. Minneapolis: Fortress, 2001.
Barclay, William B. *"Christ in You": A Study in Paul's Theology and Ethics*. Lanham, MD: University Press, 1999.
Barnett, Paul. *The Second Epistle to the Corinthians*. New International Commentary on the New Testament. Grand Rapids: Eerdmans, 1997.
Barrett, C. K. *The First Epistle to the Corinthians*. Black's New Testament Commentary. London: A. & C. Black, 1968.
———. "Pauline Controversies in the Post-Pauline Period." *New Testament Studies* 20 (1973–1974) 229–45.
Barth, Markus. *Ephesians: Introduction, Translation, and Commentary*. 2 vols. Anchor Bible 34. Garden City, NY: Doubleday, 1974.
Barth, Markus, and Helmut Blanke. *Colossians: A New Translation with Introduction and Commentary*. Translated by Astrid B. Beck. Anchor Bible 34B. New York: Doubleday, 1994.
Bauckham, Richard J. "Colossians 1:24 Again: The Apocalyptic Motif." *Evangelical Quarterly* 47 (1975) 168–70.
———. "Pseudo-Apostolic Letters." *Journal of Biblical Literature* 107 (1988) 469–94.
Bauer, Walter. *Rechtgläubigkeit und Ketzerei im ältesten Christentum*. Beiträge zur historischen Theologie 10. Tübingen: Mohr/Siebeck, 1934.
Bauer, Walter, et al. *A Greek-English Lexicon of the New Testament and Other Early Christian Literature*. 3rd ed. Chicago: University of Chicago Press, 2000.

Bibliography

Baum, Armin Daniel. *Pseudepigraphie und literarische Fälschung im frühen Christentum: Mit ausgewählten Quellentexten samt deutscher Übersetzung*. Wissenschaftliche Untersuchungen zum Neuen Testament 2/138. Tübingen: Mohr/Siebeck, 2001.

Beale, G. K. *John's Use of the Old Testament in Revelation*. Journal for the Study of the New Testament: Supplement Series 166. Sheffield: Sheffield Academic, 1999.

———. "The Old Testament Background of Reconciliation in 2 Corinthians 5–7 and Its Bearing in the Literary Problem of 2 Corinthians 6.14–7.1." *New Testament Studies* 35 (1989) 550–81.

Beisser, Friedrich. "Wann und von wem könnte der Epheserbrief verfasst worden sein?" *Kerygma und Dogma* 52 (2006) 151–64.

Beker, J. Christiaan. *Heirs of Paul: Paul's Legacy in the New Testament and in the Church Today*. Grand Rapids: Eerdmans, 1996.

Benoit, Pierre. "Rapports littéraires entre les épîtres aux Colossiens et aux Éphésiens." In *Neutestamentliche Aufsätze: Festschrift für Prof. Josef Schmid zum 70*, edited by J. Blinzler et al., 11–22. Regensburg: Pustet, 1963.

Best, Ernest. *A Critical and Exegetical Commentary on Ephesians*. International Critical Commentary. Edinburgh: T. & T. Clark, 1998.

———. "Ephesians 1.1 Again." In *Paul and Paulinism: Essays in Honour of C. K. Barrett*, edited by M. D. Hooker and S. G. Wilson, 273–79. London: SPCK, 1982.

———. *One Body in Christ: A Study in the Relationship of the Church to Christ in the Epistles of the Apostle Paul*. London: SPCK, 1955.

———. "Paul's Apostolic Authority?" *Journal for the Study of the New Testament* 27 (1986) 3–25.

———. "The Revelation to Evangelize the Gentiles." *Journal of Theological Studies* 35 (1984) 1–30.

———. "Who Used Whom? The Relationship of Ephesians and Colossians." *New Testament Studies* 43 (1997) 72–96.

Betz, Hans Dieter. *Galatians: A Commentary on Paul's Letter to the Churches in Galatia*. Hermeneia. Philadelphia: Fortress, 1979.

———. "Paul's 'Second Presence' in Colossians." In *Texts and Contexts: Biblical Texts in Their Textual and Situational Contexts*, edited by Tord Fornberg and David Hellholm, 507–18. Oslo: Scandinavian University Press, 1995.

Black, David Alan. "The Peculiarities of Ephesians and the Ephesian Address." *Grace Theological Journal* 2 (1981) 59–73.

Blackman, E. C. *Marcion and His Influence*. London: SPCK, 1948.

Blass, F., and Albert Debrunner. *A Greek Grammar of the New Testament and other Early Christian Literature*. Translated and revised by Robert W. Funk. Chicago: University Press, 1961.

Blenkinsopp, Joseph. *Isaiah 40–55: A New Translation with Introduction and Commentary*. Anchor Bible 19A. New York: Doubleday, 2002.

Bloomquist, L. Gregory. *The Function of Suffering in Philippians*. Journal for the Study of the New Testament: Supplement Series 78. Sheffield: Sheffield Academic, 1993.

Bockmuehl, Markus. *The Epistle to the Philippians*. Black's New Testament Commentary. Peabody, MA: Hendrickson, 1998.

———. *Revelation and Mystery in Ancient Judaism and Pauline Christianity*. Grand Rapids: Eerdmans, 1990.

Boers, Hendrikus. "The Form Critical Study of Paul's Letters. 1 Thessalonians as a Case Study." *New Testament Studies* 22 (1975) 140–58.

Bibliography

Boese, H. "Über eine bisher unbekannte Handschrift des Briefwechsels zwischen Paulus und den Korinthern." *Zeitschrift für die neutestamentliche Wissenschaft und die Kunde der älteren Kirche* 44 (1953) 66–76.

Boismard, M.-É. *L'Énigme de la letter aux Éphésians*. Études Bibliques. Paris: Gabalda, 1999.

Bornkamm, Günther. *Paul: Paulus*. Translated by D. M. G. Stalker. New York: Harper & Row, 1971. Originally published as *Paulus* (Stuttgart: Kohlhammer, 1969).

Bouttier, Michel. *L'Épître de Saint Paul aux Éphésiens*. Commentaire du Nouveau Testament 9b. Geneva: Labor et Fides, 1991.

Bowers, W. Paul. "A Note on Colossians 1:27a." In *Current Issues in Biblical and Patristic Interpretation*, edited by Gerald F. Hawthorne, 111–14. Grand Rapids: Eerdmans, 1975.

Bratke, E. "Ein zweiter lateinischer Text des apokryphen Briefwechsels zwischen dem Apostel Paulus und den Korinthern." *Theologische Literaturzeitung* 17 (1892) 585–88.

Brown, Raymond E. *The Churches the Apostles Left Behind*. New York: Paulist, 1984.

———. *The Semitic Background of the Term "Mystery" in the New Testament*. Philadelphia: Fortress, 1968.

Bruce, F. F. *1 and 2 Corinthians*. New Century Bible Commentary. Grand Rapids: Eerdmans, 1971.

———. *The Epistles to the Colossians, to Philemon, and to the Ephesians*. New International Commentary on the New Testament. Grand Rapids: Eerdmans, 1984.

———. *The Epistle to the Ephesians: A Verse-by-Verse Exposition*. London: Pickering & Inglis, 1961.

———. *The Epistle to the Galatians*. The New International Greek Testament Commentary. Grand Rapids: Eerdmans, 1982.

———. *Romans*. Rev. edition. Tyndale New Testament Commentaries. Leicester: InterVarsity, 1985.

———. *Philippians*. New International Biblical Commentary on the New Testament. Peabody, MA: Hendrickson, 1989.

Brueggemann, Walter. *Isaiah 40–66*. Westminster Bible Companion. Louisville: Westminster John Knox, 1998.

Bujard, Walter. *Stilanalytische Untersuchungen zum Kolosserbrief als Beitrag zur Methodik von Sprachvergleichen*. Studien zur Umwelt des Neuen Testaments 11. Göttingen: Vandenhoeck & Ruprecht, 1973.

Bultmann, Rudolf. *Der zweite Brief an die Korinther*. Göttingen: Vandenhoeck & Ruprecht, 1976.

Burnet, Régis. "Pourquoi avoir récrit l'insipide épître aux Laodicéens?" *New Testament Studies* 48 (2002) 132–41.

Byrne, Brendan. *Romans*. Sacra Pagina 6. Collegeville, MN: Liturgical, 1996.

Byrskog, Samuel. "Ephesians 4:1–16—Paraenesis and Identity Formation." In *Ethik als angewandte Ekklesiologie: Der Brief an die Epheser*, edited by Michael Wolter, 109–38. Rome: Benedictina, 2005.

Cahill, Michael. "The Neglected Parallelism in Col 1,24–25." *Theologische Literaturzeitung* 68 (1992) 142–47.

Cannon, George E. *The Use of Traditional Materials in Colossians*. Macon, GA: Mercer University Press, 1983.

Bibliography

Caragounis, Chrys C. *The Ephesian Mysterion: Meaning and Content*. Coniectanea biblica: New Testament 8. Lund: Gleerup, 1977.

Carson, D. A. "Mystery and Fulfillment: Toward a More Comprehensive Paradigm of Paul's Understanding of the Old and the New." In *Justification and Variegated Nomism*, edited by D. A. Carson et al., 2:393–436. Grand Rapids: Baker, 2004.

———. "Pseudonymity and Pseudepigraphy." In *Dictionary of New Testament Background*, edited by Craig A. Evans and Stanley E. Porter, 857–64. Downers Grove, IL: InterVarsity, 2000.

Carson, D. A., and Douglas Moo. *An Introduction to the New Testament*. 2nd ed. Grand Rapids: Zondervan, 2005.

Cassidy, Richard J. *Paul in Chains: Roman Imprisonment and the Letters of Saint Paul*. New York: Herder & Herder, 2001.

Cerfaux, Lucien. *The Church in the Theology of St. Paul*. Translated by Geoffrey Webb and Adrian Walker. New York: Herder & Herder, 1959.

———. *Recueil Lucien Cerfaux: Études d'Exégèse et d'Histoire Religieuse, réunites à l'occasion de son soixante-dixième anniversaire*. Vol. 2. Bibliotheca ephemeridum theologicarum lovaniensium 6–7. Gembloux, Belgium: Duculot, 1954.

Chae, Daniel Jong-Sang. *Paul as Apostle to the Gentiles: His Apostolic Self-Awareness and its Influence on the Soteriological Argument in Romans*. Paternoster Biblical and Theological Monographs. Carlisle: Paternoster, 1997.

Childs, Brevard S. *Isaiah*. Old Testament Library. Louisville: Westminster John Knox, 2001.

Clark, Andrew C. "Apostleship: Evidence from the New Testament and Early Christian Literature." *Vox evangelica* 19 (1989) 49–82.

Clarke, Kent D. "The Problem of Pseudonymity in Biblical Literature and Its Implications for Canon Formation." In *The Canon Debate*, edited by Lee Martin McDonald and James A. Sanders, 440–68. Peabody, MA: Hendrickson, 2002.

Collins, John N. "The Mediatorial Aspect of Paul's Role as *Diakonos*." *Australian Biblical Review* 40 (1992) 34–44.

Collins, Raymond F. "The Case of a Wandering Doxology: Rom 16,25–27." In *New Testament Textual Criticism and Exegesis: Festschrift J. Delobel*, edited by A. Denaux, 293–303. Bibliotheca ephemeridum theologicarum lovaniensium 161. Leuven: Leuven University Press, 2002.

———. *First Corinthians*. Sacra Pagina 7. Collegeville, MN: Liturgical, 1999.

———. *Letters That Paul Did Not Write: The Epistle to the Hebrews and the Pauline Pseudepigrapha*. Good News Studies 28. Wilmington, DE: Glazier, 1988.

Conzelmann, Hans. "Die Schule des Paulus." In *Theologia Crucis—Signum Crucis: Festschrift für Erich Dinkler*, edited by Carl Andresen and Günter Klein, 85–96. Tübingen: Mohr/Siebeck, 1979.

———. "Paulus und die Weisheit." *New Testament Studies* 12 (1965–1966) 231–44.

Corrigan, Gregory M. "Paul's Shame for the Gospel." *Biblical Theology Bulletin* 16 (1986) 23–27.

Coutts, John. "The Relationship of Ephesians and Colossians." *New Testament Studies* 4 (1957/58) 201–7.

Cranfield, C. E. B. *A Critical and Exegetical Commentary on The Epistle to the Romans*. 2 vols. International Critical Commentary. Edinburgh: T. & T. Clark, 1975.

Dahl, Nils A. "Form-Critical Observations on Early Christian Preaching." In *Jesus in the Memory of the Early Church*, 30–36. Minneapolis: Augsburg, 1976.

Dalton, W. J. "Pseudepigraphy in the New Testament." *Catholic Theological Review* 5 (1983) 29-35.
de Boer, Martinus C. "Images of Paul in the Post-Apostolic Period." *Catholic Biblical Quarterly* 42 (1980) 359-80.
Denniston, J. D. *The Greek Particles*. Oxford: Clarendon, 1934.
Dibelius, Martin. *Die Briefe des Apostels Paulus II: Die neun kleinen Briefe*. Handbuch zum Neuen Testament. Tübingen: Mohr/Siebeck, 1913.
Donelson, Lewis R. *Pseudepigraphy and Ethical Argument in the Pastoral Epistles*. Tübingen: Mohr/Siebeck, 1986.
Dübbers, Michael. *Christologie und Existenz im Kolosserbrief: Exegetische und semantische Untersuchungen zur Intention des Kolosserbriefes*. Wissenschaftliche Untersuchungen zum Neuen Testament 2/191. Tübingen: Mohr/Siebeck, 2005.
Dunn, James D. G. *The Epistles to the Colossians and to Philemon: A Commentary on the Greek Text*. New International Greek Testament Commentary. Grand Rapids: Eerdmans, 1996.
———. *The Epistle to the Galatians*. Black's New Testament Commentary. Peabody, MA: Hendrickson, 1993.
———. "Once More, ΠΙΣΤΙΣ ΧΡΙΣΤΟΥ." In *Pauline Theology Volume IV: Looking Back, Pressing On*, edited by E. Elizabeth Johnson and David M. Hay, 61-81. SBL Symposium 4. Atlanta: Scholars, 1997.
———. "Pauline Legacy and School." In *Dictionary of the Later New Testament and Its Developments*, edited by Ralph P. Martin and Peter H. Davids, 887-93. Downers Grove, IL: InterVarsity, 1997.
———. *Romans*. Word Biblical Commentary 38A-B. Nashville: Nelson, 1988.
———. *The Theology of Paul the Apostle*. Grand Rapids: Eerdmans, 1997.
Ehrman, Bart D. *Lost Christianities: The Battle for Scripture and the Faiths We Never Knew*. Oxford: Oxford University Press, 2003.
———. *Forged: Writing in the Name of God—Why the Bible's Authors Are Not Who We Think They Are*. New York: HarperOne, 2011.
Elliott, J. K. *The Apocryphal New Testament: A Collection of Apocryphal Christian Literature in an English Translation*. Oxford: Clarendon, 1993.
———. "The Language and Style of the Concluding Doxology to the Epistle to the Romans." *Zeitschrift für die neutestamentliche Wissenschaft und die Kunde der älteren Kirche* 72 (1981) 124-30.
Ernst, Josef. *Die Briefe an die Philipper, an Philemon, an die Kolosser, an die Epheser*. Regensburger Neues Testament. Regensburger: Pustet, 1974.
Fay, Greg. "Paul the Empowered Prisoner: Eph 3:1-13 in the Epistolary and Rhetorical Structure of Ephesians." PhD diss., Marquette University, 1994.
Fee, Gordon D. *The First Epistle to the Corinthians*. The New International Commentary on the New Testament. Grand Rapids: Eerdmans, 1987.
———. *Paul's Letter to the Philippians*. New International Commentary on the New Testament. Grand Rapids: Eerdmans, 1995.
Fischer, Karl Martin. *Tendenz und Absicht des Epheserbriefes*. Forschungen zur Religion und Literatur des Alten und Neuen Testaments 111. Göttingen: Vandenhoeck & Ruprecht, 1973.
Fitzmyer, Joseph A. *Romans: A New Translation with Introduction and Commentary*. Anchor Bible 33. New York: Doubleday, 1993.

Bibliography

Foster, Paul. "The First Contribution to the πίστις Χριστοῦ Debate: A Study of Ephesians 3.12." *Journal for the Study of the New Testament* 85 (2002) 75–96.

Fredrickson, David E. "Paul, Hardships, and Suffering." In *Paul in the Greco-Roman World: A Handbook*, edited by J. Paul Sampley, 172–97. Harrisburg: Trinity, 2003.

Fung, Ronald Y. K. *The Epistle to the Galatians*. The New International Commentary on the New Testament. Grand Rapids: Eerdmans, 1988.

———. "Revelation and Tradition: the Origins of Paul's Gospel." *Evangelical Quarterly* 57 (1985) 23–41.

Furnish, Victor Paul. *II Corinthians*. Anchor Bible 32A. Garden City, NY: Doubleday, 1984.

———. "Ephesians, Epistle to the." In *Anchor Bible Dictionary*, edited by D. N. Freedman, 2:540. New York: Doubleday, 1992.

———. "On Putting Paul in His Place." *Journal of Biblical Literature* 113 (1994) 3–17.

Gamble, Harry Y. *Textual History of the Letter to the Romans: A Study in Textual and Literary Criticism*. Studies and Documents 42. Grand Rapids: Eerdmans, 1977.

Garland, David E. *1 Corinthians*. Baker Exegetical Commentary on the New Testament. Grand Rapids: Baker, 2003.

———. *2 Corinthians*. New American Commentary 29. Nashville: Broadman & Holman, 1999.

———. *Colossians and Philemon*. NIV Application Commentary. Grand Rapids: Zondervan, 1998.

Gignilliat, Mark. "2 Corinthians 6:2: Paul's Eschatological 'Now' and Hermeneutical Invitation." *Westminster Theological Journal* 67 (2005) 147–61.

———. *Paul and Isaiah's Servants: Paul's Theological Reading of Isaiah 40–66 in 2 Corinthians 5.14–6.10*. Library of New Testament Studies 330. London: T. & T. Clark, 2007.

Gnilka, Joachim. *Der Epheserbrief*. Herders theologischer Kommentar zum Neuen Testament 10/2. Freiburg: Herder, 1971.

———. *Der Kolosserbrief*. Herders theologischer Kommentar zum Neuen Testament 10/1. Freiburg: Herder, 1980.

———. *Der Philipperbrief*. 2nd ed. Herders Theologische Kommentar zum Neuen Testament 10/3. Freiburg: Herder, 1976.

Goldingay, John. *God's Prophet, God's Servant: A Study in Jeremiah and Isaiah 40–55*. Exeter: Paternoster, 1984.

———. *The Message of Isaiah 40–55: A Literary-Theological Commentary*. London: T. & T. Clark, 2005.

Gombis, Timothy G. "Ephesians 3:2–13: Pointless Digression, or Epitome of the Triumph of God in Christ?" *Westminster Theological Journal* 66 (2004) 313–23.

Goodspeed, Edgar J. *The Formation of the New Testament*. Chicago: University of Chicago Press, 1926.

———. *The Meaning of Ephesians*. Chicago: University of Chicago Press, 1933.

Goulder, M. D. "The Visionaries of Laodicea." *Journal for the Study of the New Testament* 43 (1991) 15–39.

Grindheim, Sigurd. "What the OT Prophets Did Not Know: The Mystery of the Church in Eph 3,2–13." *Biblica* 84 (2003) 531–53.

———. "Wisdom for the Perfect: Paul's Challenge to the Corinthian Church (1 Corinthians 2:6–16)." *Journal of Biblical Literature* 121 (2002) 689–709.

Grudem, Wayne. *The Gift of Prophecy in the New Testament and Today*. Westchester, IL: Crossway, 1988.

Guthrie, Donald. "Acts and Epistles in Apocryphal Writings." In *Apostolic History and the Gospel: Biblical and Historical Essays Presented to F. F. Bruce on His 60th Birthday*, 328-45. Exeter: Paternoster, 1970.

———. *New Testament Introduction*. Rev. ed. Leicester: Apollos, 1990.

Hafemann, Scott J. "Paul's Use of the Old Testament in 2 Corinthians." *Interpretation* 52 (1998) 246-57.

———. "The Role of Suffering in the Mission of Paul." In *The Mission of the Early Church to Jews and Gentiles*, edited by Jostein Ådna and Hans Kvalbein, 165-84. Wissenschaftliche Untersuchungen zum Neuen Testament 127. Tübingen: Mohr/Siebeck, 2000.

———. "The Salvation of Israel in Romans 11:25-32: A Response to Krister Stendahl." *Ex Auditu* 4 (1988) 38-58.

———. *Suffering and Ministry in the Spirit: Paul's Defense of His Ministry in II Corinthians 2:14-3:3*. Rev. ed. Grand Rapids: Eerdmans, 1990.

Hanson, Anthony Tyrell. *The Paradox of the Cross in the Thought of Paul*. Journal for the Study of the New Testament: Supplement Series 17. Sheffield: JSOT Press, 1987.

Harding, Mark. "Disputed and Undisputed Letters of Paul." In *The Pauline Canon*, edited by Stanley E. Porter, 129-68. Pauline Studies 1. Leiden: Brill, 2004.

Harnack, Adolf von. *Marcion: Das Evangelium vom fremden Gott: Eine Monographie zur Geschichte der Grundlegung der katholischen Kirche*. 2nd ed. Texte und Untersuchungen zur Geschichte der altchrislichen Literatur 45. Leipzig: Hinrichs, 1924.

Harris, Murray J. *Colossians and Philemon*. Exegetical Guide to the Greek New Testament. Grand Rapids: Eerdmans, 1990.

———. *The Second Epistle to the Corinthians: A Commentary on the Greek Text*. New International Greek Testament Commentary. Grand Rapids: Eerdmans, 2005.

Hawthorne, Gerald F. *Philippians*. Word Biblical Commentary 43. Waco: Word, 1983.

Hay, David M. *Colossians*. Abingdon New Testament Commentaries. Nashville: Abingdon, 2000.

Hays, Richard B. *Echoes of Scripture in the Letters of Paul*. New Haven: Yale University Press, 1989.

———. "ΠΙΣΤΙΣ and Pauline Christology: What Is at Stake?" In *Pauline Theology Volume IV: Looking Back, Pressing On*, edited by E. Elizabeth Johnson and David M. Hay, 35-60. SBL Symposium 4. Atlanta: Scholars, 1997.

Heil, John Paul. *Empowerment to Walk in Love for the Unity of All in Christ*. Studies in Biblical Literature 13. Atlanta: SBL, 2007.

Hobson, Donald G. "The Authorship of Colossians." PhD diss., Claremont Graduate School, 1968.

Hodgson, Robert. "Paul the Apostle and First Century Tribulation Lists." *Zeitschrift für die neutestamentliche Wissenschaft und die Kunde der älteren Kirche* 74 (1983) 59-80.

Hoehner, Harold W. *Ephesians: An Exegetical Commentary*. Grand Rapids: Baker, 2002.

Holtz, Traugott. "Zum Selbstverständnis des Apostels Paulus." *Theologische Literaturzeitung* 91 (1966) 321-30.

Holtzmann, Heinrich Julius. *Kritik der Epheser- und Kolosserbriefe auf Grund einer Analyse ihres Verwandtschaftsverhältnisses*. Leipzig: Engelmann, 1872.

Bibliography

Houlden, J. L. *Paul's Letters from Prison: Philippians, Colossians, Philemon, and Ephesians*. Westminster Pelican Commentaries. Philadelphia: Westminster, 1977.

Hovhanessian, Vahan. *Third Corinthians. Reclaiming Paul for Christian Orthodoxy*. Studies in Biblical Literature 18. New York: Lang, 2000.

Hübner, Hans. *An Philemon, an die Kolosser, an die Epheser*. Handbuch zum Neuen Testament 12. Tübingen: Mohr/Siebeck, 1997.

Hultgren, Arland J. "Colossians." In *The Deutero-Pauline Letters: Ephesians, Colossians, 2 Thessalonians, 1-2 Timothy, Titus*, edited by Gerhard Krodel, 24-38. Proclamation Commentaries. Minneapolis: Fortress, 1993.

James, Montague Rhodes. *The Apocryphal New Testament*. Oxford: Clarendon, 1924.

Jeal, Roy R. *Integrating Theology and Ethics in Ephesians: The Ethos of Communication*. Studies in Bible and Early Christianity 43. Lewiston, NY: Mellen, 2000.

Jewett, Robert. *Romans*. Hermeneia. Minneapolis: Fortress, 2007.

Josephus. *Jewish War*. Translated by H. St. J. Thackeray. LCL. Cambridge, MA: Harvard University Press, 1961.

Kamlah, E. "Wie beurteilt Paulus sein Leiden? Ein Beitrag zur Untersuchung seiner Denkstruktur." *Zeitschrift für die neutestamentliche Wissenschaft und die Kunde der älteren Kirche* 54 (1963) 217-32.

Karakolis, Christos. "A Mystery Hidden to be Revealed?" Philological and Theological Correlations between Eph 3 and 1." In *Ethik als angewandte Ekklesiologie: Der Briefe an die Epheser*, edited by Michael Wolter, 65-108. Monographische Reihe von "Benedictina," Biblisch-Ökumenische Abteilung 17. Rome: Benedictina, 2005.

Karlsson, Gustav. "Formelhaftes in Paulusbriefen?" *Eranos* 54 (1956) 138-41.

Käsemann, Ernst. "Eine urchristliche Tauftliturgie." In *Festschrift Rudolf Bultmann zum 65. Geburtstag überreicht*, edited by E. Wolf, 133-48. Stuttgart: Kohlhammer, 1949.

Keck, Leander E. "Images of Paul in the New Testament." *Interpretation* 43 (1989) 341-51.

Kertelge, Karl. "Das Apostelamt des Paulus, sein Ursprung und seine Bedeutung." *Biblische Zeitschrift* 14 (1970) 161-81.

Kiley, Mark. *Colossians as Pseudepigraphy*. Biblical Seminar. Sheffield: JSOT Press, 1986.

Kim, Seyoon. *The Origin of Paul's Gospel*. Grand Rapids: Eerdmans, 1981.

Kitchen, Martin. *Ephesians*. New Testament Readings. London: Routledge, 1994.

Klijn, A. F. J. "The Apocryphal Correspondence between Paul and the Corinthians." *Vigiliae christianae* 17 (1963) 2-23.

Knox, John. *Marcion and the New Testament: An Essay in the Early History of the Canon*. Chicago: University of Chicago Press, 1942.

Knox, Wilfred L. *St. Paul and the Church of the Gentiles*. Cambridge: Cambridge University Press, 1939.

Kremer, Jacob. *Der Erste Brief an die Korinther*. Regensburger Neues Testament. Regensburger: Pustet, 1997.

———. "Was an den Bedrängnissen des Christus mangelt: Versuch einer bibeltheologischen Neuinterpretation von Kol 1,24." *Biblica* 82 (2001) 130-46.

———. *Was an den Leiden Christi noch mangelt: Eine interpretationsgeschichtliche und exegetische Untersuchung zu Kol. 1,24b*. Bonner Biblische Beiträge. Bonn: Hanstein, 1956.

Kruse, Colin. *The Second Epistle of Paul to the Corinthians: An Introduction and Commentary*. Tyndale New Testament Commentaries 8. Leicester: InterVarsity Press, 1987.

Kümmel, Werner Georg. *Introduction to the New Testament*. Translated by Howard Clark Kee. Rev. ed. Nashville: Abingdon, 1975.

Ladd, George Eldon. "Paul's Friends in Colossians 4:7–16." *Review and Expositor* 70 (1973) 507–14.

Lähnemann, Johannes. *Der Kolosserbrief: Komposition, Situation und Argumentation*. Studien zum Neuen Testament 3. Gütersloh: Mohn, 1971.

Lapham, Fred. *An Introduction to the New Testament Apocrypha*. London: T. & T. Clark, 2003.

Leppä, Outi. *The Making of Colossians: A Study on the Formation and Purpose of a Deutero-Pauline Letter*. Publications of the Finnish Exegetical Society 86. Göttingen: Vandenhoeck & Ruprecht, 2003.

Liddell, Henry George, Robert Scott, and Henry Stuart Jones. *A Greek-English Lexicon*. 9th ed. Oxford: Clarendon, 1940.

Lietzmann, Hans. *Die Briefe des Apostels Paulus I: An die Galater*. Handbuch zum Neuen Testament. Tübingen: Mohr/Siebeck, 1910.

Lightfoot, J. B. *St. Paul's Epistles to the Colossians and to Philemon*. London: Macmillan, 1892.

———. *St. Paul's Epistle to the Philippians: A Revised Text with Introduction, Notes, and Dissertations*. 8th ed. London: Macmillan, 1885.

Lincoln, Andrew T. *Ephesians*. Word Biblical Commentary 42. Nashville: Nelson, 1990.

Lindemann, Andreas. *Der Epheserbrief*. Zürcher Bibelkommentare NT 8. Zürich: Theologischer, 1985.

———. *Der Erste Korintherbrief*. Handbuch zum Neuen Testament 9/1. Tübingen: Mohr/Siebeck, 2000.

Lohmeyer, Ernst. *Die Briefe an die Philipper, an die Kolosser und an Philemon*. Kritisch-exegetischer Kommentar über das Neue Testament. Göttingen: Vandenhoeck & Ruprecht, 1964.

Lohse, Eduard. *Colossians and Philemon: A Commentary on the Epistles to the Colossians and to Philemon*. Translated by William R. Poehlmann and Robert J. Karris. Hermeneia. Philadelphia: Fortress, 1971.

———. *Die Briefe an die Kolosser und an Philemon*. Kritisch-exegetischer Kommentar über das Neue Testament (Meyer) 9/2. Göttingen: Vandenhoeck & Ruprecht, 1968.

———. "Pauline Theology in the Letter to the Colossians." *New Testament Studies* 15 (1968/69) 211–20.

Longenecker, Richard N. *Galatians*. Word Biblical Commentary 41. Nashville: Nelson, 1990.

Löwe, Hartmut. "Bekenntnis, Apostelamt und Kirche im Kolosserbrief." In *Kirche: Festschrift für Günther Bornkamm zum 75. Geburtstag*, edited by Dieter Lührmann and Georg Strecker, 299–314. Tübingen: Mohr/Siebeck, 1980.

Lucian. *Toxaris*. Translated by A. M. Harmon. LCL. Cambridge, MA: Harvard University Press, 1962.

MacDonald, Margaret Y. *Colossians and Ephesians*. Sacra Pagina 17. Collegeville, MN: Liturgical, 2000.

Bibliography

———. *The Pauline Churches: A Socio-historical Study of Institutionalization in the Pauline and Deutero-Pauline Writings.* Society for New Testament Studies Monograph Series 60. Cambridge: Cambridge University Press, 1988.

Marguerat, Daniel. "Paul après Paul: Une histoire de reception." *New Testament Studies* 54 (2008) 317–37.

Marrow, Stanley B. "Parrhēsia in the New Testament." *Catholic Biblical Quarterly* 44 (1982) 431–46.

Marshall, I. Howard. "Romans 16:25-27—An Apt Conclusion." In *Romans and the People of God*, edited by Sven K. Soderlund and N. T. Wright, 170–84. Grand Rapids: Eerdmans, 1999.

Martin, Ralph P. *2 Corinthians.* Word Biblical Commentary 40. Waco: Word, 1986.

———. *Colossians and Philemon.* New Century Bible Commentary. Grand Rapids: Eerdmans, 1981.

———. *Philippians.* Rev. ed. Tyndale New Testament Commentary. Leicester: Inter-Varsity, 1987.

Martyn, J. Louis. *Galatians: A New Translation with Introduction and Commentary.* Anchor Bible 33A. New York: Doubleday, 1997.

Masson, Charles. *L'épître aux Colossiens.* Commentaire du Nouveau Testament 10. Paris: Delachaux & Niestlé, 1950.

Matera, Frank J. *Galatians.* Sacra Pagina 9. Collegeville, MN: Liturgical, 1992.

Mayerhoff, Ernst Theodor. *Der Brief an die Colosser: mit vornehmlicher Berücksichtigung der drei Pastoralbriefe.* Berlin: Schultze, 1838.

Meade, David G. *Pseudonymity and Canon.* Tübingen: Mohr, 1986.

Meeks, Wayne A. "'To Walk Worthily of the Lord': Moral Formation in the Pauline School Exemplified by the Letter to Colossians." In *Hermes and Athena: Biblical Exegesis and Philosophical Theology*, edited by Eleonore Stump and Thomas P. Flint, 37–58. University of Notre Dame Studies in the Philosophy of Religion 7. Notre Dame: University of Notre Dame Press, 1993.

Merklein, Helmut. *Das kirchliche Amt nach dem Epheserbrief.* Studien zum Alten und Neuen Testament 33. Munich: Kösel, 1973.

———. "Paulinische Theologie in der Rezeption des Kolosse- und Epheserbriefes." In *Paulus in den neutestamentlichen Spätschriften: Zur Paulusrezeption im Neuen Testament*, 25–69. Quaestiones Disputatae 89. Freiburg: Herder, 1981.

Metzger, Bruce M. "Literary Forgeries and Canonical Pseudepigrapha." *Journal of Biblical Literature* 91 (1972) 3–24.

———. *A Textual Commentary on the Greek New Testament.* 2nd ed. Stuttgart: United Bible Societies, 1994.

Mitton, C. Leslie. *The Epistle to the Ephesians: Its Authorship, Origin, and Purpose.* Oxford: Clarendon, 1951.

Mommsen, Theodor, and Paul Krueger, editors. *The Digest of Justinian.* Translated by Alan Watson. Vol. 4. Philadelphia: University of Pennsylvania Press, 1985.

Moo, Douglas J. *The Epistle to the Romans.* New International Commentary on the New Testament. Grand Rapids: Eerdmans, 1996.

———. *The Letters to the Colossians and to Philemon.* Pillar New Testament Commentary. Grand Rapids: Eerdmans, 2008.

Moreschini, Claudio, and Enrico Norelli. *Early Christian Greek and Latin Literature: A Literary History.* Translated by Matthew J. O'Connell. 2 vols. Peabody, MA: Hendrickson, 2005. Originally published as *Storia della litteratura cristiana antica greca e latina* (Brescia: Morcelliana, 1995).

Morton, A. Q., and James McLeman. *Paul, the Man, and the Myth: A Study in the Authorship of Greek Prose.* New York: Harper & Row, 1966.

Motyer, J. Alec. *The Prophecy of Isaiah: An Introduction and Commentary.* Downers Grove, IL: InterVarsity, 1993.

Moule, C. F. D. *The Epistles of Paul the Apostle to the Colossians and to Philemon.* Cambridge: University Press, 1957.

———. *An Idiom Book of New Testament Greek.* 2nd ed. Cambridge: University Press, 1968.

Muddiman, John. *A Commentary on the Epistle to the Ephesians.* Black's New Testament Commentaries. London: Continuum, 2001.

Müller, Peter. *Anfänge der Paulusschule: Dargestellt am zweiten Thessalonicherbrief und am Kolosserbrief.* Abhandlungen zur Theologie des Alten und Neuen Testaments 74. Zürich: Theologischer, 1988.

Mullins, Terence Y. "Disclosure: A Literary Form in the New Testament," *Novum Testamentum* 7 (1964) 44–50.

Munck, Johannes. *Paul and the Salvation of Mankind.* Translated by Frank Clarke. London: SCM, 1959.

Neumann, Kenneth J. *The Authenticity of the Pauline Epistles in the Light of Stylostatistical Analysis.* SBL Dissertation Series 120. Atlanta: Scholars, 1990.

Nickelsburg, George. "An Ἔκτρωμα, Though Appointed from the Womb: Paul's Apostolic Self-Description in 1 Corinthians 15 and Galatians 1." *Harvard Theological Review* 79 (1986) 198–205.

Nielsen, Charles M. "The Status of Paul and His Letters in Colossians." *Perspectives in Religious Studies* 12 (1985) 103–122.

Nguyen, V. Henry T. "The Identification of Paul's Spectacle of Death Metaphor in 1 Corinthians 4.9." *New Testament Studies* 53 (2007) 489–501.

O'Brien, Peter T. *Colossians, Philemon.* Word Biblical Commentary 44. Waco: Word Books, 1982.

———. *The Epistle to the Philippians: A Commentary on the Greek Text.* New International Greek Testament Commentary. Grand Rapids: Eerdmans, 1991.

———. *The Letter to the Ephesians.* Pillar New Testament Commentary. Grand Rapids: Eerdmans, 1999.

Oakes, Peter. *Philippians: From People to Letter.* Society for New Testament Studies Monograph Series 110. Cambridge: Cambridge University Press, 2001.

Ochel, Werner. "Die Annahme einer Bearbeitung des Kolosser-Briefes im Epheser-Brief: in einer Analyse des Epheser-Briefes untersucht." PhD diss., Philipps-Universität Marburg, 1934.

Osborne, Grant R. *Romans.* IVP New Testament Commentary Series. Downers Grove, IL: InterVarsity, 2004.

Oswalt, John N. *The Book of Isaiah: Chapters 40–66.* The New International Commentary on the Old Testament. Grand Rapids: Eerdmans, 1998.

The Panarion of Epiphanius of Salamis: Book I (Sects 1–46). Translated by Frank Williams. Nag Hammadi Studies 35. Leiden: Brill, 1987.

Penny, D. N. "The Pseudo-Pauline Letters of the First Two Centuries." Ph.D. diss., Emory University, 1980.

Bibliography

Percy, Ernst. *Die Probleme der Kolosser- und Epheserbriefe*. Skrifter utgivna av Kungl. Humanistiska Vetenskapssamfundet i Lund 39. Lund: Gleerup, 1946.

Perriman, Andrew. "The Pattern of Christ's Sufferings: Colossians 1:24 and Philippians 3:10–11." *Tyndale Bulletin* 42 (1991) 62–79.

Pfitzner, Victor C. *Paul and the Agon Motif: Traditional Athletic Imagery in the Pauline Literature*. Supplements to Novum Testamentum 16. Leiden: Brill, 1967.

Pink, Karl. "Die pseudo-paulinischen Briefe I." *Biblica* 6 (1925) 68–91.

———. "Die pseudo-paulinischen Briefe II." *Biblica* 6 (1925) 179–200.

Plummer, Alfred. *A Critical and Exegetical Commentary on the Second Epistle of St. Paul to the Corinthians*. International Critical Commentary 34. Edinburgh: T. & T. Clark, 1915.

Pokorný, Petr. *Colossians: A Commentary*. Translated by Siegfried S. Schatzmann. Peabody, MA: Hendrickson, 1991.

Polhill, John B. "The Relationship between Ephesians and Colossians." *Review and Expositor* 70 (1975) 439–50.

———. "Twin Obstacles in the Christian Path: Philippians 3." *Review and Expositor* 77 (1980) 359–72.

Proudfoot, C. Merrill. "Imitation or Realistic Participation? A Study of Paul's Concept of 'Suffering with Christ.'" *Interpretation* 17 (1963) 140–60.

Reid, D. G. "Prison, Prisoner." In *Dictionary of Paul and His Letters*, edited by Gerald F. Hawthrone and Ralph P. Martin, 752–54. Downers Grove, IL: InterVarsity, 1993.

Reumann, John. "Col 1:24 ("What Is Lacking in the Afflictions of Christ"): History of Exegesis and Ecumenical Advance." *Currents in Theology and Mission* 17 (1990) 454–61.

———. "Οἰκονομια—Terms in Paul in Comparison with Lucan Heilsgeschichte." *New Testament Studies* 13 (1966–67) 147–67.

———. *Philippians: A New Translation with Introduction and Commentary*. Anchor Yale Bible 33B. New Haven: Yale, 2008.

Reynier, Chantal. *Évangile et Mystère: Les enjeux théologiques de l'épître aux Éphésiens*. Lectio Divina 149. Paris: Cerfaux, 1992.

Richards, E. Randolph. *Paul and First-Century Letter Writing: Secretaries, Composition and Collection*. Downers Grove, IL: InterVarsity, 2004.

Ridderbos, Herman N. *The Epistle of Paul to the Churches of Galatia*. The New International Commentary on the New Testament. Grand Rapids: Eerdmans, 1953.

Rigaux, B. *Saint Paul. Les Épîtres aux Thessaloniciens*. Études bibliques. Paris: Gabalda, 1956.

Rist, Martin. "III Corinthians as a Pseudepigraphic Refutation of Marcionism." *Iliff Review* 26 (1969) 49–58.

———. "Pseudepigraphy and the Early Christians." Pages 75–91 In *Studies in the New Testament and Early Christian Literature*, edited by David Edward Aune, 75–91. Leiden: Brill, 1972.

Robertson, A. T. *A Grammar of the Greek New Testament in Light of Historical Research*. 4th ed. Nashville: Broadman, 1934.

Robertson, Archibald, and Alfred Plummer. *A Critical and Exegetical Commentary on the First Epistle of St. Paul to the Corinthians*. 2nd ed. International Critical Commentary. Edinburgh: T. & T. Clark, 1914.

Robinson, D. W. B. "Who Were 'The Saints'?" *Reformed Theological Review* 22 (1963) 45–53.

Robinson, J. Armitage. *St. Paul's Epistle to the Ephesians: A Revised Text and Translation with Exposition and Notes.* 2nd ed. London: Clarke, 1904.
Rodorf, Willy. "Hérésie et Orthodoxie selon la correspondance apocryphe entre les Corinthiens et l'Apôtre Paul." In *Orthodoxie et Hérésie dans l'Église ancienne: Perspectives nouvelles,* edited by Willy Rodorf and Dirk van Damme, 21–63. Cahiers de La Revue de Théologie et de Philosophie 17. Lausanne: Cahiers de la Revue de Théologie et de Philosophie, 1993.
Sanders, Ed Parish. "Literary Dependence in Colossians." *Journal of Biblical Literature* 85 (1966) 28–45.
Sanders, Jack T. "Hymnic Elements in Ephesians 1–3." *Zeitschrift für die neutestamentliche Wissenschaft und die Kunde der älteren Kirche* 56 (1965) 214–32.
Sandnes, Karl Olav. *Paul—One of the Prophets? A Contribution to the Apostle's Self-Understanding.* Wissenschaftliche Untersuchungen zum Neuen Testament 2/43. Tübingen: Mohr/Siebeck, 1991.
Sappington, Thomas J. *Revelation and Redemption at Colossae.* Journal for the Study of the New Testament: Supplement Series 53. Sheffield: JSOT Press, 1991.
Schenk, Wolfgang. *Die Philipperbriefe des Paulus: Kommentar.* Stuttgart: Kohlhammer, 1984.
Schenke, Hans-Martin. "Das Weiterwirken des Paulus und die Pflege seines Erbes durch die Paulus-Schule." *New Testament Studies* 21 (1975) 505–18.
Schnackenburg, Rudolf. *The Epistle to the Ephesians: A Commentary.* Translated by Helen Heron. Edinburgh: T. & T. Clark, 1991.
Schneemelcher, Wilhelm. "The Acts of Paul." In *New Testament Apocrypha: Revised Edition of the Collection initiated by Edgar Hennecke,* edited by Wilhelm Schneemelcher, translated by R. McL. Wilson, 2:213–70. Louisville: Westminster John Knox, 1992.
———. "The Epistle to the Laodiceans." In *New Testament Apocrypha: Revised Edition of the Collection initiated by Edgar Hennecke,* edited by Wilhelm Schneemelcher, translated by R. McL. Wilson, 2 vols., 42–46. Louisville: Westminster John Knox, 1991–1992.
Schreiner, Thomas R. *Paul, Apostle of God's Glory in Christ: A Pauline Theology.* Downers Grove, IL: InterVarsity, 2001.
———. *Romans.* Baker Exegetical Commentary on the New Testament. Grand Rapids: Baker, 1998.
Schütz, John Howard. *Paul and the Anatomy of Apostolic Authority, with New Introduction by Wayne A. Meeks.* New Testament Library. Louisville: Westminster John Knox, 2007.
Schweizer, Eduard. *The Letter to the Colossians: A Commentary.* Translated by Andrew Chester. Minneapolis: Augsburg, 1982.
———. "The Letter to the Colossians: Neither Pauline nor Post-Pauline?" In *Pluralisme et Oecuménisme en Recherches Théologiques: Mélanges offerts au R. P. Dockx,* edited by Y. Congar et al., 3–16. Bibliotheca ephemeridum theologicarum lovaniensium. Paris: Duculot, 1976.
Seifrid, M. A. "In Christ." In *Dictionary of Paul and His Letters,* edited by Gerald F. Hawthrone and Ralph P. Martin, 433–36. Downers Grove, IL: InterVarsity, 1993.
———. "Romans." In *Commentary on the New Testament Use of the Old Testament,* edited by G. K. Beale and D. A. Carson, 607–94. Grand Rapids: Baker, 2007.
Seitz, Christopher R. "The Book of Isaiah 40–66." In *The New Interpreter's Bible,* 6:309–552. Nashville: Abingdon, 2001.

Bibliography

———. "'You Are My Servant, You Are the Israel in Whom I Will Be Glorified': The Servant Songs and the Effect of Literary Context in Isaiah." *Calvin Theological Journal* 39 (2004) 117–34.

Seneca. *Epistula Morales*. Translated by Richard M. Gummere. LCL. Cambridge, MA: Harvard University Press, 1967.

Silva, Moisés. *Philippians*. 2nd ed. Baker Exegetical Commentary on the New Testament. Grand Rapids: Baker, 2005.

Smillie, Gene R. "Ephesians 6:19–20: A Mystery for the Sake of Which the Apostle Is an Ambassador in Chains." *Trinity Journal* 18 (1997) 199–222.

Smith, Ian K. *Heavenly Perspective: A Study of the Apostle Paul's Response to a Jewish Mystical Movement at Colossae*. Library of New Testament Studies 326. London: T. & T. Clark, 2006.

Smyth, Herbert W. *Greek Grammar*. Revised by Gordon M. Messing. Cambridge, MA: Harvard University Press, 1956.

Snodgrass, Klyne. *Ephesians*. NIV Application Commentary. Grand Rapids: Zondervan, 1996.

Snyman, Andries H. "A Rhetorical Analysis of Philippians 3:1–11." *Neotestamentica* 40 (2006) 259–83.

Spencer, F. Scott. "Metaphor, Mystery and the Salvation of Israel in Romans 9–11: Paul's Appeal to Humility and Doxology." *Review and Expositor* 103 (2006) 113–38.

Speyer, Wolfgang. *Die literarische Fälschung im heidnischen und christlichen Alterum: Ein Versuch ihrer Deutung*. Handbuch der Altertumswissenschaft 1/2. Munich: Beck, 1971.

———. "Religiöse Pseudepigraphe und literarische Fälschung im Altertum." In *Pseudepigraphie in der heidnischen und jüdisch-christlichen Antike*, edited by Norbert Brox, 195–263. Darmstadt: Wissenschaftliche Buchgesellschaft, 1977.

Standhartinger, Angela. "Colossians and the Pauline School." *New Testament Studies* 50 (2004) 572–93.

———. *Studien zur Entstehungsgeschichte und Intention des Kolosserbriefs*. Supplements to Novum Testamentum 94. Leiden: Brill, 1999.

Sterling, Gregory E. "From Apostle to the Gentiles to Apostle of the Church: Images of Paul at the End of the First Century." *Zeitschrift für die neutestamentliche Wissenschaft und die Kunde der älteren Kirche* 99 (2008) 74–98.

Stettler, Hanna. "An Interpretation of Colossians 1:24 in the Framework of Paul's Mission Theology." In *The Mission of the Early Church to Jews and Gentiles*, edited by Jostein Ådna and Hans Kvalbein, 185–208. Wissenschaftliche Untersuchungen zum Neuen Testament 127. Tübingen: Mohr/Siebeck, 2000.

Strecker, Georg. "Paulus in Nachpaulinischer Zeit." *Kairos* 12 (1970) 208–16.

Sumney, Jerry L. "I Fill Up What Is Lacking in the Afflictions of Christ: Paul's Vicarious Suffering in Colossians." *Catholic Biblical Quarterly* 68 (2006) 664–80.

Tannehill, Robert C. *Dying and Rising with Christ: A Study in Pauline Theology*. Beiheft zur Zeitschrift für die neutestamentliche Wissenschaft 32. Berlin: Töpelmann, 1967.

Testuz, Michel. *Papyrus Bodmer X–XII*. Geneva: Bibliotheca Bodmeriana, 1959.

Thiselton, Anthony C. *The First Epistle to the Corinthians: A Commentary on the Greek Text*. New International Greek Testament Commentary. Grand Rapids: Eerdmans, 2000.

Thrall, Margaret E. *A Critical and Exegetical Commentary on the Second Epistle to the Corinthians*. 2 vols. International Critical Commentary. London: T. & T. Clark, 2004.

———. *Greek Particles in the New Testament: Linguistic and Exegetical Studies*. New Testament Tools and Studies 3. Grand Rapids: Eerdmans, 1962.

Thurston, Bonnie B., and Judith M. Ryan. *Philippians and Philemon*. Sacra Pagina 10. Collegeville,MN: Liturgical, 2005.

Toit, A. B. du. "Encountering Grace: Towards Understanding the Essence of Paul's Damascus Experience." *Neotestamentica* 30 (1996) 71–87.

Tooley, Wilfred. "Stewards of God: An Examination of the Terms ΟΙΚΟΝΟΜΟΣ and ΟΙΚΟΝΟΜΙΑ in the New Testament." *Scottish Journal of Theology* 19 (1966) 74–86.

Trudinger, L. Paul. "A Further Brief Note on Colossians 1:24." *Evangelical Quarterly* 45 (1973) 36–38.

Unnik, Willem Cornelis van. "The Christian's Freedom of Speech in the New Testament." In *Sparsa Collecta: The Collected Essays of W. C. van Unnik, Part 2*, 269–89. Supplements to Novum Testamentum 30. Leiden: Brill, 1980.

van Roon, A. *The Authenticity of Ephesians*. Novum Testamentum Supplements 39. Leiden: Brill, 1974.

Verhoef, Eduard. "Pseudepigraphy and Canon." *Biblische Notizen* 106 (2001) 90–98.

Viard, André. *Saint Paul. Épître aux Romains*. Sources bibliques. Paris: Gabalda, 1975.

Wagner, J. Ross. *Heralds of the Good News: Isaiah and Paul "In Concert" in the Letter to the Romans*. Supplements to Novum Testamentum 101. Leiden: Brill, 2002.

Wallace, Daniel B. *Greek Grammar beyond the Basics: An Exegetical Syntax of the New Testament*. Grand Rapids: Zondervan, 1996.

Wannamaker, Charles A. *The Epistles to the Thessalonians: A Commentary on the Greek Text*. New International Greek Testament Commentary. Grand Rapids: Eerdmans, 1990.

Wansink, Craig S. *Chained in Christ: The Experiences and Rhetoric of Paul's Imprisonments*. Journal for the Study of the New Testament: Supplement Series 130. Sheffield: Sheffield Academic, 1996.

Watts, John D. W. *Isaiah 34–66*. Word Biblical Commentary 25. Waco: Word, 1987.

Webb, William J. *Returning Home: New Covenant and Second Exodus as the Context for 2 Corinthians 6:14–7:1*. Journal for the Study of the New Testament: Supplement Series 85. Sheffield: Sheffield Academic, 1993.

Westermann, Claus. *Isaiah 40–66: A Commentary*. Translated by David M. G. Stalker. Old Testament Library. Philadelphia: Westminster, 1969.

Wikenhauser, Alfred, and Josef Schmid. *Einleitung in das Neue Testament*. 6th ed. Freiburg: Herder, 1973.

Wilckens, Ulrich. *Der Brief an die Römer*. 3 vols. 3rd ed. Evangelisch-katholischer Kommentar zum Neuen Testament 6. Zürich: Benziger, 1997.

Wilcox, Peter, and David Paton-Williams. "The Servant Songs in Deutero-Isaiah." *Journal for the Study of the Old Testament* 42 (1988) 79–102.

Wild, Robert A. "The Warrior and the Prisoner: Some Reflections on Ephesians 6:10–20." *Catholic Biblical Quarterly* 46 (1984) 284–98.

Wilder, Terry L. *Pseudonymity, the New Testament, and Deception: An Inquiry into Intention and Reception*. Lanham, MD: University Press of America, 2004.

Bibliography

Wilk, Florian. "Isaiah in 1 and 2 Corinthians." In *Isaiah in the New Testament*, edited by Steve Moyise and Maarten J. J. Menken, 133–58. London: T. & T. Clark, 2005.

Wilson, R. McLachlan. *A Critical and Exegetical Commentary on Colossians and Philemon*. International Critical Commentary. London: T. & T. Clark, 2005.

Wilson, Walter T. *The Hope of Glory: Education and Exhortation in the Epistle to the Colossians*. Supplements to Novum Testamentum 88. Leiden: Brill, 1997.

Windisch, Hans. *Paulus und Christus: Ein biblisch-religionsgeschichtlicher Vergleich*. Untersuchungen zum Neuen Testament 24. Leipzig: Hinrischs, 1934.

Witherington III, Ben. *Grace in Galatia: A Commentary on St Paul's Letter to the Galatians*. Grand Rapids: Eerdmans, 1998.

———. *The Letters to Philemon, the Colossians, and the Ephesians: A Socio-Rhetorical Commentary on the Captivity Epistles*. Grand Rapids: Eerdmans, 2007.

Wolter, Michael. *Der Brief an die Kolosser. Der Brief an Philemon*.Ökumenischer Taschenbuch-Kommentar zum Neuen Testament 12. Gütersloh: Mohn, 1993.

Wright, N. T. *The Climax of the Covenant: Christ and the Law in Pauline Theology*. Minneapolis: Fortress, 1992.

———. *The Epistles of Paul to the Colossians and to Philemon: An Introduction and Commentary*. Tyndale New Testament Commentaries. Grand Rapids: Eerdmans, 1987.

Yates, Roy. "A Note on Colossians 1:24." *Evangelical Quarterly* 42 (1970) 88–92.

Young, Edward J. *The Book of Isaiah*. 3 vols. New International Commentary on the Old Testament. Grand Rapids: Eerdmans, 1965.

Young, Frances, and David F. Ford. *Meaning and Truth in 2 Corinthians*. Grand Rapids: Eerdmans, 1988.

Index of References

OLD TESTAMENT

Genesis

49:10	34n48

Job

5:9	155n101
9:10	155n101
13:6–8	55n132
34:24	155n101

Psalms

25:1–3	55n133

Isaiah

25:8	35
26:19	35
40–66	37, 38, 39, 41, 42n82, 45, 55n133, 162, 169
40:1–2	58n148
41:8–9	38
42	43n86
42:1	38
42:6	37n58, 44, 155, 169
42:6–7	37n58
42:7	155n104
42:9–10	42n82
43:1	38
43:10	38
43:18–19	42n82
44:1	38
44:21	38
44:24	38
45:4	38
45:16–17	55n133
48:6	42n82
49	37, 38, 40, 42, 43n86, 42n81, 59, 60, 62
49:1	37, 38
49:1–6	37, 37n58, 40
49:1–8	155n104
49:2	40, 41
49:4	42n83
49:5–6	37
49:6	37n58, 40, 40n73, 44, 155, 155n104, 169
49:7	40, 41, 41n74
49:8	40
49:13	58n148
49:23	55n133
50:5–9	55n133
51:3	58n148
51:4	44
51:12	58n148
51:19	58n148
52	44
52:7	44, 151, 169
52:13–15	43, 44
52:13—53:12	40, 41n74, 42, 43, 44
52:14	43
52:15	43, 43n89, 44, 44n94
53:1	44
54:11	58n148
61:2	58n148
64:2–3	31n33
65:17	42n82
66:13	58n148

Index of References

Jeremiah

1:5	37, 37n59, 38n60
31:31–34	150n86

Ezekiel

11:17–20	150n86
36:24–28	150n86
39:25–29	150n86

Daniel

2	157n108
2:18–19	29n22
2:30	29n22
2:47	29n22
12:2	35

Hosea

13:14	35

Joel

2:28–32	150n86

~

New Testament

Mark

4:1–12	115n125

Luke

	167n146
8:29	167n146
12:47	142n56

Acts

	13, 14, 15, 16, 21n1, 22, 167n146
9:3–19	22n2
9:15–16	52n119
11:27–28	147n72
13:1–3	147n72
13:47	37n58
14:27	118n139
15:32	147n72
21:10–11	147n72
22:1–21	22n22
26:12–18	22n22
26:16–18	37n58
26:18	155n104
28:20	167n158

Romans

	2, 33, 34, 81, 105n81, 122n160, 123, 133n18, 137n33
1:1	45, 46, 46n99, 67, 83, 135n25
1:2	147
1:1–15	27n19
1:3	111
1:5	26, 34, 96, 136, 138n40, 139, 147n76
1:7	130n10, 147
1:8–15	115n128
1:9	121
1:11–12	81n4
1:13	100, 136
1:14	120
1:15	130n10
1:19	155n103
2:24	100
3:21	51, 155n103
3:22	160
3:24	152
3:26	160
3:28	51
4:13	149
4:13–14	149
5:1–2	160n116
5:2	25, 103n76, 159, 159n116
5:6	136
5:15	25, 152

Index of References

Romans (cont.)

5:17	25
6:3–11	52n119
6:4–8	149
6:11	150n88
6:23	150n88
7:12	147
8	149n81
8:9–11	104, 105, 105n81
8:9–39	149n81
8:17	149
8:17–18	52n119, 87
8:19–21	157
8:26	120, 167
8:27	99, 147
8:28	158
8:29	149
8:32	150n88
8:38	157
8:39	150n88
9–11	40n72
9:11	158
9:22	155n103
9:23	102, 102n75
9:23–24	102, 102n75, 155
10:12	155
10:15	44, 151
10:16	44
11:12	36n56, 155
11:13	34, 36n56, 45, 51, 136
11:17–24	148n79
11:25	28, 35, 45n97, 100, 103, 105, 111, 140
11:25–27	35, 37
11:32—12:5	152n93, 155n101, 164n134
11:33	113n115, 154, 155n101
12:1	107n89, 164n134
12:3	26, 27n19, 95, 95n54, 137, 138n40, 139, 152, 152n93
12:4–5	157
12:6	25
12:6–8	26
15	96n57, 97n59
15:5–6	112
15:14	106, 113
15:14–33	27n19
15:15	95, 137, 141n48, 152
15:15–16	26n17, 27, 138n40, 139
15:15–18	96
15:15–19	96
15:15–21	136, 154
15:16	27, 83n9, 96, 97, 107
15:18	25, 27, 96, 97, 111, 152
15:18–19	27
15:19	36n56, 45, 51n116, 96, 97n59, 118
15:20	25
15:21	37, 43, 44, 123
15:24–29	115n128
15:25	98
15:25–26	120
15:30	110n99, 149
15:30–31	118, 118n138, 121, 165n141
15:31	98
16	33
16:7	121
16:16	147
16:19	87
16:25	97n61, 140
16:25–26	28, 28n21, 29, 32–34, 37, 97, 98, 102n75, 105, 141, 146n70, 150n89, 163
16:25–27	32, 33n40, 33n43
16:26	34, 105, 140, 155n103, 158

1 Corinthians

	2, 34, 81, 122n160, 133
1–2	106, 114, 115
1:1	45, 46, 67, 81, 81n3, 99, 133, 135n25
1:2	147
1:4	25, 150n88

193

Index of References

1 Corinthians (cont.)

1:8	107n91
1:10	112
1:10—4:23	32n34
1:18	30, 31, 31n31
1:18—2:10	114
1:20	149
1:21	30, 31n31
1:23–24	114
1:24	31, 31n31
1:30	114, 150n88, 157
2	99, 101, 148, 148n77
2–3	108, 109
2:1	28n21, 106, 106n85, 114, 119
2:1–2	114
2:1–5	101
2:1–10	106n85, 114
2:1–16	29, 115
2:2	31
2:4–7	30
2:6	99n65, 108, 108n93
2:6–7	101
2:6–10	105, 106n84, 163
2:6–16	29, 35, 37, 98, 105
2:7	28, 29, 31, 98, 99, 102n75, 103, 105n82, 119, 156, 157
2:7–8	103
2:7–10	141
2:7–16	148
2:8	30, 31, 31n33
2:8–10	101
2:9	30, 30n28, 31
2:10	30, 30n28, 98, 99, 120, 148n78
2:11–12	30n29
2:11–13	30
2:12	30n28
2:13	30n29
2:14–16	30
3:1	108
3:1–4	108n93
3:1–13	30n27
3:5	85, 96
3:10	25, 27n19, 95, 95n54, 137, 138n40, 139, 152
3:10–17	157
3:11	146n72
3:17	147
4:1	28, 29, 31, 32, 32n34, 37, 94, 95n52, 101, 106n84, 119, 138
4:1–2	32n37, 138n40
4:2–5	32
4:5	155
4:6	53
4:8	53
4:8–13	52, 53
4:9	53, 125, 157, 157n109
4:10	53, 136
4:12	53, 109
4:14	106
4:16	164n134
4:17	106
5:3	115n127, 116, 116n131, 116n132, 116n133
5:11	86n21
6:9	149
7:14	86n21, 147
8:1	48
8:2	120n149, 167
8:13	48
9:1	22n4, 23, 23n10, 48
9:1–5	57
9:1–6	45, 48, 147
9:5	124
9:12	118
9:16	120
9:16–17	32
9:17	138n40
9:25	109
10:1	111
10:24	48
10:33	48
11:1	48
11:3	111
11:10	157n109

1 Corinthians (*cont.*)

11:23	59, 75, 75n47
12:1	111
12:8	166n143
12:12–14	157
12:20	86n21
12:26	149
12:28	147n72
13:2	28, 32n34
13:10–12	108n94
14:2	28, 32n34
15	35n52, 52, 68
15:1	48, 68
15:1–11	45, 48, 51, 146n72
15:1–12	47n103
15:3	48, 68, 75
15:3–7	51
15:3–11	147
15:5–11	124
15:6–11	148n77
15:8	22n4, 23n10, 24, 52
15:9	25, 153, 153n97
15:9–10	24, 26, 49, 124, 139, 153n97, 154n100
15:10	25, 39n67, 49, 109, 111, 138n40, 152, 153
15:11	50, 83, 147, 153n98
15:22	150n88
15:23	35n52
15:24	157
15:24–28	153n97, 157
15:50	35, 149
15:51	28, 35, 35n53, 101, 103, 105, 143n58
15:51–52	35n52
15:54–55	35n51
16:1	98
16:9	53, 118
16:17	90, 90n37, 91
16:20	147

2 Corinthians

	2, 57, 75, 81, 109n98, 123, 133
1	112
1:1	45, 67, 81, 81n3, 133, 135n25, 147
1:1–11	57
1:3–7	58n148
1:4	74
1:4–8	87, 87n25, 161
1:5	42, 58, 87, 136
1:5–7	54n129
1:5–11	52, 54n129, 57, 58
1:6	58, 75, 87, 94, 112, 136, 162
1:7	58
1:8	111
1:8–10	58
1:9	58n148, 58n151
1:10	58, 58n148
1:10–11	118, 165n141
1:11	61
1:12	25
1:12–17	82, 134
1:12—2:13	57
2:4	74
2:12	54, 118
2:14	155n103
2:14—6:10	57
2:17	96n55
3:4	160
3:5	111n104, 152
3:6	85
3:12	159, 166
4:1	161
4:2	96n55
4:4	24n10, 155
4:5	23n10, 59n156, 94
4:6	23n10
4:6–7	113
4:7	59
4:7–11	42, 93n46
4:7–12	52, 57, 59, 75
4:7–15	112
4:8–9	59
4:10	59, 92, 93n46
4:10–11	92, 93

2 Corinthians (cont.)

4:10–12	40n70
4:11	59, 92, 93n46, 136
4:12	59, 94, 162
4:14	107
4:15	25, 59, 94, 96, 136, 162
4:16	161
4:17	87, 161
5–6	163, 163n129, 167
5:3	136
5:10	142n56
5:14–17	41n80, 42
5:18–20	85
5:18—6:2	85
5:18—6:10	85, 85n17, 85n18, 96, 123, 163
5:20	166n144, 167, 167n147
6	40
6:1	25, 39n67, 42n83
6:1–10	165n140
6:2	37, 40–42, 123, 155n104
6:3–10	52, 57, 59, 85, 123
6:4	74, 85, 87, 161
6:4–10	109
6:5	109
6:10	112, 162
6:11–13	85
6:11—7:16	57
7:4	87, 159, 161, 166
7:4–7	87
7:5	115n127
8:1—9:15	57
8:4	98
8:9	25
8:22	160
8:23	124
9:1	98
9:12	90, 90n37, 98
9:13	118
9:14–15	152
10–13	50
10:1	84, 84n13, 116n133, 135
10:1—13:14	57
10:7	160
10:11	116n133
10:14–16	25
11:1	50
11:2	107
11:4	50
11:4–5	50
11:5	45, 50, 51
11:6	143n59
11:9	90, 90n37
11:13	50
11:14	50
11:23	85, 109
11:23–33	109
12:9	111n104, 152
12:11	50
12:11–12	45, 50, 51
12:15	110, 136, 162
13:2	116n133
13:10	116n133
13:11	112
13:12	147

Galatians

	2, 46, 66, 66n17, 67, 68, 77, 81, 123, 132n15
1	37, 40, 45, 68, 70, 140, 163
1–2	37, 47, 47n103, 52, 68, 68n19, 141n45, 168
1:1	22, 22n4, 45, 65n9, 66–68, 81
1:1–12	67
1:1—2:10	51
1:4	40
1:6	25
1:6–7	67
1:6–9	40, 46, 67
1:6—2:10	46, 141
1:7	40, 118
1:8–9	67
1:10	40, 53, 135n25
1:10—2:21	82, 134

Index of References

Galatians (cont.)

1:11	40, 68
1:11–12	22, 51–52, 68
1:11–16	40
1:11–17	22
1:12	140
1:13	137
1:13–14	22, 24
1:13–15	24
1:13–16	24, 26, 124
1:15	22–24, 37, 38n60, 138n40, 139, 147n76; 162
1:15–16	37, 123, 154n100, 155n104
1:16	22, 38n60, 40, 100, 136, 154
1:17	45, 46, 75, 76, 141
1:19	124
1:23–24	24
2:1–2	68
2:1–10	45, 47, 51, 52
2:2	23, 39n67, 40, 47, 100, 154
2:2–5	47
2:4	150n88
2:5	67, 68
2:6	47
2:6–9	47
2:7	23, 25, 47, 83, 147, 152
2:7–8	141
2:7–9	47, 136, 147, 154
2:8	23, 25, 47, 51, 152
2:8–9	25, 40
2:9	25, 27n19, 47, 95, 95n54, 137, 137n36, 138n40, 139, 152
2:11–12	28
2:11–14	67
2:14	68, 142n56
2:16	160
2:19	149
2:20	40, 40n70, 52, 52n119, 59, 160
2:21	25
3:4	136
3:13–29	150
3:14	150, 150n88
3:18	149, 150
3:19	134
3:20	149n82
3:22	160
3:26–28	157
3:28	150, 150n88
3:28–29	150
3:29—4:7	149
4:11	109
4:28–30	149
5:2	84, 135
5:4	25
5:10	159n112, 160
5:21	149
6:9	161
6:11	121n157
6:12	52
6:17	52, 76, 92n45, 121, 121n157, 136, 164, 164n136

Ephesians

	1–20, 28, 28n20, 34n45, 52, 62, 63, 73, 73n39, 79, 104, 128–74
1:1	128, 130, 133, 164
1:1–14	157n110
1:3	156
1:3–8	159
1:3–10	159n111
1:3–14	154, 158
1:4	157n110
1:9	28, 139, 141, 157n110
1:9–10	138, 142, 142n51, 144, 155n102, 157
1:10	141, 149n80
1:11	157n110
1:12	162
1:13	160
1:13–14	148, 150, 157

Index of References

Ephesians (*cont.*)

1:14	149, 162, 162n127
1:15	131, 134, 137, 159, 160
1:17	148, 162
1:18	149, 155
1:18–19	154
1:19	160
1:19–20	152
1:20	156
1:21	157
1:21–23	141n51
1:22–23	155n102
1:23	150
2	160n116
2:1–10	152
2:4–7	154
2:5–6	148
2:6	156
2:6–7	159
2:8	159, 160
2:8–9	153
2:10	156, 159n111
2:11	134
2:11–22	134, 141, 142, 144, 163n129
2:11—3:13	85n18
2:12	150, 169
2:13	159
2:14	159n111
2:14–16	156
2:14–18	149
2:14–22	159
2:15	156
2:15–16	155n102
2:15–22	157
2:16	150
2:17–18	160n116
2:18	148, 150, 158, 159
2:19	154
2:19–22	148
2:20	145n68, 145n69, 146, 146n72
2:21	147
3	140, 141n45, 148, 160n116
3:1	73, 134, 135, 135n25, 136, 139, 144, 151, 161, 163, 165, 166
3:1–2	137n36
3:1–7	142n51
3:1–13	2, 5, 12, 15, 18, 19, 27, 128, 133, 134n24, 139, 146, 154, 155n104, 157n110, 158, 159, 162, 163, 163n129, 163n130, 164, 173
3:2	96, 131, 133, 136, 137, 137n36, 138, 139, 144, 152
3:2–3	143
3:2–6	156
3:2–7	133, 153
3:2–12	161, 162
3:2–13	137
3:3	28, 139, 140, 140n43, 141, 142, 142n51, 168
3:3–4	76n50
3:3–6	142
3:4	12, 28, 143, 144n64, 149
3:5	7, 12n47, 19, 76n50, 139, 140, 144n64, 145, 145n68, 146, 146n70, 148, 148n78
3:6	145, 148, 148n79, 149, 149n81, 149n82, 150, 151, 163, 169
3:7	139, 143, 151, 152
3:7–8	168
3:7–9	76n50
3:7–10	152n93
3:8	12, 18, 139, 143, 146, 152, 153, 153n95, 153n96, 153n97, 153n98, 154, 154n100, 155, 155n101, 156
3:8–9	151n92, 155n104, 163
3:8–11	152

Ephesians (cont.)

3:9	28, 133, 138, 155
3:9–10	141n51
3:9–11	19
3:10	145, 149, 155–57, 163
3:11	157, 158
3:11–12	160n116
3:12	136, 145n69, 158, 159, 160n119, 163, 166
3:13	134, 136, 160–63, 165, 165n136
3:14	134, 134n24
3:14–21	155, 165
3:16	162
3:17	159, 160
3:18	145n69
3:18–19	155
3:20	152
3:21	162
4–6	164, 165
4:1	73n35, 128, 164, 164n134, 165n136, 166
4:4	148, 150
4:4–6	155n102
4:8	134
4:11	145n68, 145n69
4:12	150
4:16	150
4:21	136, 137
4:25	134
4:29	166n142
4:30	148
5:5	149
5:6	134
5:7	149
5:14	134
5:15–16	166n142
5:17	134
5:18	148
5:23	150
5:30	150
6:12	156, 157
6:13	134
6:15	151
6:17	148
6:18	165
6:19	28, 155n103, 166
6:19–20	128, 159, 165, 166, 166n142, 166n144, 168
6:20	73n35, 135, 166n145, 167n150
6:21–22	168

Philippians

	2, 54, 60n158, 64, 66, 68, 73n39, 97n60, 108n92, 116n133, 117, 121n155, 123n160
1	60n158, 70, 135n25
1:1	66, 67, 81, 147
1:5	54
1:7	25, 52, 54, 54n128, 54n129, 76n51, 121, 121n155, 138n40, 139, 166
1:9	113, 118n138
1:10	107n91
1:12	54, 69, 111, 168n153
1:12–13	70, 94
1:12–18	75, 118
1:12–26	52, 54, 54n129, 70, 82, 92n45, 134
1:13	54, 69, 76n51, 121, 121n155, 136, 166
1:13–14	54
1:14	54, 76n51, 97n60, 121, 159n112, 160, 166
1:15–18	83
1:17	54, 76n51, 87, 121, 121n155, 161, 166
1:17–18	54, 106
1:18	69, 87
1:19	54, 58, 61, 65n9, 69, 70, 118, 165n141
1:20	55, 69, 92n45, 159, 166
1:20–24	55
1:21	55, 70
1:21–23	54

Index of References

Philippians (cont.)

1:22	55, 115n127
1:22–25	75
1:22–26	70
1:23	55
1:24	55, 115n127
1:24–25	70, 94, 96
1:24–26	54
1:25	136
1:25–26	55
1:27	54, 112, 116n133, 118, 168n153
1:29	55n134, 87
1:29–30	52, 55
1:30	110
2:2	87, 112, 149
2:12	116n133
2:16	39n67, 55, 109
2:16–17	75
2:16–18	52, 55
2:17	87, 149
2:22	54
2:25	124
2:30	90, 90n37, 91, 94n50
3	77
3:3–4	160
3:4–8	86
3:6	24n11
3:7–8	56
3:8	56, 77
3:8–9	56
3:8–11	52, 56
3:9	150n88, 160
3:10	56, 88, 136, 149
3:10–11	40n70, 52n119, 54, 55n134
3:11	77
3:12	23n10
3:15	108n92
3:21	57, 110, 111
4:1	87
4:3	54
4:14	54n128
4:19	155

Colossians

	1–20, 28, 28n20, 34n45, 52, 62, 63, 65, 66, 73n39, 79, 80–133, 135, 137n33, 144, 146, 157, 162, 163, 166, 168–74
1	101, 108, 141n45
1–2	106, 108, 112, 114, 158
1:1	80, 81, 81n3, 83, 125, 133, 135n25
1:2	99, 108n95
1:4	99
1:5	96n55, 103
1:6	107
1:7	83n8, 116n129, 124
1:11	87, 102
1:12	98n64, 104, 149
1:12—2:3	7
1:14	91
1:16	157
1:18	157
1:20	85, 91
1:22	85, 91, 107, 107n90
1:23	16, 82–86, 103, 107, 120, 123–25, 135, 136, 151
1:23–25	101
1:23–29	85, 133
1:23—2:1	109
1:23—2:3	80
1:23—2:5	17, 80, 81–82, 110, 117, 127, 136, 146
1:24	5, 16, 17, 85–89, 89n32, 90, 90n37, 91–93, 93n47, 94, 94n50, 96, 109, 126, 136, 161n124, 162, 174
1:24–25	92n45
1:24–29	86, 148, 163
1:24—2:3	173
1:24—2:5	82, 87n22, 112, 115n128
1:24—2:7	15

Colossians (*cont.*)

1:25	16, 85, 93–95, 95n52, 95n54, 96, 97, 97n59, 97n60, 124, 133, 136, 138, 138n39
1:25–26	95n52, 138
1:25–27	95n52, 96
1:25–28	85, 106n85
1:25–29	96
1:26	28, 97, 98, 98n63, 99, 102n75, 105n82, 120n150, 133, 145, 146, 148n78, 155n103, 156
1:26–27	94, 98–101, 102n75, 103, 105, 105n82, 118, 120, 141
1:27	28, 96, 99, 101, 102, 102n74, 102n75, 103–5, 105n81, 144, 155, 155n103
1:27–29	85
1:28	96, 105–7, 107n90, 108, 108n92, 108n95, 109
1:28–29	101
1:29	85, 97, 109–11, 120, 152
1:29—2:1	109, 109n98, 110, 110n102
2:1	81, 82, 87n22, 109, 110, 111, 115n127, 117n134, 131, 136
2:1–3	108, 111, 114
2:2	28, 102, 112, 118, 144, 155
2:2–3	113, 113n115, 115, 157
2:3	107, 114, 156n106
2:4	110, 116
2:5	17, 87, 115, 116, 116n131, 116n132, 116n133, 143n57
2:6	85
2:8	125n167
2:10	157
2:10–12	108n95
2:11–13	125n167
2:12	111n105
2:13–14	91
2:15	157
2:16	125n167
2:19	112
3:4	102, 103, 120n150
3:10–11	157
3:11	106, 107, 150
3:14	112
3:16	102, 106
4	17, 117
4:2–6	166n142
4:3	28, 117–19, 144, 166
4:3–4	118, 120–22, 166, 166n142, 166n144, 167
4:4	80, 119, 120, 155n103, 167
4:6	120
4:7	102, 124, 124n165, 168n153
4:10	118, 121, 121n153, 122
4:12	108, 108n94, 110, 110n99
4:13	82
4:16	65, 131
4:18	80, 118, 121, 121n155, 121n157, 166

1 Thessalonians

	2
1:1	67, 81
1:2–3	121
2:1	56n137
2:1–12	82, 134
2:2	39, 55, 110, 159, 166n144, 167n150
2:4	83
2:6	125
2:6–7	45, 47, 48
2:9	109
2:11–12	106n87
2:13	96n55
2:16	100
2:18	84, 84n13, 135

Index of References

1 Thessalonians (*cont.*)

2:19–20	87, 107n91
3:2	118
3:3–7	87, 161
3:5	109
3:6–10	87
3:7	90n36
3:8	86n21
3:10	90
3:13	107, 147
4:1	120n149, 167
4:13	111
4:13–17	35
5:12	106
5:14	106
5:23	107
5:25	121
5:26	147

2 Thessalonians

	3n8, 13, 15
2:7	28

Pastoral Epistles

3n8, 10, 13, 14, 16, 34n45, 74

1 Timothy

1:6	74
1:15	153n97
3:9	28
6:21	74

2 Timothy

	73n39
1:16	167n146
2:9	167n146
2:18	74
4:6	56n138

Philemon

2, 5, 73, 117, 121n155

1	52, 60, 67, 73, 81, 135, 135n25, 136
4	121
5	147
6	113
8	159, 159n112, 166
8–9	61, 161n122, 165, 165n137
9	60, 73n35, 135, 135n25, 136
9–10	52
10	60, 61, 73n35, 76n51, 121, 121n155, 166
13	52, 60, 73n35, 76n51, 121, 121n155, 166, 166n145
19	84, 135
21	141n48, 160
22	61, 73n35
23	52, 60, 121

Hebrews

4:16	159
6:4	150n85
10:19	159

1 Peter

5:12	141n48

1 John

2:28	157

Revelation

18:20	147n72

Apostolic Fathers

1 Clement

34:8	31n33

Ignatius

To the Ephesians
3:1	75n46
21:2	153

To the Philadelphians
7:2	75n46, 165n136

To the Romans
9:2	153

To the Smyrnaeans
4:2	165n136
11:1	153

To the Trallians
10:1	165n136
12:2	75n46, 165n136
131	153

Shepherd of Hermas
9:9—10:1	75n46
69:6–8	75n46
105:5–6	75n46

Polycarp

To the Philippians
1:1	75n46
9:1–2	75n46

Martyrdom of Polycarp
2:1	75n46
14:3	75n46

New Testament Apocrypha and Pseudepigrapha

Acts of Paul
16, 71, 71n22, 71n25, 73

3 Corinthians
2, 3, 52, 62, 63, 63n1, 64, 70, 70n22, 71, 71n25, 72, 72n34, 73, 73n36, 74n45, 75–78, 80, 110, 126, 132n16, 153n97, 163, 163n130, 171–73

1	73n36
2	73n36
2:1	77
2:2	73
2:4	75, 75n47, 76n49, 83
2:34	77
2:34–35	73, 73n39, 76, 77
2:35	77

Epistle to the Laodiceans
2, 3, 52, 62, 63, 63n1, 64, 65, 65n8, 66–70, 73, 80, 83, 110, 117, 121n155, 126, 132n16, 153n97, 171–73

1	65n9, 66, 68
4	67, 68
6	68, 69
6–8	69, 70
7	65n9, 69
13	67

Gospel of Thomas
17	31n33

~

Jewish Literature

Josephus

Jewish War
4.628	61n162, 119n143

Dead Sea Scrolls

1QpHab	29n22
7:1–2	29n22

Index of References

GRAECO–ROMAN LITERATURE

Codex Justinianus
49.7.1   61n162, 119n143

Lucian

Toxaris
28   119n143

Seneca

Moral Epistles
9.8–9   119n143

www.ingramcontent.com/pod-product-compliance
Lightning Source LLC
Chambersburg PA
CBHW060609230426
43670CB00011B/2034